ETHICS

NIHIL OBSTAT

Henri DuLac, Ph.D.
Censor Deputatus

IMPRIMATUR   December 14, 1956

✠ Leo A. Pursley, D.D.
Apostolic Administrator
Diocese of Fort Wayne

ETHICS

The Introduction to Moral Science

John A. Oesterle

Department of Philosophy
University of Notre Dame

PEARSON

Custom
Publishing

Printed in the United States of America

20   18

Reproduced by Simon & Schuster Custom Publishing.

ISBN 0–536–04949–1

BA 98673

 PEARSON CUSTOM PUBLISHING
75 Arlington Street, Suite 300, Boston, MA 02116
A Pearson Education Company

To

*my mother
and the memory of
my father*

Preface

Ethics is an introduction to moral science in several ways. It is introductory in the sense that the initial questions, problems, and distinctions of moral knowledge are raised: the problem of the ultimate end, the distinction of ends and means, the notion of virtue and the distinction of its various kinds, and the problem of moral knowledge and prudence. These and other matters are fundamental and necessarily prior to the consideration and analysis of other moral and practical problems.

In a more specific sense, ethics is introductory insofar as it precedes political philosophy. Politics and ethics may be considered as parts of moral philosophy, since both consider human actions as ordered to an end. They differ in that ethics deals with actions of individual human beings as directed to an ultimate end, while politics deals with actions of the members of a political society as ordered to an ultimate end. In the study of ethics we see that the realization of an ultimate end for man demands social and political life. and in this way ethics leads to politics.

Ethics leads also to moral theology, and this is another way in which it is introductory to moral science. Ethics is based on principles known by reason alone and deals with human acts as directed to a natural end. Moral theology is based on revealed principles accepted by faith and deals with human acts as directed to a supernatural end, the vision of God. While it is true that human beings need revealed moral doctrine in order to achieve the supernatural end to which they are ordered, it is also true that moral theology presupposes the reasoned grasp of natural moral doctrine, for the truths of moral theology are not intelligible in a scientific way without a comprehension of the moral truths available to human reason. On the one hand, this book is written in such a way that it easily leads to moral theology, not by confusing ethics with moral the-

vii

ology, but by distinguishing ethics from moral theology in order
to see the complementary relationship between the two sciences.
On the other hand, the position is taken throughout the book—and
argued explicitly in several places—that ethics as a science is adequate to attain truths about the natural moral order.

This book is an introduction also in the sense that it remains, for
the most part, general in its treatment. It does not explicitly cover
material contained in what is often called "special ethics," the specific application of moral principles and distinctions to particular
problems, as in business ethics, medical ethics, and so on. Such areas
are important parts of moral doctrine, deserving of separate and extensive treatment. They are best treated, however, if the general,
fundamental principles and distinctions of moral knowledge are
first understood in their full exposition as covered by ethics. For
many persons, then, ethics is the introduction to more specialized
areas of human activity in which they will be professionally engaged.

Still another sense in which ethics should be considered as preliminary is as an introduction to the concrete order of singular action. This point needs stressing because there is a common misap-
prehension that the knowledge of ethics alone—or the knowledge of
moral theology as well—should guarantee a person's being morally
good in his actions by providing complete and certain solutions to
all courses of action to be taken here and now. In the completely
practical order of singular action, each person's rectified will is a
prerequisite for good moral action. No one, therefore, can justi-
fiably expect ethics to *make* him good. On the other hand, with a
reasoned grasp of moral doctrine, one will be much better prepared
to approach his own moral situations and problems than he would
be without any understanding of moral science.

At present there are at least four prevailing tendencies among
writers in the field of moral philosophy. One view holds that ethics
is "normative" and cannot be a science; all that one can do scientifically is to give a logical analysis of certain moral terms. Careful
analysis of terms in moral discourse is necessary, of course, and I
have sought to retain this important part of philosophical investigation. At the same time, I have attempted to keep such an analysis

in the context of ethics as a practical science, and not to present it as only a logical or semantic problem. A second position adopts a purely empirical and subjective view of ethics, as though it were nothing more than statements of likes and dislikes. The third position offers a rationalistic and sometimes purely theoretical view of ethics as a science. Finally, some Christian authors tend to give a theological exposition of moral philosophy, mixing theological and philosophical elements to a point where they are no longer distinguishable.

My aim is to recapture ethics as it was originally conceived to be a practical science based on reasoning derived from common experience, though considering speculative truths as any science must necessarily do. I have also sought to reassert the primary role of virtue in moral doctrine. Consequently, I have followed closely the order of Aristotle in his *Nicomachean Ethics*, thereby acknowledging that his work still remains the best formulation of the practical science of ethics. I have often followed just as closely the commentary on this work by St. Thomas Aquinas, who clearly had the same opinion of the worth of Aristotle's ethics as a science of natural moral doctrine. While I am thus indebted to Aristotle and St. Thomas on almost every page, I have not quoted them directly, since the soundness of what they say is evident on the only authority relevant here—reason itself. However, at the end of each chapter, I have given the appropriate references to Aristotle's *Ethics* and to the accompanying commentary of St. Thomas. The one exception is the chapter on law, which is drawn principally from the *Summa Theologiae* of St. Thomas, though I have followed a philosophical order in the exposition of law. Other readings are also cited, though purely in a suggestive manner. Some of these readings are in more or less conformity with the text itself; others are offered as contrasting views. For the most part, the selections are chosen with an eye to their easy availability.

Acknowledgments

A preliminary version of this book was used in several classes at the University of Notre Dame, and I am indebted to the students of these classes for many helpful suggestions and comments. They also contributed some of the discussion material appearing at the end of the chapters. I am indebted also to Mr. Samuel J. Kennedy, teaching fellow at Notre Dame, for reading a portion of the manuscript and offering suggestions for clarification. I am grateful also for the assistance given me by my colleagues in the Department of Philosophy, particularly Dr. Herbert Johnston and Dr. Ralph McInerny.

To Miss Natalie Lincoln of Mt. Rainier, Maryland, I am indebted in many ways over a period of many years for encouragement and stimulation in philosophical pursuits. In particular, I am grateful for the opportunity, during the summer of 1956, to present portions of the material of this book at two discussions held at her House of Studies at Austin, Brome County, Quebec, Canada.

Fr. Leo A. Arnoult, O.P., and Fr. James M. Egan, O.P., professors of theology at St. Mary's College, Notre Dame, have read considerable portions of the text and have made many valuable comments and suggestions for improvement of the material. Without their knowledge, encouragement, and helpful discussion, it would have been much more difficult to write a text on ethics as a science of natural moral doctrine, distinct from, yet ordered to, and necessary for, moral theology. I am also as fully indebted to Fr. Henri DuLac, Ph.D., who, during his stay as professor of philosophy at Notre Dame and professor of theology at St. Mary's, went far beyond the requirements of a *censor deputatus* in carefully reading the preliminary and final drafts of the manuscript. His conscientious fulfillment of this task paralleled his concern as a true friend to make many comments and suggestions for clarification and improvement of the writing.

I must also acknowledge a long outstanding debt to Fr. R. J. Belleperche, S.J., of the University of Detroit, Detroit, Michigan. The teacher who first introduced me to philosophy, he has ever since served as a model of the spirit of philosophical inquiry in my own study and teaching. In particular, I have benefited immeasurably from his own experience and knowledge as a consistently successful teacher of moral philosophy. But with respect to him and the others who have so generously helped me, I must take pains to reserve the shortcomings of the text entirely to myself.

To my wife, finally, I am indebted for her expert work in editing the manuscript. All other acknowledgment I should like to make to her has not survived her editing pencil.

J.A.O.

Contents

I

II

III

IV

V

WHEN ARE ACTIONS VOLUNTARY? . . . 64

VI

WHEN ARE ACTIONS FREE? 81

VII

VIII

IX

X

I

The science and method of ethics

*H*uman beings seek knowledge either for the sake of simply knowing or for the sake of doing or making something. The pure mathematician, for example, is interested primarily in understanding exact relations existing between quantities, magnitudes, and operations, not in application of his knowledge to the construction of a bridge or a building. The engineer, on the other hand, is interested precisely in the construction of objects such as bridges. The first kind of knowledge is called *speculative* or *theoretical* knowledge; the second kind is called *practical* knowledge. These two differ primarily by their *object*. Speculative knowledge concerns an object about which nothing is done directly, and hence the object is nonoperable. Practical knowledge, on the contrary, is concerned precisely with an object insofar as it is operable.

1

Our initial concern is to state precisely what kind of knowledge or science ethics is. In terms of the fundamental distinction we have just given, we can ask, first of all, whether ethics is speculative or practical knowledge. We can presume, in raising this question, the common understanding of ethics as a treatise on the moral life. Our question might then be phrased in the following way. Do we seek primarily a speculative knowledge of moral doctrine, or do we seek primarily the practical knowledge of how to act well morally? Is contemplation the end of ethical inquiry, or are we seeking rather to examine how human actions are to be performed? This question is not altogether simple to answer. In choosing either alternative, we run into difficulties. If we say that ethics is a speculative science, we appear to deny the fact that ethics is generally admitted to be concerned with the good life, clearly a practical matter. If we say that ethics is practical in the sense that it considers how individual acts should be done, we appear to deny that ethics is a science at all, for no science extends to the completely practical order of singular actions. Moreover, in the completely practical order where we are confronted with the problem of acting here and now, knowledge of moral principles alone is not a sufficient guide for good action, as experience amply manifests.

Purely Speculative and Completely Practical Knowing

Stating the two alternatives above in the manner in which we did, we proposed two extremes within the order of knowing. Let us call the first *purely speculative knowledge*. In purely speculative knowledge, truth is sought on the part of both the *object known* and the *knower*. The object known, such as a mathematical object, is not subject to any kind of operation or activity. Similarly, the mathematician as knower has no intention of doing anything with or about the object, at least in any proper sense of doing or making. He is, as we say, a "pure" mathematician. Such speculative knowledge is wholly removed from any practical consideration, and it is for this reason that we designate it as *purely* speculative. It is clear, from this explanation of speculative knowledge, that ethics is not a purely speculative science, for it certainly includes practical considerations.

Let us call the second alternative *completely practical knowing*. In completely practical knowing we are concerned with an object that is operable, either with doing something, such as voting for a candidate for public office, or with making something, for example a chair. In the making of the chair our knowing is ordered to the actual construction of the chair, not merely to an understanding of how to make the chair, and hence both the *manner* of knowing and the *intention* of the knower is operative. Such knowing is wholly removed from any speculative consideration, and therefore we designate it as *completely* practical knowing. Now, while this alternative might seem to approximate more closely what a treatise on the moral life should be, a moment's reflection will indicate that it is not the kind of knowing we shall be engaged in when studying ethics, for such completely practical knowing is quite distinct from any *science*. The actual *making* of something or the actual *doing* of something goes beyond the limits of any science. True enough, ethics is concerned with human action but, being a science, it cannot deal with human action as it actually occurs.

At the outset, therefore, we must eliminate two extremes of knowing from the kind of knowing that is proper to ethics. It should be noted, however, that some moral philosophers have identified ethics with one or the other of these extremes. Some have understood ethics to be a speculative and demonstrative science in the sense that mathematics or metaphysics is a science. In this view, ethics is a purely theoretical treatment of moral phenomena, approached and analyzed in a demonstrative manner similar to that in which a mathematician proceeds in Euclidean geometry. Such a conception and such a manner of approach does violence to the operable object of ethics and the practical end which it has in view. On the other hand, and perhaps as a reaction to the purely speculative treatment of ethics, some have tended to identify ethics with completely practical knowing. In so doing they have confused, among other things, the moral philosopher with the counselor. Ethics cannot tell you how to act at a given time and in particular circumstances, although, as we shall see, it will provide knowledge that will serve as a general guide for action. But completely practical knowing of what to do here and now is utterly distinct from any sort of science, speculative or practical.

The Definition of Ethics   (a)

If ethics is not a purely speculative science nor completely practical knowing, what sort of knowledge is it? We shall be able to resolve this problem by indicating why we need to study ethics and what we would like to know about moral life. This procedure will help us to understand more precisely what ethics is and, as a consequence, what kind of knowledge ethics is.

The common notion of ethics as a treatise on moral life suggests that to live well morally, i. e., to lead a good human life, is both necessary and desirable. Any human being wishes to lead as happy a life as possible, and we have no hesitancy in associating a good moral life with a happy life, for this association is one that agrees with the facts of ordinary experience and is in conformity with the traditional approach to the study of ethics from the time of the ancient Greeks. To live well morally requires at least a minimum knowledge of what it is to live well as a human being. The purpose of ethics, therefore, from the standpoint of the science itself, and from the viewpoint of the knower, is a practical one: to live well as a human being. Nothing could be more desirable nor more immediately necessary.

We may also consider, in a preliminary way, what we would like to know about moral life. In answering this question, we shall arrive at a definition of ethics, and the definition, in turn, will resolve the problem of what sort of knowledge ethics is.

Even the most superficial acquaintance with ordinary experience indicates that we live and act for the sake of achieving this or that goal or end. If we reflect upon the activities we engage in during the course of a day, we recognize that we do some things for the sake of other things, such as taking a train for the sake of arriving at a certain destination. We regard such action as worth the effort in proportion to the desirability of the end and to the effectiveness of the means for getting there. No one really denies that ethics is somehow concerned with such ends and means of human action. We thus see, first of all, that ethics is a science that deals with man as acting voluntarily for an end.

The word *voluntarily* is important for understanding what ethics means and what it is especially concerned to treat. As we shall see in detail in Chapter five, voluntary acts are acts which, in varying degrees, are under the control of the will, and such acts constitute what may be called the *material object* of the science of ethics. Such acts are distinctively *human acts*, acts willed in terms of what we know by reason. You have to know what and where a destination is before you can will to go there. These human or voluntary acts are distinguished from other acts which we can perform but which do not fall under the control of the will and the direction of reason; for example, acts of digestion. We mention the latter type of act in order to exclude it from the consideration of ethics. The material object of ethics, then, is the voluntary or human act as we have now described it.

However, ethics does not consider such human acts in haphazard fashion. We must consider these acts in a certain ordering. The word *end* now becomes important for understanding more formally what ethics means and what it especially must treat. The end to which human acts are ordered constitutes the *formal object* of ethics. We are naturally led to inquire, more specifically, what we mean by "end" and what such an end is. And this brings us to the most fundamental meaning of ethics as a science. It pertains to ethics to consider human acts as ordered to the *ultimate* end of man, that is, to the end of man as such. We may therefore propose as the definition of ethics that it is *the science which deals with those acts that proceed from the deliberative will of man, especially as they are ordered to the ultimate end of man.* Ethics is therefore the science of the ultimate end as such, for no other human science has this consideration as its formal concern. We shall have more to say about such an ultimate end in the next two chapters and in the final chapter. We speak, in the definition, of the "deliberative" will of man in order to emphasize that the will is specified in its operation by knowledge obtained through reason.

What Kind of Knowledge Is Ethics?

We can now return to the question of what kind of knowledge ethics is and, in the light of the definition of ethics we have given, resolve the question of whether ethics is speculative or practical knowledge. In a sense, we can say that ethics is both.

Let us consider, first, the sense in which ethics is practical. As a *science*, ethics is practical, and in this sense it is opposed to any speculative science. It is a practical science because it is concerned with the human act, an object that is clearly operable. Furthermore, the *mode of knowing* proper to ethics is a practical mode; that is, ethics concerns knowledge as it is ordered to operation. Contemplation, accordingly, is not the end of ethics, for we seek to know about something to be done, not simply to understand an object insofar as it is knowable. However, our intention in studying ethics is not to seek *immediately* how to act in this or that concrete situation, and in making this observation we distinguish ethics from the extreme of practical knowing described above as completely practical knowing. As we shall see later, the domain of completely practical knowing is that of either art or prudence, both of which are outside the limits of science. Art and prudence deal with the individual act here and now, whereas no science embraces the individual as such. While recognizing, then, that ethics is a practical science, let us designate it as *formally practical knowledge* to distinguish it from the completely practical knowing involved in the activity of art or of prudence.

Yet the truth attained in the science of ethics is speculative, and this is the sense in which ethics is speculative. It might seem paradoxical, at first glance, to say that we achieve speculative truth in a practical science. The paradox disappears when we contrast *speculative truth* with *practical truth* and see, as a consequence, the impossibility of attaining practical truth in any science. Let us note, first, that the common meaning of truth is the conformity of intellect with reality, of what we know with what is. It is this meaning of truth that we have in mind when we say, for example, that it is true that Washington is the capital of the United States of America. This common meaning of truth (it is not necessary, for our purpose here, to analyze the meaning of truth further) is speculative truth.

Practical truth is quite different. While the notion of truth must always indicate some relation between an intellect and an object, the relationship in practical truth is the contrary of that in speculative truth. In the case of art, for example, the relationship is one of a made object to the mind and will of the maker. For example, the shoemaker makes a shoe to conform with what he conceives a shoe to be and with what he intends and wills it to be. Practical truth, therefore, is a conforming of something made or done with the mind and right appetite of the maker or doer. Practical truth is thus a truth of action, not a truth of knowledge, and for this reason the truth attained in ethics cannot be practical truth, but must be the truth of knowledge, that is, speculative truth.

A summary answer to the question of what kind of knowledge ethics is may now be given by saying that ethics is *formally practical knowledge* and by briefly explaining what this phrase means. The words "practical knowledge" refer to the fact that ethics is a practical science, since ethical knowledge is ordered to operation. The word "formally" indicates, negatively, that the knowledge is not completely practical and, positively, that the truth attained in ethics is speculative. Thus we shall seek to know, for example, what virtue is and what its divisions are, while also seeking to understand, though in a general way, how to realize virtue in operation.

The Method of Ethics b)

The preceding remarks lead us to consider the *method* that is appropriate to the science of ethics. Since ethics is a practical science, though the truth attained is speculative, tne method will be one appropriate to a practical science. In a practical science, since knowledge is directed to knowing how something can be done, it is necessary to proceed in a *compositive* way. We shall best understand the compositive method of ethics by contrasting it with the method of a speculative science.

In a speculative science, the end sought is simply knowledge itself, the contemplation of what is true. In general, the method by which such knowledge is attained is the method of *resolution*. We use the name "resolution" because we seek to *resolve* an effect to its cause, since to know a thing in a speculative way is to know it as the effect of some cause. This resolutory method is also described as reducing the complex to something simpler, for an effect is something complex in relation to its cause. We proceed in such a fashion when we refer the ability man has to appreciate humor to its cause, the rational nature of man; the effect—ability to laugh— is seen in its cause, rationality.

The compositive method of ethics proceeds in a contrary manner, by applying causes to effects and by proceeding from the simpler to the more complex. This method is in conformity with knowing something in a practical way, namely knowing how something can be done. A practical science such as ethics is not concerned with universal principles and causes for their own sake, but for the application that can be made of them to directing operation. We do not mean that ethics applies universal principles directly to *singular* acts, for this completely compositive mode of procedure is achieved only by prudence or art in the completely practical order. For example, when you decide here and now that you should not steal this object, you are in the order of prudence and no longer merely in the order of practical science. But so far as possible in ethics, we apply common or general considerations to less and less common determinations. Thus, we seek not only to know what virtue is and what the cause of virtue is, but also to understand more in particular how to acquire virtue. Hence, we see how practical considerations always affect the knowledge we attain in ethics. This emphasis on the compositive mode in a practical science is not, however, inconsistent with the fact that the truth in ethics is achieved in a speculative mode. To a degree, therefore, the resolutive mode proper to speculative knowing is also found in ethics, but subordinated to the compositive mode that primarily characterizes ethics.

The Certitude Possible in Ethics

Allied to the question of the method of ethics is the question of the certitude of ethics. The compositive method of ethics, as we have seen, proceeds from universal principles to more particular determinations, which we have also described as proceeding from what is simple to what is complex. In ethics, then, we derive our principles from ordinary experience and then apply them to the multiplicity of human acts which can be performed. This compositive mode limits the certitude of ethics in at least two ways.

First, the subject matter of ethics is *variable*, since it consists of free human acts. (It is because the subject matter of ethics is variable that we need experience of human acts both to derive the principles of ethics and subsequently to apply them. In a speculative science, e.g., mathematics, the subject matter is not variable, and hence little experience is needed.) It is this variability of subject matter that prevents our having absolute certitude in all parts of moral knowledge. Unlike a speculative science, ethics cannot simply deduce the particular from the universal; we must take into account the particular situations to which the universal moral principle is applied. Hence, certitude of knowledge in ethics is limited by the variability of the subject matter, especially with regard to conclusions drawn from the principles, that is, with regard to the application of a principle to particular matters.

Second, even the universal principles in ethics have an element of uncertainty about them. We have already mentioned that the principles of ethics are derived from our experience of human affairs, but it is not in this respect that the universal principles of ethics lack certainty. Indeed, in this precise respect there is certainty about the principles of ethics, for we obtain them by induction. The uncertainty about the principles of ethics arises from the fact that they are remote from action, the end of a practical science. Universal reasoning in ethics, though often certain in itself, is insufficient and lacking in certitude in relation to particular action. The reason is that in going from the universal to particular determinations we have to take into account more and more the circumstances surrounding human action, about which there is less certainty. For example, the principle *stealing is wrong* is certain (when sufficiently defined and explained), but its certainty may be diminished in trying to apply it to complex human actions.

The certitude of a practical science such as ethics, therefore, is not as great as that of a purely speculative science, nor should we presume it to be so. To avoid possible misunderstanding, however, we do not mean to deny certainty in all respects to ethics, for to the extent we can attain speculative truth about moral doctrine, we can have certitude. The certitude becomes qualified, as we have indicated, in relation to the order of action and insofar as ethics is a practical science. Here, also, a possible misunderstanding about the order of concrete action should be eliminated. The general position we are taking does not assume that when we act here and now we are always in a state of uncertainty. We normally have what can be called *practical* certainty when we act in particular circumstances. This practical certainty comes not from the knowledge we have about the act to be performed, but from the ordering of the will to the end sought. This is the certitude proper to prudence, and derives from the disposition of the appetite.

Ethics and Moral Theology

Theology, as a science, draws conclusions from principles that are given by God in revelation and are accepted on faith by man. St. Paul, for example, argues from the resurrection of Christ to the general resurrection. Moral theology is one part of theology, and it treats of human acts as they are ordered to a supernatural end. the intuitive vision of God. Ethics, as we have seen, is that part of philosophy which treats of human acts as they are ordered to a natural ultimate end. Through revelation we learn that man, because of his elevation to the supernatural order, wherein he operates through both grace and reason as principles of direction, should order all his actions to a supernatural end. This being the case, a question arises not only about the relation of ethics to moral theology, but also about the adequacy of ethics as a science of moral action, at least for a Christian.

Let us consider first the question of the relationship between ethics and moral theology. Formally speaking, ethics and moral theology are specifically different sciences. They have distinct objects and they proceed from specifically distinct principles; ethics from principles known by reason to be evident and true, moral theology from principles accepted as true on faith through revelation. This formal difference between sciences is in no way compromised by the fact that man is ordered ultimately to a supernatural end. The addition of revealed knowledge and of the supernatural order of grace does not invalidate the knowledge we can have of the natural moral order. A whole new dimension is added, but the natural order is not thereby eliminated.

The question still remains, however, as to whether ethics is adequate as a science of moral action if man is ordered to an end that is wholly beyond a natural ultimate end known by reason. We do not propose to answer this question in any detail here, for we shall consider it more fully in the last chapter of the book; and indeed it can be faced comprehensively only when a final resolution is sought about the problem of a natural ultimate end. Here we are concerned only to show that, so far as the demands of a practical science are concerned, ethics is true knowledge about what we can know by reason with respect to the natural moral order. Ethics is adequate, in other words, as formally practical knowledge. With regard to the completely practical order—the order of acting here and now in singular circumstances—man needs the proportionate means of grace to attain the good of the supernatural order and the complete good of the natural order as well. In this respect ethics is inadequate, but so also is moral theology in the sense that no science as science is ever adequate in relation to the completely practical order where rectitude of appetite is necessary for performing singular acts.

Only one additional point need be made now. It is true that the Christian has the tremendous advantage and privilege of being assured through revelation what his ultimate end fully and truly is, and what the precise means are for attaining it. The salvation of a human being does not depend on his acquiring either the science of moral theology or of ethics. But the Christian who seeks an integral education should accept the required means of achieving such an education and should observe the order of learning. The grasp of moral theology as a science presupposes the grasp of ethics as a science, since moral theology presumes the understanding of moral truths known by reason in order to employ such truths for its own development as a science, for example the analysis and definition of a human act. Hence, a person who seeks to be an educated Christian cannot dispense with the grasp of natural moral truth in the light of reason itself.

Consequently, ethics is not only adequate in the sense described, but desirable and necessary as well. With respect to the Christian who seeks to be educated fully as a human being, ethics is both desirable and necessary for the sake of understanding well the truths of moral theology and for communicating with the non-

Christian with whom he can share only the truths of the natural moral order. With respect to the non-Christian, the truths of ethics are as necessary for him as for the Christian; in addition, in grasping sound moral doctrine, the non-Christian may become disposed to accept the truths of Christian revelation.

REVIEW QUESTIONS

1. Explain the distinction between speculative knowledge and practical knowledge.
2. Describe purely speculative knowledge.
3. Describe completely practical knowing.
4. Why cannot ethics be purely speculative knowledge?
5. Why cannot ethics be completely practical knowing?
6. What is the material object of ethics?
7. What is the formal object of ethics?
8. State and explain the definition of ethics.
9. Why must ethics be a practical science?
10. In what sense can it be said that ethics is also speculative?
11. Distinguish between speculative truth and practical truth.
12. What does the phrase *formally practical knowledge* mean?
13. Explain the method of ethics. How does it differ from the method of a speculative science?
14. Why is the subject matter of ethics variable?
15. Are the principles of ethics certain? Explain.
16. To what extent is certitude possible in ethics?
17. What is moral theology?
18. How are moral theology and ethics distinct as sciences?
19. Is ethics adequate as a science?
20. How is ethics both desirable and necessary?

DISCUSSION

1. The distinction between speculative and practical knowledge is untenable. There is no knowledge that is not in some way ordered to activity of some kind or to some practical consideration. No knowledge can be sought merely for its own sake, for what we

know we put to use sooner or later. All knowledge, therefore, is practical at least to some extent.

2. The distinction between speculative and practical science is invalid. Every science proves statements of one kind or another, whether its object is knowledge itself or activity. Consequently, every science is speculative, including ethics, which has activity as its object.

3. If ethics is to be regarded as a practical science, it must be concerned with an operable object, that is, action. But action is always individual, for it is this act or that act which is done. No science, however, deals with the individual as individual. Therefore, either ethics is a speculative science or it is not a science at all.

4. Ethics cannot guide a person's action completely in a particular situation under particular circumstances, for such knowing is completely practical. On the other hand, ethics cannot be a purely theoretical treatment of moral phenomena. Therefore, ethics can only be understood as a history of moral opinions held by different authorities at various times.

5. No acts of a human being are wholly rational and voluntary, for a human being acts as a unified whole and not just as a part. But there are no distinct rational or voluntary parts of a human being, and even if there were, they would be conditioned by other factors of human activity, both conscious and unconscious. The definition of ethics which limits ethics to the voluntary acts of a human being is, therefore, inadequate if not altogether wrong.

6. The common meaning of truth is a conforming of what we know with what is. Since ethics is a practical science, its truth must be a conforming of what we know with action. Consequently, the truth of ethics is practical, not speculative.

7. The compositive method consists in applying universal principles immediately to singular actions. But this method is achieved only by prudence in the completely practical order. Since ethics is a science, its method cannot be compositive. On the other hand, the method of ethics cannot be resolutive either, for this method belongs to a speculative science and ethics is a practical science. Therefore, ethics has no proper method.

8. Every science, speculative or practical, has to proceed from principles that are true and certain. But the principles of ethics are not certain, for the variability of the subject matter of ethics excludes certainty. Hence, ethics is not really a science.

9. Whatever certainty may be attributed to ethics as a science is qualified when principles are applied to action. In the concrete or-

der, consequently, one's knowledge of how to act is no longer certain. Therefore, one can never act with certainty in the completely practical order.

10. The ultimate end for Christians is a supernatural end given by revelation and accepted by faith. Moreover, a human being is elevated by grace to a supernatural mode of action. Ethics, as natural moral knowledge, is therefore insufficient and inadequate for a Christian as a science of moral doctrine.

SUGGESTED READINGS

Aristotle, *Nicomachean Ethics*, Book I, chaps. 1-3. Consult *Introduction to Aristotle*, edited by R. P. McKeon. New York: Modern Library, 1947, pp. 308-543.

St. Thomas Aquinas, *Commentary on Aristotle's Ethics*, Lessons I-III, *in X Libros Ethicorum Aristotelis ad Nicomachum*, edited by A. Pirotta. Turin: Marietta, 1934.

Albert, Denise and Peterfreund, *Great Traditions in Ethics*. New York: American Book Co., 1953, chap. XV, "Ethics as Emotive Expression," pp. 324-349.

Ayer, A., *Language, Truth, and Logic*. New York: Dover Publications, 1946, chap. VI, pp. 103-112.

Bourke, V., *Ethics*. New York: Macmillan, 1951, chap. I, pp. 3-25.

Cronin, M., *The Science of Ethics*. Dublin: Gill, 1939, Vol. I, chap. I, pp. 1-27.

Dewey, J., *The Quest for Certainty*. New York: Minton, Balch and Co., 1929, chap. X, pp. 255-284. Consult Albert Denise and Peterfreund, *op. cit.*, chap. XIII, pp. 279-303.

Kant, I., *Foundations of the Metaphysics of Morals*, preface and secs. I-III. Consult Melden, A., *Ethical Theories*. Englewood Cliffs: Prentice-Hall, 1955, pp. 292-340.

Nowell-Smith, P., *Ethics*. London: Penguin Books, 1954, chaps. 1-2, pp. 11-35.

Renard, H., *The Philosophy of Morality*. Milwaukee: Bruce, 1953, Intro. pp. 1-10.

Sidgwick, H., *The Methods of Ethics*, Book I, chap. 3; Book III, chaps. 13-14. Consult Melden, A., *Ethical Theories*, pp. 425-457.

Stevenson, C., *Ethics and Language*. New Haven: Yale University Press, 1946, chaps. I-II, pp. 1-36.

Tsanoff, R., *Ethics*. New York: Harper, 1947, chap. I, pp. 3-22.

Wheelwright, P., *A Critical Introduction to Ethics*. New York: Odyssey Press, 1949, chaps. 1-2, pp. 3-60.

II

The problem of the ultimate end

Since any science begins with principles upon which all other knowledge attained in the science depends, we shall begin with a consideration of the first principle of ethics. The first principle of a practical science must be related to action, and since ethics deals with human action, whatever is the principle of human action will be the first principle of ethics. This principle, evident from our experience, is that all human acts are directed to some good. Following the method of ethics, let us investigate what this principle means so that we shall be able to see how and to what extent it can direct our activity. In this chapter we shall use an inductive and dialectical approach to investigate the first principle of ethics and to establish the fundamental terms used in ethics.

In arriving at a definition of ethics in Chapter I,

we spoke of ethics as the science which considers man as acting voluntarily for an end. When we say now that all human actions are directed to some good, we intend to associate the word "good" with the word "end." The meaning of "good," as we first use it in ethics, is very broad. It signifies anything that appears desirable to us, for the most common aspect about anything we designate as "good" is that it attracts our desire or appetite. Whatever is good, consequently, can be identified with whatever is desirable, and this identification is confirmed daily in our ordinary experience. We do whatever we do because of what we desire, and what we desire we have apprehended as good for us. Hence, the first principle of ethics states a most universal point that we find immediately applicable to every action of our life: *all men seek the good.*

Nevertheless, at least three objections can be raised against this basic principle of ethics. First, the principle is so universal it seems meaningless. The universal formulation of the principle misleads us into thinking that it tells us much when, in fact, it tells us very little. Even if the principle is admitted to be true, it is without any real value because of its extreme generality.

We must grant, in replying to this objection, that any first principle, whether in a speculative science or in a practical science, tells us very little and precisely for the reason that it is only a starting point, and hence it must be as universal as possible. The content of its meaning develops only as we see how all other moral knowledge depends upon it. Like the principle of contradiction, it says very little initially, and yet nothing else is true unless it is true. Without the self-evident truth that all men desire the good, nothing else would even be understood in ethics. The full meaning and relevance, then, of the first principle of ethics will be seen at the completion of ethics, not at the beginning.

Another objection to the principle is that we often desire what seems to be evil rather than what is good. This objection, however, is not a relevant difficulty, for it fails to take into account how broad the initial meaning of "good" is. As we have noted, we identify the meaning of "good" with "desirable." We have also noted that this identification agrees with the facts of experience, for everyone does seek the good in the sense that he seeks what he desires. The principle states no more than this. Whether what is actually sought in this or that case is really good and really desirable is another question. The point is that no one desires what is in fact evil except under the appearance of good. The objection does raise an important difficulty, not about the principle, but about the application of the principle to complex situations. The question of what is really good and desirable and what is not is one of the most important questions in ethics. However, we can begin to answer it only as we acquire moral knowledge. Indeed, the question cannot even arise unless we first see the universal truth of the principle that no one seeks anything except insofar as it appears desirable to him.

The third objection is as follows. If we state that all men seek the good, we imply that all human actions must be for an end, since everything we seek is in terms of some end as it appears good. Now the objection can be made that the good, taken as an end, cannot be a *cause* of action, for an end is what is last in an action. It is in this sense we say that the end of a race does not occur until the finish line is crossed. But a cause must refer to something that happens first, otherwise the action would not begin, and so an end does not appear to be a cause, but rather an effect. The end and the good, therefore, must be distinguished from each other and, if so, it does not follow that all human acts are for an end.

In this objection, there is a failure to understand how the good, precisely as an end, is a cause. It is true, in one sense, that an end is last in execution, for it is the last thing to happen. But in another sense the end is first, not in the order of execution, but in the order of intention. The one who performs an action must first intend something, and it is in this sense that the end is a cause. Consequently, while the runner will not gain victory until he crosses the finish line, nevertheless he would not run at all unless he first willed to gain the victory. Hence, the end and the good can be associated with each other, and all human acts are still for an end in the sense in which we have explained it.

The last objection is important on two scores. First, it brings out the important distinction between an end that is last in execution and an end that is first in intention, a basic distinction in ethics. Secondly, this objection leads us to investigate further the meaning of "end" as a good that is desired. Ethics, as a practical science, properly begins with an analysis of the end to which human action is ordered. First, however, we must make the general distinction between ends and means.

Ends and Means

The common meaning of an end is *that for the sake of which an agent acts.* We sometimes use the word "purpose" to express this meaning of end, but the normal use of the word "purpose" is narrower than the use of the word "end." An agent can act for an end with or without being explicitly aware of it, and hence we can legitimately speak of every action being ordered to some end. If we were to substitute "purpose" in the previous sentence, we would become involved in unnecessary difficulty and need of clarification, since "purpose" usually means acting consciously for an end.

The statements "all men seek the good" and "all men act for an end" are materially the same, but formally different. They are the same in the sense that the appetite—both the will and the sense appetite—of man is attracted by any end as a good, real or apparent. The difference is that, formally speaking, the good is the *object* of the appetite whereas the end *moves* the appetite. *What* we desire is a good; we *act for it* because we wish to attain it. An automobile appears as a good to us, but we work and earn money to buy it for ourselves. Subject to this qualification of meaning, "good" and "end" can be used interchangeably.

Now it is a matter of ordinary experience that we do some things for the sake of others. We earn money to buy the car. We are thus led to acknowledge a general difference between a *means* and an *end.* In our example, a car is an end, since we use the money to get the car. Money, on the other hand, is a means, since we wish it, not for the sake of itself, but for something else. The primary distinction between an end and a means, therefore, is the difference between something sought for itself and something sought for the sake of something else.

It is evident, also from experience, that some things can be an end in one respect and a means in another. Clothes, for example, can be an end with respect to money; clothes can also be a means with respect to something else as an end, for example, good appearance.

Then, again, good appearance can be a means in relation to getting a better position which, in turn, can be a means to getting something else. Could we continue endlessly willing *this* thing as an end, and then as a means to *that* thing, then *that* thing as a means to something else, and so on? If we literally meant *endlessly*, we would not be able to will any thing as an end, that is, simply for the sake of itself. But unless we will something simply for the sake of itself, we shall not be able to will any thing else as a means toward it. If we could not will any thing as an end and therefore could not will any thing as a means, i.e., if we are not able to will any thing at all, then we could not act in any fashion whatsoever.

We are led, therefore, to acknowledge that there must be at least one thing—possibly more—which must be willed for itself and not for something else. We are likewise led to acknowledge that there must be at least one end—possibly more—which is never a means. Let us call such an end an *ultimate end.*

Is there also something which is never willed for itself, but only for the sake of something else? Is there, in other words, something which is a means but never an end? Money might seem to be an example. In itself, it has no value; its worth lies in what it can be used for, namely, buying things. If there are things like this, then they will be means which never become ends. Let us call them *pure means.*

We have, then, three distinctions which are made evident from ordinary experience:

An ultimate end:	Something willed only for itself.
An end-means:	Something willed for itself, but also for other things.
A pure means:	Something willed only for the sake of other things.

The Ultimate End

It is to the ultimate end that we must turn our attention in the beginning of ethics. If there is some end for everything that we do and for the sake of which we will everything else, clearly such an end matters most and will be the greatest good of all; otherwise, we would not will everything else for it. The only question is whether there is such an ultimate end for all human action.

There is a sense in which the question seems easy to answer. We suggested such an answer when we said that unless there was something for which everything else is willed, nothing could be willed or done at all. How would it be possible *always* to be willing something for the sake of something else? There has to be some ultimate goal at which to aim, otherwise, as we have seen, we would not will or do anything at all. On the other hand, even if we grant that there must be some ultimate end, must it be one and the same end always and in all circumstances? We note two things from experience which seem to suggest a negative answer to this question. First, we do not always seem to have the same end in view in our actions; we shift from one thing we want more than anything else to something else we want more than anything else. Secondly, it often seems as though there is no *one* thing that is more desirable than everything else.

An even graver difficulty is whether, granting each one of us does have one end for which he does everything else, it follows that everyone has the same end. There seems to be an extraordinary diversity of such ends for different persons. Yet, if we take the position that there is such diversity of ultimate ends, how can there be any real science of ethics? As we have already noted, a practical science like ethics must have a common and objective principle from which to start, but if there is only diversity and relativity about its very starting point, ethics cannot be scientific in any legitimate meaning of the term. It would not be worth our while merely to catalogue sentimental preferences for ultimate ends. Nevertheless, can we deny that there is a great deal of diversity about that for the sake of which we will everything else? Let us try to answer these questions and difficulties by investigating more precisely what an ultimate end means as it is considered in ethics.

As we have already remarked, the common meaning of *ultimate end* is that for which all other things are willed. How universal is the "all" in this phrase? Do we mean "all" absolutely or relatively? We can speak, for example, of the ultimate end of an army, or of the military order. Such an end—victory—is an ultimate end in the sense that all military activity, in defense or attack, is ordered to victory, but such an ultimate end is relative to only one sphere of activity. There is, to take another example, an ultimate end in the political order, the common good of the political society. But this end also, though ultimate in its order, and more ultimate than the military because it is more fundamental, still seems to be relative to a distinct sphere of activity.

We can speak, however, of an ultimate end in the moral order, and when we do we seem to be referring to an ultimate end without qualification. But to be sure that we understand fully what such an ultimate end is, we must keep distinct any *relative* ultimate end, such as victory in war, from an *absolute* ultimate end—something that is an end beyond that of any particular order. It may well be that relative ultimate ends are closely connected with such an absolute ultimate end, perhaps in some way being even a part of such an end, but a difference always remains between an end proper to one order and an end transcending all particular orders. We can state this same point by saying that we are seeking to establish the end of man, not as he is a soldier, an artist, or a statesman, but as he is a man without qualification.

There is a difference to be noted also between the end consid- ered on the part of the *object* and the end considered on the part of the *subject*, that is, the agent as attaining and possessing the ob- ject. Thus, in the case of a candidate running for public office—the governorship of a state, for example—the office is an end in the sense of end as an object. The candidate's actual attaining and pos- sessing this office, upon election, is the end with respect to the subject seeking it. Hence, the object in which an ultimate end con- sists is not the same as the attainment and possession of that object.

We can now return to our main problem of whether there is an absolute ultimate end for human action. We can now give an argu- ment to show that there must be some absolute ultimate end for all human life, and in this argument we shall be speaking of the end with respect to the subject seeking it, not with respect to the end considered on the part of the object. This argument has been already suggested, but we can now express it more fully, although in a simplified form.

If there were no end of any kind at all, nothing would be willed or desired. Nothing could be desired as an end, because there would be none; nothing could be desired as a means, because if there is no end nothing can be desired as a means. But since we do in fact desire things, it is impossible that there be no end at all. Some end, therefore, must exist. But if there were no ultimate end, there would be no other kind of end either. Therefore, there is at least an absolute ultimate end, whether there are other ends or not; otherwise, nothing at all could be desired, and this is certainly contrary to the facts of experience.

This argument is a negative one insofar as it shows that unless one admits an absolute ultimate end, one is reduced to the absurdity of denying all desire. This kind of argument is used to prove only *that* there is such an end. Before we go on to consider the more important question of *what* such an ultimate end is, we must acknowledge that difficulties can be raised against the argument we have given. Some of them can be met only as we proceed further in ethics, but one of them can be removed now. The argument as given does not imply that one must always be actually thinking of the absolute ultimate end in every desire he has and in every action he does. It is neither necessary nor possible that one do so. Everyone, however, will be at least *implicitly* directed toward some ultimate end. And whenever a major decision has to be faced or a crisis resolved, we shall then explicitly give our attention to whatever we want above everything else. The situation is analogous to walking along a road. We are aware, without explicitly taking into account at each step of the journey, what our destination is. When we come to a crossroad, we find ourselves making a deliberate choice in terms of the end of our journey. It is the same in life taken as a whole. We have some ultimate end in view, but we do not have to advert to it all the time. We do advert to it, however, when we have major decisions to make.

What Is the Ultimate End?

There is one sense in which it is easy to answer the question of *what* the ultimate end of human life is. Everyone agrees that happiness is the ultimate end; everyone agrees, that is, in the sense that everyone in fact *wills* happiness above everything else. We can therefore restate our first principle of ethics to read *all men seek happiness*. True enough, this way of expressing the principle adds little to the prior formulation, *all men seek the good*; nevertheless, an additional point is made. This point is that no human being can avoid seeking happiness as his ultimate end or, to state the point positively, every human being desires his complete well-being, i.e., his happiness. This is a fact about human nature readily observed by anyone in his own desires and action and observable in the desires and action of everyone else.

Difficulties arise when we try to state more precisely what happiness means and especially when we try to understand in what happiness consists. We understand happiness, first of all, in a general way as the complete good. By the complete good, we mean that which fully satisfies our will. When we say, then, that everyone seeks happiness as the ultimate end, we mean simply that everyone desires complete satisfaction. Everyone desires happiness in this sense, and this part of the problem is not difficult to resolve.

The real difficulty begins in trying to establish in what happiness consists. It is easy enough to say everyone wishes complete happiness, but it is not easy to determine the *object* of happiness. What we now wish to know, therefore, is what definite thing or object the general notion of happiness refers to. What is it that will produce happiness in us? According to this understanding of happiness, not all men seek happiness, since not all men know where to look for happiness or know objectively what constitutes happiness. There is, indeed, great diversity among men about the objective realization of happiness, contrary to the universal acceptance of the general notion of happiness as the complete satisfaction of all desire.

In seeking to establish the objective realization of happiness, we must follow a mode of inquiry appropriate to ethics by using an inductive approach. We begin, in an inductive approach, with what is more knowable to us, the singular event or the observed fact. In the present case, the starting point is the opinions men hold on this matter, for a sound opinion is based on observed facts. By means of investigating various opinions, we may be able to arrive at some determination of the object or activity in which happiness is realized. But not all opinions on this matter need be investigated, otherwise our task would be endless. We need to take into account only those views on happiness which appear to be reasonable and worthy of consideration.

Opinions on What Happiness Is

The opinion that happiness consists in a life of *pleasure* deserves attention first because it seems to be the opinion most men hold, either expressly in what they say or at least implicitly in what they do. It is easy to understand why such a view is held since pleasure, in its strict meaning, is the satisfaction of the senses, and sense satisfaction is obvious and immediate. Thus, we delight spontaneously in the taste of food and drink, in the hearing of beautiful sounds, in the seeing of beautiful sights, and so on. We experience powerful urges impelling us to delight in sense pleasure of all kinds. The immediacy and vehemence of sense delight is probably the main reason so many identify happiness with pleasure. The ethical theory advocating the life of pleasure as happiness is known as *hedonism*, a name taken from the Greek meaning "pleasure."

This opinion runs into difficulties on several scores. The most serious difficulty is that pleasure does not satisfy the whole of man, nor even the best part of man. Man, in fact, shares sense pleasure with animals, and since it is evident that man can be happy in a way that an animal cannot be, pleasure would not seem to provide the sort of happiness suitable to a human being. Another difficulty is that any pleasure is shortlived; it may be intense, but it never lasts. In seeking happiness, however, we wish to attain something that will not be intermittent and transitory but, if possible, continual and as long lasting as possible. Finally, any sense pleasure is necessarily restricted and at best a decidedly limited good. In fact, when sense pleasure is carried to excess, it turns into its contrary, pain, and no one regards pain as productive of happiness.

Another opinion claiming many adherents is one maintaining that *wealth* produces happiness. Perhaps there are few who would categorically state that wealth is identical with happiness, but there appear to be many who *act* as though they sought wealth above everything else. It is not uncommon to find persons who will sacrifice health, comfort, honor, friends—almost anything—for the sake of wealth. In a highly industrial society, wealth assumes a proportionately great importance and therefore may be easily presumed to constitute happiness more than anything else.

Nevertheless, it is not difficult to see that wealth of itself will not produce happiness, much less be identified with happiness. Natural wealth, consisting in such things as clothing, food, and shelter, cannot be identified with happiness, for these things are chosen in order to survive and therefore they operate more as a means, whereas happiness is admittedly an end. Artificial wealth, chiefly in the form of money, holds even less claim since it is only a means to natural wealth, itself primarily a means. On any score, wealth cannot be identified with happiness or with any end; the surprising thing is that so many persons seem to act as though wealth could be an ultimate end. Perhaps they are really thinking of something like social security or provision for retirement in old age. Viewed in this way, wealth might be regarded as an end, though certainly not the ultimate end. At best, wealth or financial security can only provide an opportunity for realizing happiness. A sign that wealth is quite distinct from happiness is the fact that often persons with great wealth are notably unhappy, and unhappy in proportion as they are burdened with responsibilities and problems arising from their wealth.

Some men appear to do everything for the sake of *power*, and hence they think having power brings complete satisfaction. This tendency is most evident in the political sphere. In a totalitarian state, for example, the impression is given that everything is subordinated to the absolute exercise of power by the ruler or rulers over subjects. On a lesser scale, a person may also seek power above everything else, for example, in commercial associations, in unions, or even in purely domestic affairs.

Difficulties easily arise about the selection of power as that which constitutes happiness. Like wealth, it is more a means than an end. One seeks power not really for its own sake but as a means of achieving something else. But there is a more serious difficulty about selecting power as the ultimate end. Power implies the beginning of action, not its completion; with power, one is *on the way* to realizing something, rather than actually having the realization. Furthermore, it is evident that power can be used for good or evil, and often the exercise of power produces the very opposite of happiness—misery.

Health seems to be held by some as constituting happiness. While few would explicitly say health is identical with happiness, nevertheless a certain number of persons act as though health were the ultimate good, whether health is understood very generally as physical well-being or more specifically as good appearance, good muscular condition, and so on. In modern times, the emphasis given to beauty aids, vitamin pills, and body treatment gives the general impression that physical well-being most of all constitutes happiness for many persons.

The difficulty about making health or the good of the body generally the equivalent of happiness is that, like sense pleasure, it is limited and transitory. Health is never so well developed that illness cannot strike suddenly. Good appearance can be maintained only so long, and not all the time at that. At best, we can never be fully satisfied, no matter how well developed the body becomes. The reason is not difficult to find, for a human being is more than just a body; his specifically human enjoyment is related more to the living principle in man which we call a *soul*. There is no denying, of course, that a good condition of the body is important and necessary, yet to attach more importance to bodily goods than to goods pertaining to the soul is to invite genuine unhappiness sooner or later.

For this reason others have looked to some good of the soul for the answer to what happiness consists in. *Honor* or *good reputation*, though properly an external good, nevertheless appears to have a close relation to the good of the soul. It is certainly a higher good than any good of the body, a good, in fact, which implies a certain nobility of character. There seems to be reason for thinking that a person held in high honor is one who has achieved genuine happiness. Hence some persons, particularly in the political sphere, seem to will everything else for the attainment of honor.

However, it is difficult to see how happiness could consist in honor. By honor we mean, strictly, a sign of excellence paid to a person; accordingly, honor is more of a consequence following upon a person's good state than the state itself. It may well be connected with happiness, but it would not seem of itself to constitute happiness. Furthermore, honor is not precisely an end for which a person should strive; it is a recognition other persons should pay to him because of some other good he has.

The consideration of honor leads one to think of something like *virtue*. Virtue, like honor, belongs to the distinctively human part of man; it is a good of the soul rather than of the body. It is even better than honor, since honor is paid to those who have virtue of one kind or another. Some have thought, therefore, that virtue constitutes happiness, and there seems to be considerable reason for such an opinion. If we understand virtue correctly, and not in a narrow, puritanical sense, it is not difficult to see how virtue might be considered as the highest good, as something sought for itself and not for something else. We say, for example, that "virtue is its own reward."

But even virtue does not seem to constitute the supreme good in which happiness is realized. The common meaning of virtue is a good habit of operation, but presumably a man can have good habits without being in a state of happiness. A further difficulty is the fact that virtue is ordered to activity and therefore appears to be still a means to something else. Nevertheless, it is undoubtedly true that virtue is more necessary for happiness than something like honor or any good of the body. Hence, although it may be that virtue is not happiness, happiness may not be possible at all without virtue.

Some maintain that *knowledge* constitutes happiness. The reason for selecting knowledge is that it appears to be the most valuable thing a human being can acquire. Moreover, man seems to be, more than anything else, a knowing being; it is the possession of knowledge that particularly distinguishes man from any other living thing in the universe, especially the kind of knowledge we call speculative or theoretical. Man alone can contemplate and therefore, this opinion maintains, the unique quality of being able to achieve contemplation of truth constitutes happiness for man. Furthermore, the possession of knowledge seems to be permanent and satisfying to a degree not found in the other possibilities we have considered.

Attractive though this opinion may be, we cannot accept it if it runs counter to the facts of experience. The facts of experience do not seem to suggest that persons who have the most knowledge and who devote their time and effort primarily to acquiring knowledge are necessarily the happiest persons. It is quite possible for the scholar, the scientist, or the philosopher to be in a decidedly unhappy state. Furthermore, as experience again suggests, the acquiring of knowledge, especially speculative knowledge, is difficult and even painful for man. Indeed, contemplation may be too high an end for man to seek; it certainly appears to be so for most human beings. Nevertheless, like virtue, knowledge of some kind at least seems to have an intimate connection with human happiness, unless we were to take seriously the common saying "ignorance is bliss."

Summary of Opinions on Happiness

No one of the foregoing opinions seems to answer the question of what happiness consists in. Every view we have considered seems to fall short for one reason or another. Perhaps there are other views and opinions which might give the answer as to *where* and *in what* real happiness can be found. The list of opinions we have given may not be exhaustive, yet it is hard to think of anything else which would not fall, in some fashion, in the list we have considered. Indeed, if we summarize the opinions under the following triparte division of good, it seems apparent that we have considered all the main possibilities.

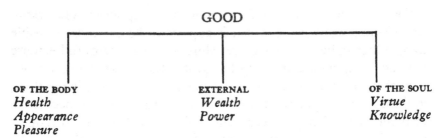

GOOD

OF THE BODY	EXTERNAL	OF THE SOUL
Health	*Wealth*	*Virtue*
Appearance	*Power*	*Knowledge*
Pleasure		

Undoubtedly we have not considered all possible answers which might be given, but it seems we have at least examined the three principal divisions one can make of the good. We have listed the most representative answers in each of the three divisions, which seem to represent an exhaustive division of the good. And surely happiness must be found in *some* good.

We seem to be in a peculiar situation. Our investigation appears to lead us to conclude that we cannot find out in what happiness consists. Presumably, then, we are not able to attain real happiness.

Yet, such a position is impossible on at least two scores. We already know there must be some ultimate end, and everyone agrees—at least verbally—that such an end is happiness. *That* there is such an end cannot be in real doubt; *what* it is constitutes the problem. Secondly, everyone by nature acts, at least implicitly, for such an end. Without some such end as a principle of operation no one would act at all.

Perhaps the explanation is that happiness is not merely *one* of the possibilities we have listed, but *all* of them. It would seem difficult, in fact, to be happy without including all of them, at least to some extent. If this is the case, then "one" ultimate end does not mean one in the sense of one in particular, but one generally. Here again, however, the facts of experience are suggestive, this time in terms of a warning. No one really acts in terms of something general: it is not enough to aim for happiness generally. No archer ever hit a target in general, nor is anyone ever really happy in general.

Our difficulty must be that we do not yet know enough to establish precisely in what happiness consists. Let us make a fresh start, therefore, and see if by other means we can find out definitely in what and how happiness is realized.

REVIEW QUESTIONS

1. What is the first principle of ethics and how do we arrive at it?
2. How can the first principle of ethics be reconciled with the fact that men often do evil acts?
3. Explain how the good, as end, is a cause of action.
4. What is the relation between "all men seek the good" and "all men act for an end"?
5. Can every end also be a means? Explain.
6. What is the meaning of ultimate end in ethics?
7. Distinguish between end considered on the part of the object and end considered on the part of the subject.
8. Is it possible to deny that there must be an absolute ultimate end? Explain.
9. What is the relation between "all men seek the good" and "all men seek happiness"?

10. In what sense do all men seek happiness? In what sense do all men not seek happiness?

11. Most men identify happiness with pleasure. Accept or reject with comment.

12. Give arguments for and against the identification of wealth with happiness.

13. Give arguments for and against the identification of health with happiness.

14. Give arguments for and against the identification of knowledge with happiness.

15. If any important opinion on what constitutes human happiness has been omitted, state it and indicate why it should be considered. If no important position has been omitted, indicate why the given list of opinions is adequate.

DISCUSSION

1. There is no evidence for concluding that there is an ultimate end for human life. Human beings live and reproduce because of some blind instinct which we cannot know. Indeed, we can have no adequate understanding of human nature, nor can we explain anything about man's many actions other than that he simply exists for a short period of time. Therefore, man has no end of any kind, much less an ultimate end.

2. Action implies an end. A series of actions implies a series of ends. A series of ends implies an ultimate end. Therefore, there must be an ultimate end.

3. Not all persons desire happiness. Some seek their own degeneration and destruction, as psychiatrists report. Therefore, the position that all men seek happiness is not true, and certainly is not self-evident.

4. The position that all men seek the good seems evident if we suppose that no one would do a certain act if he knew that as a result of that act something evil would happen. Nevertheless, experience amply manifests that at times men do perform acts which are admittedly evil. Since this is so, it cannot be true that all men seek the good.

5. Many persons seem to perform many of their acts by instinct or on the spur of the moment. In these instances, they have no thought of any end at all. Not only, then, is there no ultimate end for all human action, but there is not even an end of any kind for many acts done by human beings.

6. Every means has an end. Every action we perform is directed toward some end and, in turn, some ends are means to further ends. This is true even for living things other than human beings. For example, a plant reproduces in order to propagate the species, and the species exists to maintain some other form of life. The whole process cannot be cyclical, since no end generates its own means. Therefore, we have to acknowledge an ultimate end, not only for human beings, but for all living things as well.

7. Men can discover what is good or evil only by trial-and-error method. In the trial-and-error method, we do not know what is good or evil until we see how the action turns out. Consequently, we cannot know whether an end is good until we finally achieve it. If we cannot know whether the end is good, it makes no sense to say that all men seek the good.

8. In order to act for an ultimate end, one must will that ultimate end, for the end is the purpose for which a man acts. However, in order to will the ultimate end, one must know the ultimate end. But some men do not know or acknowledge any ultimate end for which they are striving. Nevertheless, such men do act, and thus there need not be an ultimate end for all action.

SUGGESTED READINGS

Aristotle, *Ethics*, Book I, chaps. 4-5.
St. Thomas, Commentary, Book I, Lessons IV-V.
St. Thomas, *Summa Contra Gentiles*, Book III, chaps. 1-3. Consult *On the Truth of the Catholic Faith, Summa Contra Gentiles*, Book III, Part I, translated by V. Bourke. New York: Doubleday, Image Books, 1956.

Adler, M., *A Dialectic of Morals*. South Bend: Notre Dame, 1941, chaps. II-III, pp. 12-46.
Bourke, *Ethics*, chap. II, pp. 27-35, 47-48.
Cronin, *The Science of Ethics*, Vol. I, chap. III, pp. 46-54.
Miltner, C., *The Elements of Ethics*. New York: Macmillan, 1941, chap. II, pp. 11-19.
Renard, *The Philosophy of Morality*, chap. I, pp. 11-27.
Stevenson, *Ethics and Language*, chap. VIII, pp. 174-205.
Ward, L., *Christian Ethics*. St. Louis: Herder, 1952, chap. 3, pp. 31-42.
Wild, J., *Introduction to Realistic Philosophy*. New York: Harper, 1948, chap. 2, pp. 39-46.

III

The problem of happiness

In the preceding chapter, we solved one problem and raised another. One problem about the ultimate end was solved in recognizing *that* there must be some ultimate end for all human action. In seeking to establish more precisely *what* such an ultimate end is, we raised another problem which we did not solve. True enough, we know that the ultimate end must be happiness, but this is an understanding of happiness only in the general sense of complete satisfaction of all desire. The problem which remains to be solved is what constitutes happiness. This is what we mean now by the problem of happiness.

We also listed a variety of opinions on what constitutes happiness. The disagreement arising from these opinions sharpens the issue of what happiness really consists in. Our preliminary problem is to see whether this disagreement can be resolved to any extent. As a start in this direction, let us first note the agreement underlying the disagreement, for there cannot be legitimate disagreement without a common starting point. The common starting point is the agreement that happiness is possible for man; otherwise there would be no opinions on what this happiness is. There is also agreement—although only implicit in some opinions—that happiness will consist in something which satisfies man as a human being. Even those opinions which specify happiness as something common to man and animal, such as pleasure, nevertheless presume that happiness of this kind will be realized in a manner appropriate to a human being. Let us, therefore, begin to resolve the problem of happiness by investigating what sort of being a man is. The moral problem of what happiness consists in presupposes at least a minimum knowledge of the nature of a human being. We shall only summarize here some of the material covered fully and comprehensively in philosophical psychology. Again, we shall use primarily an inductive approach.

Characteristics Indicate Types

We may take it for granted that any kind of thing, especially any kind of living thing, has some distinguishing mark about it. The ability to fly, for example, characterizes most birds. The ability to swim is a trait especially appropriate to fish. The ability to spin webs distinguishes the spider. Such characteristics, of course, may not be the most important possessed by these beings, nor are they necessarily peculiar to them. Still, they are characteristics which reveal a good deal about the kind of being each thing is.

Even within the human order, persons differ from each other in the special traits they possess. A carpenter is such by virtue of a building skill he has. An engineer is one who constructs fortifications, bridges, and the like. A teacher is one who possesses the art of assisting a student to learn. A doctor is one who can consistently restore patients to health. In these and countless other instances, we designate men in relation to the respective functions they perform. But should there not be some basic function or characteristic which belongs to all men in virtue of which they act distinctively as men? And, if they perform such a function well, would they not achieve—at least in the most primary way—happiness? Would they not be happy. then, not merely as carpenters, engineers, teachers, or doctors, but simply and completely as men?

A human being is admittedly a complex being, and it might be rash to suppose we could single out any one trait or function more characteristic than any other. Modern psychological research ranges over a vast area of instinct, sensation, imagination, emotion, learning, genetics, and problem-solving. We easily gain the impression that man is so complex in his structure and activity that he cannot be analyzed as just one sort of being, distinctive and different from other living beings.

Nevertheless, there clearly seems to be a sense in which a human being is a whole and unified being, for in both popular and scientific speech we speak of a man in such a way as to distinguish him as one kind of being, quite different from a dog, a monkey, or any other living being. Moreover, the many characteristics man alone appears to possess differ considerably from each other and reveal varying aspects about human life. Some clearly are more important and revealing than others; the act of scratching one's ear, for example, is hardly on a par with the act of grasping a mathematical demonstration. Dreaming is an activity engaged in by human beings generally and even by some animals, but the interpretation of dreams is a distinctively human characteristic, far superior to the mere having of dreams. Undoubtedly man is a highly complex being and has an extraordinary variety of behavior; all the more reason, then, for supposing some aspects of his being and behavior are more typical of him than others.

Let us put the matter in a slightly different way. Is it reasonable to suppose that teachers, doctors, engineers, and carpenters have distinctive functions but that man himself has no characteristic or distinctive functions? Is it reasonable to suppose that although the human eye or the human ear have characteristic functions, man as a whole has none? Could a human being exist without any activity characteristic of his nature as such? Assuming, therefore, that there are such characteristics typifying man as a whole, it is not difficult to see that ascertaining what such human characteristics are will help greatly to establish in what human happiness consists. Let us see if we can establish what one characteristic most of all specifies human nature. In other words, we are asking only the following simple question: What is the characteristic function of man as man, and not merely man as carpenter?

What Characterizes Man as Man?

If we consider a living thing merely as living, we would say its characteristic function is growth, or metabolism, or reproduction. In giving such a characteristic and defining it carefully, we would distinguish any living thing from any non-living thing; such a characteristic we wish to establish in man. Of course, human beings are also living beings, but they are not distinctively human by virtue of some characteristic proper to life as such; any such characteristic is too general to distinguish man as man. Man and plants are both living beings, but they differ considerably. Their difference, therefore, must be in the kind of life they have.

All men experience a life of sensation, and they possess this form of life in a way no plant life exhibits at all. By a life of sensation, we mean a form of knowing occurring in connection with stimulation of certain bodily organs as in seeing, hearing, touching, and the like. We include also under sensitive life the whole area of emotional experience, that is, the whole domain of sense desire. While such characteristics distinguish a human being from any plant, they do not distinguish a human being from animals.

Human beings, however, possess a form of life no animal has at all. The term "intelligence" is too broad to specify the kind of living activity by which man, for example, expresses himself grammatically, for we recognize a kind of animal intelligence as well. When the ape reaches some bananas by piling boxes on top of each other, we ascribe a kind of intelligence to the ape. But when one human being asks another human being to hand him a banana, we recognize a form of intelligence different in kind from that which we ascribe to the ape. For human beings, reaching for bananas is a trivial incident in intelligent activity.

The form of life which human beings peculiarly possess, enabling them to communicate thought, make works of art, and associate with each other politically is a life of reason. Without going into psychological analysis in detail, it is enough, for our purpose in ethics, to understand this life of reason in terms of its most obvious manifestations, such as the ability to use language significantly or to lead a political life. This rational principle in a human being extends also to whatever other parts of human life are guided by reason, as well as to the very activity of reason itself.

We can express more specifically this latter distinction between what is guided by reason and the activity of reason itself by noting the difference between voluntary activity and rational activity. We shall take "voluntary activity" in the strict sense to mean our activity of willing; by "rational activity" we mean, of course, the activity of thinking. When we say both are included under the rational principle in a human being, we mean both activities manifest the rational principle, though in different ways. The activity of thinking manifests what is at once the highest and most proper activity of a human being, and hence we associate the name "rational" with this highest principle in man. Voluntary activity is also a proper activity of man, but it follows upon rational activity insofar as we will in virtue of what we know. Hence, in the broad sense of the term "rational," both rational activity and voluntary activity share in the rational principle in man.

Just as rational activity has its counterpart in voluntary activity, so our knowing through sense organs has its counterpart in emotional activity. Just as we desire things as a consequence of what we know through our reason, so we desire things as a consequence of what we know through our senses. Why do I desire to be just in my dealings with other persons? It is because I understand being just as a quality I should have. Why do I desire the tasteful preparation of food? It is because I sense the quality of taste in food.

Before returning to the main problem of what human happiness is, let us illustrate by means of a chart the relationships between the different activities and powers of a human being. In this way we can grasp readily the various relations of activities in a human being and, at the same time, understand their order.

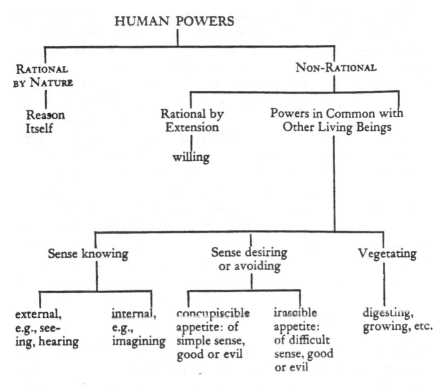

HUMAN POWERS

RATIONAL BY NATURE — NON-RATIONAL

Reason Itself | Rational by Extension (willing) | Powers in Common with Other Living Beings

Sense knowing | Sense desiring or avoiding | Vegetating

external, e.g., seeing, hearing | internal, e.g., imagining | concupiscible appetite: of simple sense, good or evil | irascible appetite: of difficult sense, good or evil | digesting, growing, etc.

Note 1: The full explanation and expansion of this chart belongs to psychology. The general indication of the divisions and relations suffices for ethics.

Note 2: The powers of willing and sense desiring can come under the control of reason in certain ways, and can therefore be understood as "rational by participation."

Note 3: In the broad sense of the term, "non-rational" applies to all powers except that of reason itself.

Preliminary Summary on Happiness

Our main problem is to establish in what human happiness con sists. The outline we have given of the various human powers, which are principles of activity in us, points to the answer. Let us giv this answer by summarizing the foregoing material in terms of th following argument.

If the function of a carpenter as carpenter is to build well, and if the function of a teacher as teacher is to teach well, then the function of man as man is to live well. To live well as a human being is to live a life of reason, by which a human being not only engages in the acts of reason itself, but directs his other acts through reason. Hence, the good life of man—the happy life of man—appears to consist in the activity of reason and the good use of reason to direct other acts. In other words, human happiness consists in the activity of reason in accordance with virtue. We add "in accordance with virtue" to emphasize that the activity of reason and the activity of other powers directed by reason must be *good*, i.e., performed with the excellence proper to each kind of activity.

Is this view of human happiness adequate? It might still seem too general to be acceptable, for we have a right to expect the notion of what happiness consists in to be specific enough to answer satisfactorily the most fundamental question in ethics. Perhaps we can best evaluate this view of happiness by comparing it with the other views on happiness listed in the previous chapter.

There is at least one respect in which all views agree. They all maintain, in effect, that happiness or the good life is nothing else basically but acting well. For, although some say pleasure is happiness, others virtue, and so on, they all think the view they advance will realize good or desirable activity, and that it is in such activity happiness is primarily found.

They agree in another respect as well. Any activity they propose is immanent, not transitive. In transitive activity, such as making a chair, we modify material external to ourselves. Such action is never for the sake of itself, but for the sake of the thing made. Immanent activity, however, remains within us and, in a quite literal sense, modifies us. Such activity perfects us and is, accordingly, activity for the sake of itself. Now, although the opinions differ on what precise object realizes happiness, they agree that happiness must be found in immanent activity, benefiting ourselves rather than some external object. Happiness is first and foremost a state of interior well being; even those who designate an external object like wealth do so primarily because of the enjoyment resulting from the possession of wealth.

Comparison with Other Views

The view holding that happiness is found in virtue is a position close to the one we have given. This view rightly estimates the importance of virtue for happiness, but at the same time it exaggerates the role of virtue in not seeing it as still a means toward happiness. Furthermore, when we say happiness is the activity of reason in accordance with virtue, we imply the activity of virtue as well, whereas to say simply that happiness is virtue may mean only the possession of virtue without the exercising of it. If our notion of happiness is correct, men are happy not merely when they are virtuous, but when they act virtuously.

The opinion that happiness consists in knowledge is also close to the position we are advancing. Obviously, the life of reason consists principally in knowledge, and it is hard to see how anyone could be really happy without knowledge, at least to some extent. On the other hand, knowledge alone would hardly seem to constitute happiness for a human being. Man is not wholly an intellectual being. If there is a sense in which we can be *more* than human, perhaps happiness would be a wholly intellectual activity; such happiness, however, would be above human nature rather than proper to it.

There are the views holding happiness to consist in one or another goods of the body, such as pleasure or health. It is perhaps sufficiently clear now that human happiness could not consist primarily in any such good. Nevertheless, it should be clear also that human happiness can hardly exist without taking such goods into account. Consequently, although happiness does not consist *primarily* in such goods, it does require them *secondarily*. But to say they are required secondarily is to admit they must be ordered by something other and better than they are, and what would this be other than the life of reason according to virtue? With this clarification, we can see how something like pleasure need not be opposed to virtue as so many persons suppose. The contrary, fact, is the case, for virtuous activity is pleasure of the finest kind. For those who act virtuously things are pleasant which are really pleasant by nature, whereas enjoyment of the pleasures of sen without the moderation of reason becomes vicious, and sometimes even painful, as one who has gone to excess in the enjoyment of food and drink knows.

There are, finally, those who think happiness consists in some external good, such as honor or wealth. Those who think happiness consists in honor are right to the extent that no one would be more honored than one who truly attains happiness. But at most, as we have already pointed out, honor would be a sign of happiness rather than happiness itself. As for wealth, no one seriously maintains that wealth in and by itself constitutes happiness. They mean, rather, that wealth is indispensable for happiness and more so than anything else. Now, while even this view is exaggerated, hardly anyone would deny the necessity of at least some wealth secondarily, just as goods of the body are required in a secondary manner. After all, it is difficult—if not humanly impossible—to be happy when destitute. But to use any amount of wealth well without being used by it requires the sort of moderation proper to reason and virtuous activity, and so we come back to the view of happiness that we are advancing.

A Further Difficulty about Happiness

Let us summarize the position we have developed about happiness as the ultimate end of human life. We have seen that human beings *cannot help* desiring happiness in the sense of wishing to attain the satisfaction of all desire, but we saw also that it was difficult to determine in what happiness consists. We investigated various opinions on what happiness is, typical views which have been held from ancient to modern times. After a consideration of these views, we argued from the nature of man and his characteristic activity to the notion of human happiness as a life or activity of reason in accordance with virtue. We defined virtue only in general terms as the disposition to act well regularly. We compared this notion with the other views on happiness to note the agreement and disagreement. Even in the disagreement, we found support for our notion of happiness insofar as whatever good is contained in the other views requires and presupposes the guiding principle of reason and virtue. At the same time, we were led to expand our own view of happiness. We now understand happiness to be realized primarily in a life of reason in accordance with virtue, and secondarily in goods of the body and external goods.

The question we raised before must be raised again. Do we have an adequate and satisfactory understanding of what constitutes human happiness? Will human beings really be happy if they achieve this state of existence? A grave difficulty still seems to remain.

This further difficulty can be formulated in more than one way. One way to state it is to ask whether we ever in fact attain such happiness. Can all of us—or most of us—or even only a few of us—attain a mode of life so well-developed that we truly live a life of reason and follow the guidance of reason in all our activities? Before attempting to answer this question, let us remove a possible misunderstanding about happiness as we have conceived it. To live a life of reason does not mean living a life of abstract thought more or less isolated from other activities of life. Man's nature is an intimate union of intellectual, sensitive, emotional, and vegetative life. These types of life are distinct, to be sure, yet they are united in the whole which is man, each modifying and influencing to some degree the other. It is *man* who acts, not the soul or the body alone, nor any power of man taken by itself. To live the life of reason in accordance with virtue means that man in his whole being exercises all his powers fully, but in a certain order such that the life of reason is primary and is the directing and guiding principle of all other human acts. The question still remains, however: Do we attain such a well developed and ordered form of life?

Let us suppose we can attain such happiness. The difficulty, in a sense, merely becomes graver: can we *maintain* it? The facts of experience reveal that life is full of sudden changes, surprises, and adversities to such an extent that a man might be happy one day in the manner we have described and thoroughly miserable the next day because of circumstances wholly outside his control. It is not at all impossible for a man to attain this sort of happiness and then, in a short period of time, lose his fortune, his family, his health, and perhaps even his virtue. It seems rash, therefore, to conclude that any man can be really happy so long as he continues to live, since the next day may bring disaster. It thus seems as though a man cannot be certain of attaining happiness, and especially maintaining it, until he dies. But could we call a dead man happy?

Let us even suppose we not only could attain such happiness, but could maintain it as well. The most serious difficulty of all then arises: Is this happiness really *complete* after all? In posing this question, we seem to run into a paradox. If we can attain such happiness and are able to maintain it, then presumably we would have realized our ultimate end and completed our life without, in fact, our life being completed. In other words, can we ever be completely happy and still continue to live? To state this final question most sharply, can we ever reach a stage in life at which nothing else remains to be desired? If our desires remain unsatisfied in any respect, we cannot have realized the ultimate end, since the attainment of the absolute ultimate end seems to require the complete satisfaction of all desire. On the other hand, if we do not ever reach such a stage in life, do we ever really attain happiness, after all? Are we doomed to pursue an end that remains forever unattainable? Is complete happiness only a myth, and are we deceived into believing it is something real we can attain? Surely this cannot be the case, for not only would life be utterly unintelligible, but actually impossible as well. We cannot live at all without acting for ends, and therefore for some ultimate end.

Apparently, then, our understanding of what happiness as the ultimate end consists in is still inadequate and incomplete. Nevertheless, we have made some progress and have achieved some understanding of happiness as the ultimate end. But our search for complete happiness, far from being ended, seems only to have begun.

REVIEW QUESTIONS

1. To what extent is there general agreement about happiness as the ultimate end?
2. What are the three grades of life and what is their relation to the problem of happiness?
3. Summarize the more obvious manifestations of a life of reason.
4. Distinguish between the activity of reason and being guided by reason.
5. Explain what is meant by "rational by participation."

6. What is the function of a human being precisely as a human being?

7. In what does human happiness appear to consist primarily?

8. What is the distinction between immanent and transitive activity, and what relevance has it for the problem of happiness?

9. In what sort of good is human happiness found primarily? In what sort of good is human happiness found secondarily?

10. What difficulty is there about *attaining* human happiness?

11. What difficulty is there about *maintaining* human happiness?

12. What is the difficulty about human happiness, as understood in this chapter, being complete happiness?

DISCUSSION

1. A human being is complex, performing a great variety of activities. All of these activities reveal what kind of being man is, hence they are all distinctively human characteristics. But no one of them distinguishes a human being more than any other. Therefore, none can be a basis for knowing what happiness is any more than another.

2. The fundamental question in ethics boils down to *What do I like?* Whatever I like will be happiness for me. I cannot prove to anyone else who does not share my taste that what I like is better than what he likes. The problem of happiness is thus reduced to a purely subjective choice of what each one likes. Consequently, happiness is different for each individual, and there is no way of establishing what happiness ought to be and that it is the same for all human beings.

3. Man's various powers and activities must depend upon a primary principle of operation in man. In this primary principle of operation, happiness will be realized. But the primary principle of human operation is reason. Therefore, human happiness is found in a life of reason, that is, in a life of knowledge.

4. It is true that man as a carpenter or as a teacher has a special ability, and that from these special abilities certain skillful actions follow. But there is no man in general, for every man is either a carpenter or a teacher or something else. Consequently, there is no action of man in general. And, if there is no action of man in general, there is no happiness for man in general. Therefore, human happiness is varied according to the different types of men who exist.

5. Happiness implies complete satisfaction of all desires, for if there is anything which we still desire we are to that extent unhappy. But at no time in human experience is anyone without at least some desire for something he has not yet attained. Therefore, no one should seek

happiness as an ultimate end, since no one should seek what is impossible to attain.

SUGGESTED READINGS

Aristotle, *Ethics*, Book I, chaps. 7-12.
St. Thomas, *Commentary*, Book I, Lessons IX-XVIII.
St. Thomas, *Summa Contra Gentiles*, Book III, chaps. 26-36.
Plato, *Philebus*. Consult *The Dialogues of Plato*, translated by B. Jowett, two Vols. New York: Random House, 1937.

Adler, *A Dialectic of Morals*, chap. IV, pp. 47-68.
Albert, Denise and Peterfreund, *Great Traditions in Ethics*, chap. IV, pp. 60-80.
Bourke, *Ethics*, chap. II, pp. 35-40.
Mill, J. S., *Utilitarianism*, chaps. I-IV. Consult Melden, A., *Ethical Theories*, pp. 365-392.
Miltner, *The Elements of Ethics*, chap. III, pp. 20-35.
Renard, *The Philosophy of Morality*, chap. I, pp. 27-48.
Tsanoff, *Ethics*, chap. 4, pp. 68-83.
Wheelwright, *A Critical Introduction to Ethics*, chap. 3, pp. 63-93.

IV

Virtue in general

*T*aking it for granted that human happiness consists primarily in a life of reason according to virtue, but realizing that we need to have a more comprehensive understanding of this notion of happiness, we shall now investigate more in detail what we mean by virtue. If we are right about the general notion of human happiness, virtue is required for the realization of happiness; hence, by understanding virtue more precisely, we shall better understand happiness.

We have already given a nominal definition of virtue as the disposition to act well in a regular manner. Let us begin to formulate a more essential definition by investigating the different kinds of virtue. It will be helpful to recall in this connection the division of powers we gave in the preceding chapter: vegetative, sensitive, and rational powers. As far as virtue is concerned, we may dismiss at once the vegetative powers, for no one speaks of human virtue in connection with any of our strictly vegetative activities, nor are vegetative powers susceptible of the type of perfection proper to virtuous activity. Since the virtue we are concerned with is human virtue, and since the characteristically human powers are rational, virtue will be concerned with rational activity. However, rational activity includes both what is rational by nature—the operation of reason itself—and what is rational by participation—the activity of appetite following upon reason. Therefore, there will be two principal kinds of virtue.

One kind is a perfection of the power of reason itself: we call such virtue *intellectual virtue*. The other kind is a development of the appetitive powers which are rational by participation: we call such virtue *moral virtue*. In calling both kinds virtue, we recognize that the name "virtue" does not retain wholly the same meaning, and is therefore analogous. Moral virtue is "virtue" in the primary meaning of the word, while intellectual virtue is virtue only in a secondary sense. When we speak of virtue unqualifiedly, we have moral virtue in mind, and this usage is in conformity with common practice.

It is not relevant here to develop in any detail the difference between moral and intellectual virtue, although the distinction is important and will be considered in a later chapter. Our concern now is to consider the division of virtue into moral and intellectual only insofar as it helps us to understand virtue in general. Let us proceed by asking how we come to have virtues at all, moral or intellectual. What is the cause of virtue and why do we need moral and intellectual virtues?

From the standpoint of *final* cause, the purpose of virtue is to dispose us to act more perfectly and in a distinctively human manner. Our powers are by nature indeterminate; they operate well or badly and either for good or evil. Our powers develop and are strengthened by the steadying influence of virtue so that we become disposed to act well regularly. Regular, good action is therefore the immediate purpose of virtue, and we need such firm dispositions of our intellectual and moral powers to lead a human life well.

Our immediate concern, however, is with the *efficient* cause of virtue, the cause of the coming to be of virtue. Here we must take into account the distinction between intellectual and moral virtue, for the efficient cause of each is different.

Intellectual virtue, by which we achieve good thinking, is generated and increased by instruction. The reason for specifying instruction as the efficient cause is that intellectual virtue is ordered to knowledge, for we need to think well in order to acquire knowledge. The surest and quickest means of acquiring knowledge is by instruction, for one who wishes to know can benefit more readily by being instructed by one who already has knowledge. It is true that knowledge can be acquired also by discovery without instruction in the usual sense of the term. Indeed, everyone must begin to acquire knowledge by discovery since any instruction presupposes some knowledge on the part of the learner. Furthermore, some types of knowledge can be acquired only by discovery on the part of each person himself. However, most persons acquire their knowledge primarily by instruction, and they acquire it in a more orderly manner this way. In the process of acquiring knowledge, intellectual virtue is formed and developed, as we shall see later.

The Efficient Cause of Moral Virtue

Moral virtue, however, is acquired by practice and not, strictly speaking, by instruction. There are two reasons why the efficient cause of moral virtue is practice rather than instruction. The first reason is that moral virtue cannot be taught, in the proper sense of the term, since virtue is not a matter of knowledge but of action, and teaching is not directly related to action. Secondly, moral virtue is located in the appetitive powers of man, in which there are inclinations or "drives" toward something desirable. The well-formed striving for something desirable can be developed only by practice and exercise. The situation is similar to throwing a forward pass well. Instruction about throwing a forward pass is not enough to do it well; exercise and practice are needed to realize this ability in an individual.

In recognizing that the efficient cause of moral virtue is practice, we see that no moral virtue is natural to us in the sense of arising

in us by nature. Everyone must acquire moral virtue through re-
peated performance of singular acts. It is true to say, then, that no
one is born good in the sense of being morally virtuous by nature.
It is also true to say that no one is born bad in the sense of having
bad moral qualities by nature. The infant has yet to come to be as
far as his moral condition is concerned.

We acquire virtues by first performing the acts which lead to
their formation. We *are not* brave before we *do* brave acts. We
must first act in a brave manner in order to become brave. Similarly, a man does not become a builder until he first builds, and
builds enough to become a good builder. Nor, to be truly brave, is it
enough to perform a few brave acts haphazardly. To be truly brave,
i.e., to have the virtue of fortitude by which you act bravely whenever danger threatens, you must perform brave acts to a point
where you become habituated to act bravely whenever the occasion requires.

Furthermore, once virtue is acquired, it cannot be simply taken
for granted but must be exercised to be maintained, a point of
practical significance often overlooked. Practice is therefore the
efficient cause not only of bringing moral virtue into existence, but
of maintaining it in existence as well. Just as the tennis player cannot
remain a good tennis player without practice, so neither can a man
remain virtuous without exercising the virtue. Likewise, just as
bad or careless tennis playing will ruin a good tennis player, so a
man can lose a virtue by bad or careless moral action. The person
who makes excuses for occasional indulgences in bad action or who
takes the "just-this-once" attitude suffers not only in the single
act concerned but in his entire moral being. The tennis player who
handles a return play carelessly suffers not only in that single play
but as a tennis player wholly. He is on the way to becoming a bad
tennis player unless he checks his faulty playing, just as a person
performing a deliberately bad act is, unless he checks himself, on the
way to becoming a bad man morally.

Since moral virtues are generated by the acts we perform, it is
clear that our acts must be of such a kind as to bring about the
virtue in us. But how can we perform good acts to bring about the
virtue in us if we need virtue to perform good acts? The answer

is that we can perform some good acts without already having the virtue, but we cannot perform them with facility and promptness until we form the virtue in us. This point leads us to the practical recognition of the need of performing good acts as early as possible in life; hence, the special need of sound moral training and guidance by parents when we are young. It is hardly an exaggeration to say that the development of virtue in a person depends as much on his parents or guardians as on himself. In addition, there are various other extrinsic influences that help to form virtue in us, such as teachers, good friends, and the enjoyment of good literature, music and painting.

We may take it as evident, then, that moral virtue comes to be only by practice and exercise of good acts on our part to a sufficient degree to form the disposition in us to act in such a manner regularly. It is evident, too, that practice is not only the cause of the coming to be of virtue, but of maintaining virtue as well.

What Determines "Good" Action?

In establishing the efficient cause of moral virtue, we have been speaking in a general fashion of virtue and of "good" action. We must try to state more specifically what makes a moral action "good," for we need to understand good acts sufficiently in order to give a satisfactory definition of virtue.

It is almost a truism to say we must act according to "right reason." Speaking generally, the good of anything consists in its action being suitable to its nature. This common principle emphasizes the point that what anything does should be suitable to what it is; in the case of man, since he is by nature rational more than anything else, he should act according to "right reason." We shall have occasion later to see the full meaning and force of this principle and how it serves as our guide to good action, but it would be premature to consider it now when we have not yet formulated the definition of virtue. Stating the principle now, however, indicates the direction we should follow in arriving at the definition of virtue.

Let us proceed in this direction by approaching inductively the question of what we mean by good action in the moral order. It is evident, from many examples, that almost anything is weakened or destroyed by "too little" or "too much." An obvious instance is found in health. Too much food, for example, can destroy health; too little food can weaken and also destroy health. The right amount of food produces, safeguards, and even increases one's health. In general, we could say that the "good" of our health is the measure of the food we should eat.

The situation is similar with respect to moral virtue. There can be "too much" and "too little"—not of the virtue itself, but of that about which the virtue is exercised. Let us illustrate with the virtue of fortitude, which is chiefly concerned with exercising control over fear. A person who fears everything is a coward; either he never acquires the virtue of fortitude or, if he has acquired it, he destroys or loses it through "too much" fear. On the other hand, a person who fears nothing at all is rash and foolhardy; he destroys the virtue of fortitude—if he has it—by "too little" fear, for the brave man is *not* the one who fears nothing at all but who *moderates* his fear.

That which determines the "good" action of virtue, then, is that which is neither "too much" nor "too little," and that which is neither of these is that which is in the *mean*. Moral virtue, therefore, consists in the mean, for the mean is the measure of the goodness of virtuous action.

When we examine the moral virtues in detail later, we shall have occasion to see how the mean works out for each of the virtues. We shall only indicate here the common reason why virtue consists in a mean. Moral virtue is a perfection of the appetitive powers of man in relation to this or that definite type of object, e.g., fortitude concerns objects producing fear. The measure or rule of the goodness of an action consists in the conformity of such an action with reason in the sense that reason rightly ordered measures what is virtuous in action. The opposite, which we call "evil," consists in departing from this rule. Now we can depart from the rule in two ways, either by exceeding the measure—"too much"— or by falling short of the measure—"too little." Hence, the good of moral virtue, the proper ordering of the movement of our appetitive powers, consists in conformity with the rule of reason which, in turn, means neither too much nor too little of the object and the accompanying desires with which the virtue is concerned. For example, in fortitude we need to regulate our passion of fear in relation to some fear-producing object so that we experience neither too much nor too little of it, but just the right amount— that is, the mean.

Moral virtue, then, is concerned with the will and the passions, i.e., the operations of these appetitive powers, as its *matter* or *object*, but it derives its goodness from the rule of reason. If we consider moral virtue in relation to its matter, then moral virtue consists in a mean, namely the mean between excess and defect in the movement of our passions and of our will. But if we consider moral virtue in relation to reason as its rule, then virtue does not consist in a mean so much as in an *extreme* in the sense that the good of reason, when realized in the movement of desire, is a perfection and hence an extreme in the order of excellence. We can illustrate this important point—often misunderstood in moral theory—with the following diagram.

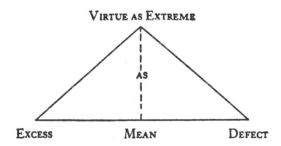

If we look only at the base line of the triangle, we see how virtue consists in a mean. This line represents the *matter* with which virtue is concerned, namely the operations of our appetites as they are concerned with various objects. In this respect, we can have too much movement or too little, and the mean is that which lies in the middle. If we look at the top of the triangle, we see how virtue is an extreme of excellence, rising above the excess and defect. The mean of virtue, therefore, is not a mean of mediocrity but a mean of perfection.

The Variability of the Mean of Virtue

The notion of the mean of virtue is easily subject to misunderstanding. We have tried to eliminate one misunderstanding—the one supposing that the mean of virtue is identified with the mediocre. We are *perfected* by virtue, not reduced to what is merely ordinary.

Another easy misunderstanding of the mean of virtue is to suppose that it is fixed or rigid. An arithmetical mean is determined in this way, but not the mean of virtue. The reason that the moral mean is variable is evident from experience itself. In all human action and passion, the mean depends on a variety of circumstances. Now, it is quite possible that what tends toward an excess or a defect according to one set of circumstances may be the mean according to another set. What may be a brave act in domestic circumstances may not be brave on the battlefield. Hence, the rule of reason cannot apply without regard for the circumstances surrounding the act.

Furthermore, the mean of virtue depends upon individual differences among persons. What may be temperate for one person may not be temperate for another. Just as, in the athletic order, a wrestler needs more food and exercise for his strength and health than a bookkeeper, so, in the moral order, a person more advanced in virtue has a higher mean than a person less advanced, and the latter higher than one merely beginning to acquire virtue. Likewise, temperamental traits may dispose one person toward the mean in one way, whereas in another person they may dispose him toward the mean in a somewhat different way. The social and economic environment also influences the mean of virtue, not only for a people as a whole but for different individuals as well.

Although there is this variability in the mean of virtue, it does not follow that the mean is purely relative in the sense that there is no objective foundation for the mean. For this person at this time and in these circumstances, the mean of a particular virtue is objectively determinable; yet, it is still variable in the sense that it may not be a mean for another person or even for himself under different circumstances. It is, incidentally, the rule of reason which supplies this variability; without the moderating rule of reason, the will and the passions would incline to move always toward an excess or a defect in a manner at once rigid and destructive. The detailed examination of the virtues later will help us to see in particular how the rule of reason brings out the best in our appetitive movements by inducing both determination and moderation in their activity.

Pleasure and Pain in Relation to Virtue

It is evident also from our experience that our actions and passions are accompanied by either pleasure or pain. When we attain a good we desire, and avoid some evil, pleasure follows; when we meet with an evil we wish to avoid and fail to attain some good we seek, pain follows. Since our actions and passions always have a reference to pleasure and pain, and since virtue concerns actions and passions, virtue is necessarily concerned with pleasure and pain.

This point should be understood accurately, for the relation of virtue to pleasure and pain has been misunderstood in ancient as well as in modern times. A common misconception is the view that man cannot be virtuous unless he is wholly lacking in passion, that is, he should not experience, as far as possible, the movements of different passions. This view is attributed principally to the Stoic philosophers of the third century, B.C., hence, the common meaning of "stoical"; but it is a view which has been held in varying degrees by a variety of persons at different times, and is still held today. Closely allied to this position is one holding an opposition between virtue and pleasure, a view Americans are familiar with in the Puritan tradition.

The truth in the foregoing positions is that men can become bad by pursuing pleasure and avoiding pain. But they do so, not so much by simply pursuing pleasure and avoiding pain, as by doing it in the wrong way. The truth these positions do not bring out is that virtue does not exclude all passion and pleasure, but only inordinate passion and pleasure. The passions, after all, belong to the nature of man, and hence the good of man requires that the activity of the passions play an integral part in human life. When we say they must play an integral part, we rule out an opposite misconception about the relation of virtue and pleasure, the view holding virtue to be a life of pleasure as such, or a life of pleasure pursued above everything else. This view, too, has been held both in ancient times by the Epicurean philosophers, from which derives our word, *epicure*, and in modern times as well.

That virtue must be concerned with pleasure and pain can be seen in the fact that we naturally tend toward those activities in which we find pleasure and avoid those which are painful. This is a fact evident from our ordinary experience. The connection with virtue occurs when we are faced with the need of regulating pleasure and pain. It is hard, for example, to resist the inclination to explosive anger in the face of evil. It is even harder to resist the excessive desire for pleasure. Through virtue, we manage anger and pleasure, not by obliterating the movements of passion or by simply giving way to them, but by regulating them to serve us in a human way.

The Definition of Virtue: The Genus

We come at last to the formulation of the definition of virtue. We have said a good deal about virtue already, and it might be supposed we have sufficiently defined it. Actually, however, we have not gone much beyond the nominal definition of virtue as a regular way of acting well according to a certain mean. In the light of the preceding remarks, we can now state a more essential definition of virtue.

In any precise formulation of a definition, we usually consider first the *genus*. The genus specifies what the thing we are defining has in common with other things. If we were defining *dog*, for example, we should likely think of "animal" first. "Animal" is the genus of *dog*, for *dog* has animality in common with cat, horse, and so on. What would be the genus of *virtue?* What does virtue share most immediately with other things like it?

We already understand how virtue is a good of the soul. More specifically, virtue is a principle of operations in the soul. What principles of operations, then, do we have? Quite clearly we sometimes act from passion, and hence passion is a principle of operation in us. For example, we act because of joy or sorrow, love or hatred. We already know that there is a close connection between virtue and the passions. But is the connection close enough to call passion the genus of virtue? Would we say, as we would have to say if passion is the genus of virtue, that virtue is a *kind* of passion?

Phrasing the matter this way, we can see that passion cannot be the genus of virtue. We cannot say that virtue *is* passion in the sense in which we say dog is animal; rather, virtue regulates or directs passion. The person who is emotional is not, by that very fact, virtuous; he is virtuous only if he regulates his emotions in a certain way. Furthermore, if passion were the genus of virtue, then animals would have virtues in the same way men have, since animals have emotions. But we cannot speak of a "just" dog or a "temperate" dog, except by sheer equivocation. Passion, therefore, cannot be the genus of virtue.

A power is also a principle of operation in us, yet we cannot make power stand as the genus of virtue. Whatever power we specify, whether vegetative, sensitive, or intellectual, we cannot say that virtue *is* power, at least in the sense of being a kind of power. Furthermore, we have our powers by nature. We are born with them and they can develop in us in a purely natural way. But no one is born with virtue, as we have had occasion to note already. We must acquire virtues by performing certain acts, and while acts—and virtues, too, for that matter—presuppose powers in us, this is not the same thing as saying that acts or virtues *are* powers. It is hardly necessary to mention that act is not the genus of virtue, for an act is not a principle of operation at all, but the operation itself.

Since virtue is a principle of operation in us, and since virtue is neither a passion nor a power, it can only be the one other principle of operation in us, namely *habit*. The word "habit," unfortunately, has lost some of the vigor of its original meaning. To most persons, "habit" suggests a more or less mechanical manner of operation arising from a mechanical repetition of acts. At best, such a meaning of "habit" indicates only one of its aspects—a decidedly lesser aspect.

In order to bring out the proper perfection of habit, let us consider the relation of habit to human powers and acts. We are aware that we perform a variety of acts. At this very moment, I am performing an act of seeing, an act of understanding, and an act of breathing. We arrive at knowledge of our different powers by knowing the different acts we do. If I can see this page of paper at this instant, I have the capability of producing this act of seeing. By "power," we mean, basically, nothing other than this capability of performing acts of a certain kind.

The first thing to note about habit, therefore, is that it is a mean between power and act, that is, it is the modification of a power to act in a certain way. If we were to try to define *habit* and were looking for the genus of habit, we would discover that *disposition* is the genus of habit. Any habit, then, is a disposition of a power to act in a certain way. Stated more fully, a habit is a firm or steady disposition of a power to act regularly in a certain way. By wording the definition this way we eliminate mere tendencies to act in this or that fashion, and by adding "regular" we bring out the fact that habitual action is steady and orderly.

In this way, we grasp the perfection that habit gives us. If we did not have habits, our individual acts would be done haphazardly and our powers would not be strengthened and developed so as to operate easily and effectively. The ordinary example of driving an automobile is an instance of this point. Without the habit, the operation of driving an automobile would be as inefficient and awkward as when we first started to drive. A good automobile driver is one who constantly, which is to say habitually, drives well; he has that perfection in virtue of the habit formed in him. Habit, therefore, is a principle of operation permitting us to operate well and efficiently in a variety of circumstances. We do not imply that we should always act from habit, for there are times when situations demand acts not related to any habit. We mean that, by and large, habit disposes us to act better in most situations than we should be able to do without habit. Habit, as we have now explained the term, is the genus of virtue.

The Definition of Virtue: The Difference

The full perfection of habit can be seen only by completing the definition of virtue. In addition to the genus, we need the *difference*, the characteristic which distinguishes virtue from anything else in the same genus. What *kind* of habit is virtue? To answer this question is to give the difference which belongs to the definition of virtue.

The simplest way to answer this question is to say that virtue is a *good* habit. A good habit, of course, is opposed to a bad habit. The division of *habit* into good and bad gives us the division into virtue and vice. As the goodness of virtue consists in perfecting and developing both our actions and our nature, so the evil of vice consists in the opposite effect, the deterioration of our acts and our nature. In either case, habit remains, for we shall inevitably become firmly disposed either to act well or badly. The person who is learning to drive an automobile will necessarily end up disposed to drive well or badly. The person who is growing up as a human being will necessarily become disposed, for example, to treat his fellow-man justly or unjustly.

It is evident from our experience that we inevitably develop habits. The reason is perhaps equally evident. If by nature we were wholly determined in our actions in such a way that we could not act otherwise than we do, we would not need habits. But human beings are endowed by nature only with powers of acting which, of themselves, are not determined to act one way rather than another. Hence, we cannot avoid developing habits; moreover, we need them. When we say we cannot avoid developing habits, we are saying something about the sort of nature we have; when we say we need them, we mean the good habits, the virtues. And the reason here is evident, too, for we are not by nature perfect. Indeed, in the moral order, we are neither good nor bad by nature; we must acquire moral goodness, especially by the formation of good habits in us.

It is not enough, however, to speak of virtue as a good habit; we need to explain in what the goodness of virtue precisely consists. To put the matter in terms of a question: When is a habit a virtue and not a vice? If we answer merely that a habit is a virtue when good acts are performed, we might seem to beg the question. We begin to resolve the question of what the difference of virtue means and consists in by returning to a matter we have already discussed, the mean of virtue. In general we can say that the goodness of virtue consists in attaining the mean between an excess and a defect. But whereas we discussed this point before only in a general manner, we must now try to understand more specifically what the mean of virtue is and how it is applied to particular instances. First of all, we must distinguish two senses of the mean of virtue, the objective mean and the relative mean, a distinction we touched upon earlier without explaining it fully.

The *objective* mean is the point equally distant from both extremes; this sort of mean is the arithmetical mean. For example, the mean between six and two is four, since four differs by two from either six or two. Such a mean is called "objective" for two reasons. The more obvious reason is that such a mean is found on the part of the object or thing. The second reason is that such a mean is the same in all respects. Four is the mean between six and two at all times, in all places, and under all circumstances.

The *relative* mean is that sort of mean which is neither too much nor too little but "just enough." The very language describing the relative mean is itself relative, for this mean is relative to this or that person, at this or that time, in this or that circumstance. It is obvious that this kind of mean cannot be simply defined, nor should we expect it to be. Yet, the importance of the relative mean is paramount in the moral order and, although it will be understood in relation to an objective mean, it should never be confused with it.

Let us take an example to illustrate the objective mean and the relative mean. Suits can be classified into large, medium, and small sizes. Medium sizes are based on the objective mean, the average between extremes. But a medium size will not exactly fit Mr. Jones, even if he is of average build. He needs a suit that will fit *him*, and the objective mean in this case will have to be tailored to the relative mean or size proper to him. Hence, the right size for Mr. Jones is the size that is neither too large nor too small for him. And because there is variation in size, however slight, among all men even of average build, the mean size will vary for each man. The relative mean, therefore, is relative to the person who is to attain his mean between extremes, and while there is a "too much" that is too much for anyone and a "too little" that is too little for anyone it does not follow that there is a mean that is the same for everyone.

It is such a relative mean that belongs to moral virtue. Moral virtue, as we have seen, is concerned with actions and passions. Now it is evident from experience that we can indulge too much in the emotions. We can become, for example, too angry. When we so act as to succumb entirely or almost entirely to emotion, we are feeling the emotions too much. On the other hand, as experience again bears out, we can also not be angry enough, and then we shall not be feeling the emotions enough. We are endowed with emotions in order to make use of them, if not wisely, at least as well as possible.

The emotions or passions, then, are virtuous actions in us when we realize the mean in their activity. We do this when we experience them at the right time, about the right matters, toward the right persons, with the right motives, and in the right way. To achieve this state is to achieve the mean which is virtue. This is no easy matter, but then the best in human action is not easy. Virtue is not an easy way out, as some mistakenly think, for there is really only one way to be virtuous: the right way. Vice is the easy way out, for there is not one bad way, but many. The fact that virtue is difficult to achieve is not unrelated to the fact that virtue is a perfection.

The Complete Definition of Virtue

By bringing together the genus and the difference of the definition of virtue, we can now give the complete definition of virtue. *Virtue is a habit inclining us to choose the relative mean between extremes of excess and defect.* A few additional remarks are necessary for a full understanding of this definition of virtue.

We state in the definition that virtue is a habit consisting in a choice. We are presupposing, without explaining now, that we choose the acts which are virtuous. We are justified in making this presupposition because we are aware from experience that we freely elect the acts we do. In a later chapter, however, we shall have to examine the basis for this presupposition as well as establish precisely what we mean by "choice." We need to mention choice in connection with habit, however, to make as specific as possible the kind of habit virtue is, for some habits operate in us without choice, whereas moral habit is impossible without choice.

A virtue is a mean between extremes in two senses. It is a mean, first, in the sense that it is a mean between two bad habits, i.e., extremes, both of which are vices. The one vice is the bad habit of excess; the other the bad habit of defect. But virtue is also a mean in a second and more important sense in that it brings about the mean in our actions and passions. In this respect virtue guides our actions and directs our passions in such a way that they are done and felt neither too much nor too little. The importance of virtue, accordingly, lies not so much in its status as a mean between vices—the first respect—as in its realization of the mean in our specific acts and emotions—the second respect. In this second respect, virtue is a perfection, as we have already noted; a perfection in the sense that it realizes what is right and best in our action. As to what determines "right" and "best" action, we have yet to consider this point fully. We know in a general way that this determination is made by right practical reason, and in a later chapter we shall examine this matter fully.

It is hardly necessary to emphasize that although we have arrived at a definition of virtue, we must do more than merely construct definitions and make general statements. Following the mode appropriate to a practical science, we must apply the general statements to specific matters; we must, in this instance, apply the definition of virtue to specific virtues. This matter, too, will be taken up in a subsequent chapter.

There remains only one point to make for the present: the special need we have for virtues. We have already referred to this matter in a general way, but now we can give three specific reasons.

First, we need virtue for consistency and stability in operation. We become well-conditioned morally through possession of virtue. Our acts, by nature indeterminate, become by means of virtue definite and steady in purpose. Secondly, we need virtue for readiness and promptness in good operation. Virtue facilitates human operation in all kinds of circumstances. Thirdly, we need virtue for the full enjoyment of good operation. This is achieved by good habit, which renders the operation so effective that habit comes to be a second nature in us. This very suitability and fittingness of good habit in us is a cause of enjoyment, and it is in this way that enjoyment of action is a sign of the existence of virtue in us.

REVIEW QUESTIONS

1. Why are there two principal kinds of virtue?
2. Does virtue mean the same thing in the two principal kinds?
3. What is the immediate purpose of virtue?
4. What is the efficient cause of intellectual virtue?
5. What is the efficient cause of moral virtue?
6. How is virtue maintained once it is acquired?
7. What extrinsic influences help develop virtue?
8. Explain how and why virtue consists in a mean.
9. Explain how and why virtue consists in an extreme.
10. How is the mean of virtue variable?
11. How is virtue concerned with pleasure and pain?
12. What are the possibilities for the genus of virtue and how do we arrive at the right one?
13. Explain what *habit* means and indicate how it is a perfection of human acts.
14. Distinguish between an objective mean and a relative mean.
15. State the full definition of virtue. Explain what the difference stated in the definition means.
16. Why do we need virtues?

DISCUSSION

1. To acquire virtue, you must perform the acts which produce virtue; for example, to be brave you must perform brave acts. But you cannot perform brave acts without being brave, and if you are brave you do not need to become what you already are. Therefore, you do not become brave by performing brave acts or acquire virtue by performing virtuous acts.

2. Since virtue is a mean between extremes in the sense that it is neither "too much" nor "too little," it follows that the virtuous man is one in whom there is neither too much nor too little virtue.

3. One can imagine human activity as a curved road that is higher in the middle and lower at the sides. If one were to roll a ball along this road, keeping it in the center would be very difficult; for the ball would tend to roll down into the gutters on both sides. The activity of virtue is like keeping the ball in the center so that it will not roll

into the gutters of vice. This is a good analogy to show how virtue is difficult to acquire.

4. The notion that moral virtue is the mean is unsatisfactory. According to this view, the virtuous man is supposed to travel the road of life by keeping away from the ditches on either side. He is supposed to be brave by not being rash or cowardly. Actually, the virtuous man is one who knows when to be rash or when to be scared as well as when to be courageous. There are times when one must be extreme; therefore, virtue is not always in the mean.

5. If we do not know what moral good we are seeking, we shall not be able to attain that good. If we cannot attain moral good, we cannot be virtuous. Therefore, knowledge, not practice, is the efficient cause of virtue.

6. Habit diminishes the rational element present in any act, for the more habituated we become, the less responsible we are for our actions. How can it be said, then, that acts proceeding from habits, which lessen responsibility, are morally better than acts in which reason alone is the directing principle?

7. We learn in psychology that the powers of intellect and will have unlimited capacity because they are immaterial or spiritual powers. Virtue as a mean determines and limits a power because it prevents a power from going to excess or defect. Insofar as virtue limits a power with unlimited capacity, it is an imperfection. Therefore, the more virtuous we try to become, the more imperfect we are as human beings.

8. Virtue has been defined as "a good quality of the mind, by which we live righteously, of which no one can make bad use, which God makes in us without us." Compare this definition with the one we have given.

SUGGESTED READINGS

Aristotle, *Ethics*, Book I, chap. 13; Book II, chaps. 1-9.

St. Thomas, *Commentary*, Book I, Lessons XIX-XX; Book II, Lessons I-XI.

St. Thomas, *Summa Theologiae*, I-II, Questions 49-56; Question 64, Articles 1-2. Consult *Basic Writings of St. Thomas Aquinas*, edited by A. C. Pegis. New York: Random House, 1945, two vols.

Plato, *Meno*.

Adler, *A Dialectic of Morals*, chap. VI, pp. 74-107.

Butler, J., *A Dissertation upon the Nature of Virtue.* Consult Melden, *Ethical Theories*, pp. 241-246.

Gilson, E., *Moral Values and the Moral Life.* St. Louis: Herder, 1941, chap. V, pp. 134-150.

James, W., *Psychology.* New York: Holt, 1905, chap. 10.

Nowell-Smith, *Ethics*, chap. 17, pp. 245-259.

Wheelwright, *A Critical Introduction to Ethics*, chap. 9, Sec. 2, pp. 229-247.

Wild, *Introduction to Realistic Philosophy*, chap. 3, pp. 58-81.

V

When are actions voluntary?

Our discussion of virtue in general has shown how virtue is concerned with actions and passions, with what we do and how we feel. Our moral life is inseparably bound up with our emotions and how we experience them. But not every emotional experience, nor every act we perform, is a *moral* act, much less an act of virtue. We do not attach moral praise or blame to a person so emotionally aroused that he no longer has any real control over his action. For example, a person beside himself with fear is generally held not accountable for his acts to the extent that he is overcome by panic; the drowning person who lunges at the throat of his rescuer does not intend the death of the one trying to save him.

While it is quite true to say that virtue is concerned with action and passion, still it is not concerned with every instance of action and passion, and consequently we must establish how, when, and to what extent it is. Prior to any consideration of the virtues in detail we must investigate when an action or passion is good or bad in a moral sense, what makes human acts distinctively human, and what is the measure of morality. If it is true, as experience suggests, that we praise or blame a person for his action in proportion as he is accountable for what he does or feels, then we can say that it is only when a person acts or feels *voluntarily* that he deserves praise or blame. We do not hold a person accountable for his actions unless he wills, at least to some degree, to perform the actions and experience the emotions. By associating the term "voluntary" with human willing, we limit it to human experience, not taking into account a wider meaning of it that extends to a kind of sense desiring found in animal life.

The voluntariness of an act, then, is the necessary condition of an act's being morally good or bad. Consequently, if we are to understand the moral order accurately, we must investigate when our acts are voluntary and when they are not. It might seem surprising, at first glance, to say that some of our acts are not voluntary, for we tend to suppose that all the acts we perform are somehow voluntary. It is advisable, therefore, to examine involuntary acts first. An added advantage to this procedure is that once we determine what acts are involuntary, we can dismiss them altogether in order to distinguish better and more clearly the acts which matter for moral life and happiness, the voluntary acts.

The word "involuntary" is negative in meaning, but the meaning is not the same as the negative expression "non-voluntary." The prefix "in" in the word "involuntary" implies a privative meaning, namely, that kind of negative meaning which denies a quality that should belong to a certain thing or subject. Hence, we can speak of "involuntary" in relation to a human being, since he can and should perform voluntary acts, whereas we do not apply the word to a plant, although a plant can be called "non-voluntary." We act involuntarily, then, when we fail to will as we could or should. Some of the acts we perform are also non-voluntary, but they are not our concern here. With regard to the involuntary acts, we can ask how it is possible to act without willing or intending the act. In general, there are two ways in which we can so act: by *compulsion* and by *ignorance*.

Acts of Compulsion

It is generally recognized that an act which happens as a result of force or violence is not a voluntary act. Let us take obvious examples of such occurrences: you are pushed out of a window, you are knocked down by a falling branch, you are blown about by a hurricane. From such examples, we arrive at the common meaning of an act of compulsion. An act of compulsion occurs when the cause of the action is external to the agent to such an extent that the agent in no way contributes to the happening of the action.

The examples and this common meaning of compulsion lead us to recognize the important distinction between an extrinsic and an intrinsic principle of action in man. The exertion of physical force upon man is an extrinsic principle of action. The will of man is an intrinsic principle of action. However, it does not follow from this distinction that everything which comes from a cause outside an agent is a case of compulsion, for one may be able to resist, at least to some degree, the effect of force. What matters is whether the will is operating or not. If some sort of force is being exercised on man and if the will in no way is concurring in the result, then the act in question is one of compulsion.

In terms of the distinction thus clarified many acts are seen at once to be purely acts of compulsion, and it would be idle to list more instances of the kind given above. Other acts, however, raise a doubt as to whether they are real cases of compulsion or not. We are familiar, for example, with the painful spectacle of the seizure by a government of the relatives of a human being and its coercion of him to do certain things under pressure of torturing his relatives if he does not comply. The kidnapper acts in a similar way with respect to the relatives of the person he has kidnapped. There is no doubt, of course, about the voluntariness of the action of the kidnapper or of the representatives of such a government, but would their victims be acting voluntarily under such threats? Compulsion of a kind certainly seems to be present in these cases, yet actions of this kind are not the same as the first examples we considered. The difference is that in the second type, although compulsion is being exercised on the persons in question, in a sense they act voluntarily as well by either complying or resisting.

A parallel situation arises when something good, rather than evil, predominates. A man may be compelled to go into bankruptcy in order to make some kind of settlement of his debts and so realize, to a degree at least, the good of justice. He may not, of his own accord, wish to go into bankruptcy, yet the circumstances "force" him to do so. The quotation marks around the word "force" indicate this is not the same sort of force implied in the strict act of compulsion; yet, neither is the act wholly free. The case of bankruptcy, or of kidnapping, is an instance of what we might describe as a *mixed act*, an act in which both compulsion and voluntariness are present. At the end of this chapter, we shall refer again to such mixed acts. For now it is sufficient to note that not all of our acts are wholly involuntary or wholly voluntary. Many of the acts we perform arise from both extrinsic and intrinsic principles of action; moreover, there can be an almost infinite variety of combination of the two influences in mixed acts.

Moral Violence

Our consideration of acts of compulsion is not complete, however. It is easy enough to see that acts done out of physical force with the will in no way co-operating are involuntary acts. But reference to mixed acts requires us to consider another type of compulsion that must be distinguished from physical force: moral violence. By moral violence we mean compulsion arising from overpowering emotional influence. This type of involuntary act is not always easy to analyze, and sometimes it is hard to distinguish it from the voluntary act, particularly in individual acts. But its importance and role in human action is extensive.

The emotion of fear, when strongly aroused, is perhaps the clearest instance of moral violence. By fear, we mean that sort of emotional disturbance which arises from the apprehension of some evil or danger difficult to avoid. The state of moral violence occurs when what we perceive through the senses so arouses the emotions that the direction and control by reason and the will is seriously attacked and, to a degree at least, overthrown. For example, a person trapped in a burning room may be so overcome by fear that he no longer acts in a rational and voluntary manner. Acts of this kind seem to be done as much under compulsion as those under physical force. Yet there is a difference. In physical compulsion the cause of the action is wholly extrinsic to the agent, whereas in moral violence the cause of the action is, in part at least, intrinsic to the agent. However, the commanding intrinsic principle in this case is not the will but the overpowering arousal of another intrinsic principle of operation in man, the emotion.

We must acknowledge at once, as we did with physical force, that not every act done out of fear is an act of compulsion. It is only when fear reaches or approximates the stage of something like hysteria and wholly prevents the will from effectively operating that we have strict moral violence, i.e., an act of compulsion. But if we act out of fear of punishment without the overthrowing of a minimum control of reason and will, such an act is not one of moral violence. It would be a voluntary act even though considerable fear may be present.

Fear, of course, is not the only source of moral violence. Excessive anger is just as typical a case of moral violence. Here, again, we must distinguish between an act in which anger is so strong as to overthrow the control of reason and will, and an act in which anger may be considerably aroused without the loss of a minimum of control. As with fear and anger, so with all the emotions in varying degrees. The distinction between an act of moral violence and a voluntary act is an important one not only for the student of ethics but also for the student of psychology, psychiatry, and law.

The modern phenomenon of what is called "brain washing" puts into sharp focus the importance of distinguishing between voluntary acts and acts of violence. Employed skillfully, this vicious process combines mental and emotional pressure to such a degree that a human being is really no longer master of his own internal acts of knowing and desiring. In a variety of ways a human being can be psychologically, morally, and physically pressured to break contact so completely with his normal external environment and even with his normal process of thinking and desiring that eventually he becomes completely disoriented and disorganized. Reduced violently to an inhuman condition—inhuman precisely to the extent his acts are rendered involuntary—a person can be gradually "fed back" information so that he incorporates this information into his thinking. Such "brain washing" is a device invented in contemporary times to destroy the moral person as far as possible. Hence, it is a new and utterly vicious form of moral violence which, if pursued long and thoroughly enough, is almost certain to break a human person morally and psychologically.

Acts of Ignorance

Common experience suggests that, in addition to physical compulsion and moral violence, *ignorance* can also make an act involuntary. You often say, for example, that you would not have done such and such an act had you known better at the time. As an agent you acted out of ignorance, and since you would have acted otherwise had you known, it seems evident enough that ignorance can cause acts to be involuntary.

By ignorance here we do not mean any sort of lack of knowledge, for such a meaning is much wider than the meaning of ignorance as it is relevant to a moral consideration. The broad meaning of ignorance is equated with non-knowing of any kind. The restricted meaning of ignorance with which we are concerned in ethics is a lack of knowledge in a person *when he can and should have such knowledge*. In the broad meaning of ignorance, a child is ignorant of Hegel's philosophy; in the restricted sense of the term, the child is not ignorant in this respect, since he neither can nor should have knowledge of Hegel's philosophy. Furthermore, ignorance in the moral context is ignorance about practical affairs, not speculative matters. As we know, the practical order is concerned with action aimed at some good we desire. Our individual acts are immediately ordered to attaining our good or end; it is knowledge of this kind we seek in ethics, and it is ignorance about such matters we wish to avoid.

Now it is possible to be ignorant about what we ought to do

or avoid in order to attain our good, but ignorance of this kind would not seem to make our acts involuntary. The reason is that we cannot escape the basic moral obligation of finding out what we ought to do or avoid in order to attain our proper good. We can be ignorant in this respect only by deliberately refusing to know what we could know. Ignorance in this way can happen to us only by negligence on our part. But acts of refusing to know and of being negligent spring from our will and are therefore voluntary. There is, in other words, such a thing as *voluntary ignorance*, but this is exactly the opposite of ignorance that makes an act involuntary.

The question we wish to consider, therefore, is the following one. When does ignorance make an act involuntary and how does this ignorance differ from voluntary ignorance? This question can be answered primarily by distinguishing between *consequent* ignorance and *antecedent* ignorance. The words "consequent" and "antecedent" refer to the relation between a state of ignorance and the act of willing. If a state of ignorance is consequent to the act of willing—if ignorance follows upon the act of willing and therefore is, to some degree at least, willed by us—then such ignorance is voluntary. We are all familiar with occasions when we expressly will to remain in ignorance about certain duties which should be performed. To pretend, in such cases, that ignorance really excuses us is simply to deceive ourselves.

Antecedent ignorance, as the name suggests, indicates a state of ignorance preceding the act of willing. Such ignorance is the cause of willing and doing something one would not will and do if knowledge were present. This is acting *because of* ignorance, and it is in this way that ignorance can make an act involuntary.

The distinction between consequent and antecedent ignorance is clear enough analytically, but it is not always clear which type of ignorance is present in individual cases. Sometimes, indeed, it seems as though ignorance is neither consequent nor antecedent but simultaneous with the act of willing—an ignorance concomitant with the act of willing. Can we distinguish more precisely when ignorance makes our act involuntary and when not?

A practical sign is often useful in this respect. If you feel pain or regret because of an act you have performed, it is a sign your act was done simply through ignorance, i.e., you would not have done it had you known. The ignorance is in no way willed by you; it was truly antecedent to your act of willing. Your genuinely regretting the act is a clear sign you acted against your will—against your will, that is, when formed by knowledge—and thus your act to that extent is involuntary. For example, if you shot someone accidentally, ignorant of the fact that the gun was loaded, a feeling of remorse would be a sign of your having acted involuntarily, whereas your not regretting the act is a sign you were not in ignorance about what you were doing. To be sure, you could also regret an act you performed without ignorance, but this is a later act of repentance, and your feeling of regret then arises from a different cause.

Ignorance of Circumstances

The example of shooting someone accidentally because of ignorance that the gun was loaded leads us to recognize another distinction between voluntary and involuntary ignorance. This distinction is based on the difference between ignorance of general principles and ignorance of circumstances surrounding an individual act. One can hardly claim that he does not know that the willful shooting of innocent persons is wrong. There can hardly be *excusable* ignorance about so fundamental a general principle. However, we can easily and sometimes unavoidably fall into ignorance about the circumstances of this or that particular act we perform, and it is in this way that ignorance can make our acts involuntary.

By circumstances, we mean the singular conditions of human acts. Since the singular conditions of human acts can be almost infinite in number, we need to narrow this definition to include only those circumstances which affect an act morally. It is a circumstance of a particular act that a human being wore a white shirt; it is a moral circumstance that he carried and used a pistol. A circumstance becomes moral to the degree that it affects directly the goodness or badness of the action done. Even the moral circumstances may be numerous in any particular act. Let us summarize them in terms of relevant questions which can be asked about any significant human act.

WHEN *is the act done?*

This circumstance of the time of the act refers not only to dates and hours but to special periods of time, such as night or day, during a catastrophe, or a time of war or peace. The length of time involved in an act may be a relevant moral circumstance. Of course, one may be ignorant of the circumstance of time, and to that extent the act will be involuntary. For example, a stranger in town might be ignorant of the fact that from 3:00 to 6:00 P. M. a certain street has one-way traffic.

WHERE *is the act done?*

The place of the act may affect the act morally. The distinction between a public and a private place is sometimes a relevant moral circumstance. Murder in a cathedral adds a special degree of gravity to an action already seriously wrong, but the murderer may be ignorant of the fact that a cathedral is a consecrated place of worship and that murder there is worse than elsewhere.

How *is the act done?*

The manner in which an act is carried out can affect the action for better or worse. A boxer, while intending to fight cleanly, may fight in an excessively rough manner out of passion and excitement. He might, as a consequence, strike a fatal blow through ignorance of the fact that his manner of fighting has become excessive and that his blow would be a fatal one.

WHY *is the act done?*

This question concerns the motive or purpose the agent has in mind in doing the act. Why is he doing what he is doing? The primary importance of this circumstance in an act is evident, but by that very fact it is hard to see how one might be ignorant about his own motive for acting. Still, one can have a certain intention in mind and at the same time not know that it will bring about the opposite of what one intends. A doctor, for example, intends the saving and restoring of health in the patient, but he may be unaware of the fact that in a certain case surgery will produce complications resulting in death.

Who is doing the act?

This is a question of the efficient cause of the act, the agent himself. It might not seem possible for the agent to be ignorant of himself and of who he is. Yet if we understand that this circumstance can refer not only to who a person is by name but also to the sort of person he is or to a certain state of life he possesses, ignorance of such facts is possible. A person may be ignorant of the fact that as a gentleman he should extend certain acts of courtesy to a lady, or he may be ignorant of the fact that in virtue of a certain position he holds he carries a special responsibility for his actions.

By what means is the act done?

The means or instrument by which an act is accomplished can affect the act morally. This circumstance usually concerns the instrumental cause of the act. Thus, a gun is the instrument used in the shooting of someone; ignorance of the fact that the gun is loaded can lead to tragic consequences, although it renders the act involuntary.

What is the action done?

This circumstance concerns the effect of the act with regard to the quality and quantity of the act, and also the person to whom the action is done. Theft is an action about which no one can be in voluntary ignorance as to its wrongness. Indeed, what makes theft a bad act is not a circumstance of the act but the nature of the act itself. The effect of the act, however, involves something over and beyond the nature of the act itself. Hence, stealing is wrong in itself, and is not a question of circumstance, but stealing in large or small amount, or stealing a rare object or a state document, is a certain effect of the act of stealing about which a person may or may not be in ignorance. To take another instance, a person may be ignorant about what is being done in the sense that he does not know that a person he is about to strike has a lame arm, or has had a recent heart attack, or is a near-sighted professor. Similarly, a wife late at night might shoot her husband, mistaking him for a burglar.

These seven questions of moral circumstances can be further summarized under three headings:

1. Some circumstances concern an act considered *in itself*. These are the circumstances of *When, Where,* and *How.*

2. Some circumstances concern an act considered *in its causes*. The circumstance of *Why* is the final cause of the act, the extrinsic end for which the act is performed. The circumstance of *Who* is the principal efficient cause of the act, while the circumstance of *By what means* is the instrumental cause.

3. One circumstance considers the act *in its effect*. This is the circumstance of *What*, which concerns particularly the quality and quantity of the act.

We have listed these moral circumstances in the context of ignorance, that is, in the context of how it is possible to be ignorant about circumstances. We have introduced the consideration of moral circumstances this way because we can become more forcefully aware of them through seeing how they can make our acts involuntary. Of course, moral circumstances also contribute positively to the goodness or badness of our acts to the extent that we are aware of them. Our immediate point, however, is to make clear how ignorance can diminish the voluntariness of our actions, and we are emphasizing that it is particularly because of these circumstances that we fall into ignorance. Since we are considering ignorance only as it is antecedent to our willing this or that act, such ignorance of circumstances renders acts involuntary in this or that respect.

Not all moral circumstances are equally important or relevant. Some of them may not be pertinent at all in many of our acts. However, one circumstance is always relevant and is also the most important one for determining the moral goodness or badness of acts, apart from the nature of the act itself. This circumstance is the *why* of the act, and its importance derives from the fact that it motivates the agent to act in the first place. We shall have occasion to refer again to all moral circumstances and to this one in particular when we discuss the morality of human action in detail.

Voluntary Acts

Our ultimate concern in this chapter is to arrive at a distinct notion of the voluntary act. We have discussed *involuntary* acts at some length in order to arrive at a fuller and clearer notion of *voluntary* acts. Let us summarize what we now know about involuntary acts and, in the light of this summary, arrive at a definition of the voluntary act.

There are two main types of involuntary acts: acts done under compulsion and acts done out of ignorance. They are both involuntary to the extent that neither proceeds from the proper intrinsic principle of voluntary action in man, the will. There are, however, important differences to be noted between various involuntary acts.

Among acts of compulsion, the acts of physical force are not the same as acts of moral violence. Acts of physical force arise wholly external to the agent. Acts of moral violence arise within the agent in the sense that they spring from the emotions, but they are still external to the intrinsic principle of the will. They force the will by an internal pressure, whereas acts of physical force do so by external pressure.

Acts committed through ignorance are involuntary in the sense that we cannot will what we do not know. We refer, of course, to antecedent ignorance, the sort of ignorance which excuses one from moral blame in an act. For this reason, antecedent ignorance is invincible ignorance. Consequent ignorance, on the other hand, is willed ignorance and therefore a voluntary act. It is vincible ignorance, ignorance which accuses one of moral blame in an act and for which one is responsible.

Acts of antecedent ignorance resemble acts of moral violence in that both arise within the agent. Whereas the acts of moral violence force or overthrow the control of the will, acts of ignorance do not force or overthrow the will but render it defective in operation. The will operates effectively only in virtue of tending toward something as known by the intellect. For example, you cannot truly love a person without knowing something about his character. The will operates defectively when there is a defect in the intellect, and the defect of the intellect in this case is ignorance. Since there is a causal relation between what we know and what we will, a defect in the one causes a defect in the other. Consequently, acts of ignorance are involuntary acts in a strict meaning of "involuntary," that is, a privation in the act itself of willing.

We understand voluntary acts, therefore, by removing the involuntary acts of compulsion and ignorance. Our positive notion of a voluntary act is presented in the following definition: *A voluntary act is an act whose moving principle is the will of the agent with knowledge of the particular circumstances.* The first half of the definition eliminates acts of compulsion, both physical and moral. The second half of the definition removes acts of ignorance which, in the moral order, are particularly concerned with the circumstances of the act. In the next chapter, we shall consider the voluntary act in detail, particularly the voluntary act of choice.

Mixed Acts

It would be incomplete and perhaps misleading to reduce all acts simply to voluntary or involuntary, although there is a sense in which every act is primarily one or the other. Yet, there appear to be acts which combine both voluntary and involuntary aspects, and we have already referred to such acts as "mixed acts." We shall conclude this chapter with a few remarks about such acts and the importance of distinguishing them from purely voluntary and purely involuntary acts.

Actually, comparatively few acts we perform appear to be purely involuntary and purely voluntary. To be blown about by a tornado seems to be a clear case of a purely involuntary act. To will something with full knowledge in a particular situation seems to be a clear case of a purely voluntary act. Between such types are the acts which, in varying degrees, combine both voluntary and involuntary elements. It is perhaps primarily a matter of terminology whether to call all of these acts mixed, or only those acts in which there appears to be something of a balance between voluntary and involuntary aspects. Common usage of the terms "voluntary" and "involuntary" suggests that voluntary acts are not only those which are wholly voluntary but also those which, while not purely voluntary, are at least primarily voluntary; the same principle applies to involuntary acts.

It is important, however, to retain the distinction of mixed acts when it refers to acts which combine both voluntary and involuntary elements to a great extent. The value of the distinction lies in its preventing our being driven to two moral extremes. Some moralists, for example, tend to make practically all our acts so voluntary that one would be driven to scrupulosity in action. In such a view, one holds himself responsible indiscriminately for everything he does even though many things cannot be foreseen or intended. One can thus be driven even to the extreme of holding oneself responsible for good he could not possibly have attained or evil he in no way causes.

On the other hand, some psychologists and psychiatrists diminish voluntariness of action to such an extent that no real difference remains between the voluntary and involuntary. The view can become so extreme that human acts are considered never to rise above the morass of subconscious and wholly conditioned reactions. All responsibility is eliminated; so, for that matter, are all distinctively human acts.

The truth in either extreme is that there are purely voluntary acts and purely involuntary acts, but for the most part we do not act wholly voluntarily or wholly involuntarily. Many of our acts are rather what we would call "mixed acts" in the sense of being an almost equal combination of voluntary and involuntary aspects; while most of these mixed acts might still be regarded as voluntary rather than involuntary, they are sufficiently diminished in voluntariness to be distinguished from the usual meaning of a voluntary act. In concrete cases of individual acts, the determination of the exact ratio of voluntary and involuntary may be so complicated that it defies precise analysis. As a consequence of this complexity, we see the need of good moral and psychological guidance. Similarly, we see the need of understanding sufficiently the distinctively human acts we perform before we analyze them morally. Consequently, we must investigate more fully what precisely constitutes human acts *as human* before we analyze them morally.

REVIEW QUESTIONS

1. What is the difference between "involuntary" and "non-voluntary"?

2. What is an act of compulsion?

3. Is every act arising from a cause extrinsic to the agent an act of compulsion? Explain.

4. What is the difference between physical force and moral violence?

5. Is every act done because of fear an act of moral violence? Explain.

6. Describe the phenomenon of "brain washing" and analyze it morally.

7. What is the meaning of "ignorance" in ethics?

8. Distinguish between antecedent and consequent ignorance.

9. What is a circumstance and when is it moral?

10. Is there any difference between ignorance of general principles and ignorance of circumstances? Explain.

11. List the different kinds of moral circumstance and explain each with an original illustration.

12. Which moral circumstance is the most important? Why?

13. What is the definition of a voluntary act?

14. What is a mixed act? Is this classification distinct from voluntary and involuntary acts?

DISCUSSION

1. Everything which is caused by something outside an agent is an act of compulsion. The drafting of a man into military service arises from a cause outside the one who is drafted. Therefore, it is an act of compulsion.

2. Not all our acts are either voluntary only or involuntary only. One can will to do an act and at the same time resist pressure or even comply with it. Some of our acts, therefore, are both voluntary and involuntary.

3. A separate classification of mixed acts is meaningless. An act is either voluntary or involuntary. No act can be 40 per cent voluntary and 60 per cent involuntary. Hence, every so-called mixed act reduces to a voluntary act more or less diminished in voluntariness.

4. If a person manifests regret because of having performed a certain act, it does not necessarily mean that he was in ignorance about the act. Quite often, in fact, a person regrets having performed a certain act even though he was fully aware of what the consequences

would be. Feeling regret later, consequently, is not a sign of having done an act when ignorant.

5. There is no wholly voluntary act. A wholly voluntary act is one in which there is complete knowledge and full consent. But no one can know all the circumstances surrounding a particular act he is about to perform. Therefore, ignorance is always present and no act can be purely voluntary.

6. A man is driving a truck which he knows has faulty tires. He is driving along a highway at a fast rate of speed when one of the tires blows out. He is unable to control the truck, which swerves off the road injuring a pedestrian seriously. Is this act voluntary, involuntary, or mixed?

7. An engineer is directing the construction of a bridge. The contractor decides to cheat and orders the engineer to put in spans of single strength instead of double strength. Before the actual time comes to erect the spans, the contractor is temporarily called away. The engineer realizes that the blueprint should be followed, but realizes also he will lose his job if he does not follow the orders of his boss. He erects the single strength spans. How voluntary or involuntary is his act?

8. A person participates in a game of "Russian Roulette." He shoots himself not knowing there is a cartridge in the chamber. What kind of ignorance is involved and is the act voluntary?

9. Frank, weighing 250 pounds, stands over Bill, weighing 150 pounds, with an axe commanding Bill to shoot Jim. If Bill does not shoot Jim, Frank will split Bill's skull. If Bill shoots Jim, he will be spared by Frank. Bill shoots Jim. How voluntary is Bill's act?

10. Dr. Brown testified as follows. "The victim of brain washing is confused by hours and hours of questioning. He is brought to the brink of despair by semi-starvation, lack of rest, cold living quarters, and humiliation. Attempts are made to make the victim deny his most sacred principles: his wife, if he has one, is slandered, his parents are ridiculed, his religion is assailed, and his country is attacked. Then doubt after doubt is planted in his mind about everything he holds. He is then fed back certain selected information, and since this is the only information he receives, he begins slowly, sometimes not so slowly, to incorporate this information into his thinking, and is accordingly transformed."

When Dr. Brown was asked whether there would be justice in court-martialing a soldier subject to this treatment, he declined comment. What would your comment be from the standpoint of the voluntariness of the action?

SUGGESTED READINGS

Aristotle, *Ethics,* Book III, chap. 1.
St. Thomas, *Commentary*, Book III, Lessons I-IV.
St. Thomas, *Summa Theologiae*, I-II, Questions 6-7.

Bourke, *Ethics*, chap. III, pp. 67-77, 85-98.
Cronin, *The Science of Ethics*, Vol. I, chap. II, pp. 28-45.
Gilson, *Moral Values and the Moral Life*, chap. II, pp. 52-70.
Miltner, *The Elements of Ethics*, chap. VII, pp. 72-87.
Renard, *The Philosophy of Morality*, chap. II, pp. 81-95.
Wild, *Introduction to Realistic Philosophy*, chap. 4, pp. 82-96.

VI

When are actions free?

*H*aving distinguished voluntary acts from involuntary acts, we must now examine the voluntary act which is especially relevant for ethics, the act of choice. In defining virtue in general in Chapter IV we spoke of virtue as that kind of habit whose proper act consists in choosing the mean between extremes. In stating this definition we remarked that we would have to explain more precisely what we mean by an act of choice, and we are now in a position to distinguish choice from other voluntary acts. Indeed, the character of a person depends more upon what he chooses than upon any other type of act he performs. Furthermore, as we know from experience, we attribute freedom to our acts in proportion as we are able to choose one thing rather than another.

Let us begin by stating that while every act of

choice is voluntary, not every voluntary act is strictly a free act or an act of choice. By a voluntary act, as we defined it in the preceding chapter, we mean any act under the control of the will; choice, on the other hand, refers to one specific kind of act performed and controlled by the will. To put the matter in more familiar terms, when we speak of having "freedom of the will" we are referring to the act of choosing; the other acts that we will, to the extent they do not refer to choice, are not acts of "free will." We are so accustomed, however, to think of the will in terms of *freedom* of the will that it may seem strange to speak of acts of the will which are not free. Our first task is to distinguish voluntary acts which are not free from those which are free.

Voluntary Acts Other than Choice

Perhaps the most obvious instance of a voluntary act that is not really free is one performed by a child when he acts out of impulse. A child is often very insistent about what he wants—for example, something to eat—and he will go to great and usually loud extremes to be satisfied. We often speak of children after they have reached a certain age as being very "self-willed," that is, as being very intent on getting what they seek. Although we recognize that such promptings come largely from the sense appetite, still we rightly ascribe voluntariness to these acts. We do not, however, ascribe freedom to their acts or suppose that they are really making acts of choice in any strict meaning of the term. They simply want what they want when they want it, and such acts are voluntary, at least in a broad sense of the term.

Acts of simple desire, then, are not acts of choice. It is true that both an act of desire and an act of choice imply a tendency toward something viewed as good or satisfying. But the act of desire springs more immediately from the emotions with the will more or less concurring in the desire, whereas choice presupposes the will as operating in a much more determinate manner. Desire is always concerned with pleasure when the object desired is present or with pain if it is absent, for pleasure or plain always accompanies the emotions. Choice, however, is not necessarily connected with pleasure or pain.

We choose in terms of good or evil rather than pleasure or pain, since all acts of the will are concerned with seeking or avoiding what the intellect grasps as good or evil. If pleasure or pain is present in an act of choice, we tend to choose one or the other, not merely because of pleasure or pain but because an object is viewed and willed as a good to be desired or an evil to be avoided. Sometimes, in fact, we even choose what is painful, not because it is painful but because of some good that can be achieved through it.

What seems to distinguish choice, then, from an act of simple desire or from acting on impulse is the manner in which the will acts. In the act of simple desire, the will tends to follow the promptings of the sense appetite, while in the act of choice the will directs and controls our emotions and impulses. Consequently, while we might speak of all these acts as voluntary, still the act of choice is clearly *more* a voluntary act than the others. Comparatively speaking, an act of choice is purely a voluntary act, whereas the others are more like mixed or partly voluntary acts—in any case not properly free acts.

Can we say, then, that all purely voluntary acts are free acts or acts of choice? A purely voluntary act is one arising solely from the will, unswayed by sense desire even though some emotional activity may be present. As we have already stated, the will acts properly insofar as it is formed by the intellect. Hence, a purely voluntary act is any movement of the will toward a good as known by the intellect apart from what is known and desired by the senses. Is every act of this kind an act of choice?

Not even all purely voluntary acts are acts of choice. We can will things—we might say, in a sense, "wish for things"—which we cannot in any way choose. You can, for example, wish to be a foot taller than you are. You can, in other words, wish for what is impossible, but you can never choose what is really impossible. This clarification helps us to see that an act of choice must refer to what you can in some way bring about through your own power and operation. Hence, while you can will or wish for anything at all, even for what is wholly impossible, you can choose only what is realizable by you.

Simple willing and the act of choice, therefore, are both purely voluntary acts, yet they are quite distinct from each other. The distinction between the two is most clearly put by noting that simple willing refers to an end, something sought for the sake of itself, while choice is directed to means, something sought for the sake of something else. This is why we can will or wish to be a foot taller than we are, but cannot choose anything in relation to becoming a foot taller than we are since there is no means available. To state the same distinction in terms of what is possible rather than something impossible, we will to be healthy and we choose the means to become healthy; likewise, we will happiness and we choose means of attaining happiness.

Deliberation and Choice

We have now distinguished choice in a general way from other voluntary acts. We still need to understand more of the nature of choice itself, first because the act of choice is often misunderstood, and second because freedom of the will properly resides in the acts of choice we make. Unless we grasp this matter sufficiently, we shall be seriously deficient and even erroneous in our understanding of the moral action of man.

To understand precisely what the act of choice is in man and particularly how it differs from other voluntary acts, we must see how an act of choice presupposes an act of deliberation. Just as the operation of the will in general follows upon that of the intellect, so a specific act of the will follows upon a specific act of the intellect. The act of choice thus follows upon the act of deliberating, an act of the intellect. By seeing what the act of deliberation is we shall realize how and why an act of choice presupposes it. We shall then come to understand better the nature of choice itself.

We deliberate when we take counsel about something to be done. Deliberation is a work of practical reason; we consider and evaluate reasons for or against doing something. Consequently, we do not properly deliberate about ends but about means, for unless there is something already given as an object of desire there is nothing to deliberate about by way of seeking to achieve this object of desire. The health of the patient is the end given for the doctor; he does not deliberate about whether the patient should be cured but whether this or that means will restore health.

The connection of deliberation with choice becomes obvious. We cannot exercise a choice except in terms of deliberating, however small the deliberation may be in many cases. Thus, we reach a decision by deliberation; our choice is the selection of what we have deliberated about. Deliberation belongs to reason, choice to the will. They are so intimately connected that they cooperate to perform what seems to be only one act, yet a distinction always remains between them.

The Complete Human Act

Deliberation and choice are really only two parts or steps of the complete moral and voluntary act we perform. We have mentioned these specifically because of their importance in the moral life of man. However, we cannot fully understand either of them unless we see them in relation to other acts which precede and follow them. The inclusion of all these acts makes up the complete, complex moral act. By examining this complex act we shall understand fully the complete human act, and specifically how and when an act is free.

Since the complete human act is concerned with ends and means, we shall summarize it in terms of (I) steps concerned with the end, (II) steps concerned with the means, and (III) steps concerned with carrying out the complete act, the execution.

I. CONCERNING THE END

Intellect	Will
1. *Apprehension* of an end	2. *Willing* the end
3. *Judgment* about the end	4. *Intention* of the end

II. CONCERNING THE MEANS

5. *Deliberation* about the means	6. *Consent* to the means
7. *Practical Judgment* of choice to be made	8. *Choice* of a means

III. CONCERNING EXECUTION

9. *Command* to execute choice	10. *Use* of powers to execute
11. *Judgment* of end as attained	12. *Enjoyment* of the attained end

Our reason for outlining these steps is to see fully the complex voluntary act which characterizes human acts as human. Our more ultimate concern is to see precisely in what freedom of the will consists, since moral freedom of action is especially important for ethics. We know already that choice consists in a free act, but it is not yet clear whether choice alone makes an act free.

This outline of the complete human act should not be understood too rigidly. For example, not all twelve steps are involved in every moral act we perform. Many practical situations are simple and do not require all the steps indicated in the outline. But a difficult practical situation may involve all twelve parts, and in such cases it is advantageous to know them and to realize, when we cannot resolve a practical problem, just where we are in the process and which step is holding us up.

The analytic distinction of the steps in this outline form does not imply that we are always aware of each step as we go through the process. It is not necessary nor even desirable always to reflect on each step of the complex human act for every moral act we do. Many times we go through the different steps habitually and quite unreflectingly, particularly when we must act quickly. But reflection and extensive consideration at this or that step of the act becomes necessary and desirable whenever a serious moral situation faces us. Awareness of the different steps on such occasions is extremely helpful. You need not pause upon or even pass through all twelve steps in so relatively a trivial matter as whether to buy a hat this afternoon, although for some persons buying a hat may be surprisingly complicated. On the other hand, you would likely go through the twelve steps carefully and reflectively if you are trying to resolve the practical matter of whether to go to college.

The numbering of the steps in the act does not mean they always follow precisely in that order. As we have already remarked, in relatively simple matters some steps may be eliminated altogether; thus, if only one means is available, little or no deliberation will take place. On the other hand, sometimes in difficult situations one may go back to earlier steps or vacillate between one step of the intellect and its corresponding step of the will before the practical problem is finally resolved.

Consideration of the Steps in Detail

1. *Apprehension of an end.* We cannot will anything except in relation to what we know. The first step, consequently, must be an act of the intellect. In this step we simply grasp some object as an end and thus propose it to the will.

2. *Willing the end.* In the initial act of the will, we will what we would like to have without necessarily strongly desiring it. This first step of the will, as complementing the first step of the intellect, is therefore an inefficacious desire for an end known and proposed by the intellect. We have already spoken of this simple willing as an instance of a voluntary act that is not strictly free. We now see this initial willing as the first of a series of willed acts making up the complex moral act.

3. *Judgment about the end.* Once we know something as an end and have some desire for it, it follows that the next step is a judgment as to whether we can attain this object of our desire. We have already indicated how we can will even what is impossible, and it is at this third step that we judge whether what we will is possible or impossible. If we judge a desired end as impossible, the moral act ends at this third step. If we judge it as possible, we can go further.

4. *Intention of the end.* At this point, we now efficaciously desire the end; we really intend it. We have gone beyond the stage of simply willing something and are now strongly intent upon attaining the object. We are therefore disposed to find the means of satisfying a strong desire.

Before we pass on to the steps concerned with the means, we might look at the first four steps as a whole, as illustrated by an example; a simple illustration will avoid the complication of a more serious situation. Since I know what a suit is, I can at any given time will to have a suit. The first two steps thus occur almost simultaneously. Can I get a suit at this time? The judgment about getting a suit is usually not a difficult one to make, since ordinarily there is nothing impossible about buying a suit. On the other hand, if there should be some difficulty at this particular time or if I judge that the suit is not worth the effort, I can judge that buying a suit here and now is not feasible; in such a case the complex act would cease. But if it is feasible to buy a suit now and if I seriously intend to have one now, then the question of means immediately arises. The first moral climax of the moral act occurs with the *intending* of the end, for the sort of end we intend indicates the sort of person morally we are.

5. *Deliberation about the means.* We have already discussed this particular act at some length and have contrasted it with other acts. We need mention now only that we deliberate by reasoning about the means available, discarding the inappropriate or bad ones and evaluating those which appear to be appropriate and good for attaining the end desired. Deliberation is a kind of taking counsel, which one may do with oneself or by consulting others. The principle in deliberation or counsel is the given end, which precedes in intention but comes afterward in realization. As an inquiry into the means available, counsel proceeds by way of resolution from the principle and finally terminates in step 7 with a judgment of the choice to be made.

6. *Consent to the means.* This act of the will follows upon deliberation to the extent that deliberation remains somewhat general. The consent by the will applies the result of deliberation in a particular and personal way: you consent to the means available as far as you are concerned. This consent, however, remains general in the sense that usually not just one means is consented to, but several.

7. *Practical judgment of choice to be made.* In this step we judge one definite means to be taken rather than any other. It is the judgment of practical reasoning that this particular course of action is to be taken. This final decision made by the intellect as to what is to be done specifies formally the complementary act of the will which follows—the act of choice. It is thus the termination of the inquiry of counsel initiated in step 5, and hence is known also as the judgment of counsel.

8. *Choice of a definite means.* The connection between the practical judgment and the choice of the will is usually so close that the two seem to be one step; in a later refinement we shall see how they do form one step. However, they remain distinct in the sense that they belong to diverse powers. As we have seen earlier in the chapter, the act of choice is what we usually call the act of free will, yet we shall see shortly in detail the sense in which the free act is not

exclusively an act of the will. The practical judgment of the intellect—the preceding step—formally specifies the act of choice in the will.

Steps 7 and 8 form the second climax of the complex moral act. Once we begin to deliberate about the means available and consent to the means suitable, we are at the heart of the moral situation. It is here we make the final decision that matters and the choice that carries the final responsibility so far as the selection of means is concerned. In importance, it parallels steps 3 and 4 as related to the end originally desired.

To continue with the simple illustration with the suit, once I have the serious intention of buying a suit, deliberation about the means follows. The matter of money may be important, especially if I do not have it readily available. I may have other debts to pay. I may prefer to get it at one store, but at another store I have a charge account. I may wish to buy it today rather than next week, and if I go downtown today I have the question of means of transportation to consider. I consent to all the means available, today rather than next week, this store rather than another, this means of transportation rather than that. Any one of these means or even some other may become the relevant one about which the final decision and last practical judgment must be made. Let us suppose, as is often the case, that the question of money is the most relevant one to settle and upon which the final decision really rests. Unless this matter is settled, nothing happens one way or another. Thus, I judge finally that I can borrow the money from a friend to buy the suit at the store I prefer. This judgment made, I finally choose this means, even though it may be a difficult choice to make inasmuch as I am hesitant to borrow money. But once the choice is firmly and fully made, I am then concerned with carrying out the choice.

9. *Command to execute the choice.* In the remaining steps, we carry out what we have decided and chosen. These steps now require, in addition to the intellect and the will, other powers both internal and external. First, however, command as an act of the intellect is necessary. A command is an order to do something; it is a declaration on the part of reason that something is now to be done by way of carrying out the deliberate choice.

10. *Use of powers to carry out the command.* The will is the cause of the exercise of powers in us, and so we can speak of the will's using other powers to carry out the command dictated by reason. Hence, knowing what is to be done, we carry it out by making use of whatever powers are necessary to accomplish the action.

11. *Judgment of the end as attained.* With the carrying out through the will of the activity needed to attain the good sought and with the actual attaining of the good desired, we now understand and judge the fittingness of the object in relation to the end originally intended. This is the intellectual possession of the good desired. This judgment of possessing the good determines the will in its last step in the complex moral act.

12. *Enjoyment of the attained end.* This is the completion of the complex human act and, if a successful completion, an act of enjoyment in the possession of the good. It is the delight resulting from the knowledge that the end sought is at last attained and possessed. If, of course, the end is not finally attained after all, the opposite of enjoyment, sorrow, results.

The last four steps are really consequences of a moral decision and choice already made. In one sense, then, these last four steps add little to the morality of the act since once the choice is made, the remaining steps only carry it out. Nevertheless, the order of execution is important from another standpoint, that of actually accomplishing what we have decided and chosen to do. It may be said, then, that the order of execution reflects the moral order which properly resides in man interiorly. To put the matter in another way, steps 5 to 8—presuming the first four steps—constitute the interior morality of the complex act and steps 9 to 12 the exterior morality. It is to this latter area of morality that positive law also applies.

In the example of buying a suit, although it is true that the last practical judgment and choice are the most important steps, still I do not yet have the suit simply by making the choice. I must, so to speak, rouse myself to external activity by following out the command of reason, by moving myself to borrow the money, by going downtown to the store, and so on. When I finally wear the suit and realize that it is really mine, the final act of enjoyment takes place.

Practical Judgment and Conscience

Our ultimate concern in this chapter is to establish when and how our acts are free. The *fact* of human freedom is obvious; the precise *understanding* of what freedom consists in is difficult. Those denying human freedom usually do so because of the difficulty on the level of analysis. In other words, no one really questions the fact of human freedom, for no one can avoid acting freely at certain times. The difficulty is in trying to explain human freedom which, for some, appears inexplicable. Although freedom of the will is primarily a topic for psychology, we shall consider it in a general way in an ethical context.

It should be noted, first, that the expression "freedom of the will" is imprecise and even misleading. The free act is actually produced by both the intellect and the will. To see how this is so, let us return to steps 7 and 8 in the complex human act. To a certain extent, steps 5 and 6 are also relevant, but we shall speak principally of the two acts of practical judgment and choice.

The situation at this stage of the complex moral act is the following. You are about to make a particular and personal judgment, for example, "I will repay this loan of twenty dollars." Let us recall what is presupposed as you make this judgment. You have, implicitly at least, willed and intended the end—repayment of a debt—because you know that in justice debts should be paid. You may have deliberated about the means of paying, the time, the place, and the manner, and have consented to such means. You then say to yourself in the form of a particular judgment that you will repay the twenty dollars. You recognize what you should do in this case, and this is the judgment of moral conscience.

This judgment of conscience, which merely says that you ought to pay this debt, is an instance falling under the universal judgment that all debts ought to be paid. It is not yet the judgment of the practical intellect in step 7, but is presupposed to it. The practical judgment of the choice to be made—step 7—is always a judgment influenced by the appetite. Let us therefore consider the judgment of conscience apart from the judgment of choice.

It is necessary to insist that conscience is a judgment of the practical intellect. The precise meaning and role of conscience has been obscured in popular understanding. The common description of conscience under the figurative expression of the "still small voice" has turned out to be misleading for those who took the expression literally and then dismissed the whole notion of conscience as a superstitious element carried over from the ancient past. Similarly, when it is said that our conscience "hurts," we should recognize the expression as metaphorical and look for the literal meaning it seeks to convey.

Even the dictionary meaning of conscience is imprecise in defining conscience as a "faculty or power or principle conceived to decide as to the moral quality of one's own thoughts or acts, enjoining what is good." Conscience is not a faculty nor a power nor even a principle. If it were a faculty or power, it would have to be the intellect itself. If it were a principle, it would have to be a principle in the way in which virtue is a principle; but conscience is not a virtue nor any principle of action. More accurately stated, conscience is a judgment made by the intellect; it is therefore an *act* of the intellect by which one judges the rightness or wrongness of an individual action. It is the application of knowledge to concrete moral action. This is conscience in the *subjective* sense of the term: your judgment of what you should do in a particular case. *Objective* conscience is also a particular judgment about a concrete action; it differs from subjective conscience in that it does not involve you personally. The judgment that this act of repaying a debt now is a good act is a judgment of objective conscience. It is subjective when applied to you directly and personally: *I* should repay this debt now.

We shall consider this matter more extensively in the next chapter when we discuss the norm of morality, for questions of rightness and wrongness of conscience can be determined only in relation to some standard by which we can evaluate moral judgments of individual actions. For the moment, let us only emphasize that conscience is an act of knowledge, a judgment of the intellect; it is not something arising primarily from fear or any other emotion, or even from the will. It is utterly removed from anything superstitious. It is not something which a psychologist or a psychiatrist can remove or explain away, for there is no way to prevent our making judgments about what is right and what is wrong. What the psychiatrist can do is help someone make better, i.e., more rational, judgments about what is right and what is wrong by employing sound psychological and moral principles.

One further point about conscience that will lead us back to the consideration of steps 7 and 8 of the complete human act—the judgment of choice and the free act of the will. By means of conscience, an act of knowledge alone, you judge what you should do in a particular case, a judgment made in relation to moral principles. Does it follow that you will do here and now what you judge you should do? From your own experience, you know that you still may not do what you know you should do. Too often, undoubtedly, you have willed and acted contrary to what you know you should do, which is to say, you have acted "against your conscience." Just how does this occur? To answer this question, we must now consider the judgment of choice and the ensuing free act of the will, the choice itself.

Judgment of Choice and the Free Act of the Will

The distinction between conscience and judgment of choice perhaps may be stated more clearly in the following way. In a broader sense of the term, a judgment of conscience is an act made only by the intellect as to what should be done. The judgment of choice, including conscience in a narrower sense of the term, is an act of the practical intellect made in conjunction with the act of choice in the will. These latter two aspects are so intimately connected that it is more accurate to say that judgment of choice is one act which flows from both the intellect and the will, for the judgment of the practical intellect is made under the influence of appetite.

Let us return once more to our example. The judgment that you should repay the loan of twenty dollars this afternoon when you meet your friend is a judgment of conscience based on the objective judgment that this debt should be paid. This is not yet the judgment of choice. You only know it is right for you to repay the loan; you may yet choose otherwise. If you meet the friend and do not repay him, you choose otherwise. In this case, the distinction between judgment of conscience and the judgment-and-choice finally made still remains.

It is unfortunate that a negative or bad situation so clearly distinguishes these two aspects. It is because one chooses contrary to what one has judged as right that we see clearly the difference between judgment of conscience and judgment of choice. Actually, the two aspects are just as distinguishable, though not so obviously, in the case where one chooses to do what one has judged as right. The fact that choosing contrary to what one judges as right more obviously distinguishes the two aspects, tends to lead to an impoverished and even misleading notion of freedom of human acts.

This misleading notion of freedom of human acts—a notion widely accepted—is that the perfection of freedom consists in doing merely what one *pleases*, that is, one is free to do whatever one wishes and, in a sense, regardless of what one knows to be right. A person is considered to be just as free in acting contrary to what he knows as in acting in conformity with what he knows. Indeed, some even consider the latter case not to be freedom at all. The misconception, then, can be stated more readily in the following form: to do what one *ought* to do because he knows what he ought to do is regarded as *not* acting freely. But a moment's reflection should show us that to choose what we know we should do is to act in conformity with a better meaning of freedom than to choose to do what we know we should not do. In the latter case, one may be simply enslaved by his passions.

Let us try to put the matter in such a way as to avoid all misunderstanding, since the preceding paragraph may still leave the meaning of human freedom ambiguous. Although the statement is true that we are most of all free when we choose to do what we know we should do, still this point might be understood in so simple a fashion that one might conclude that acts of freedom are always acts of strict obligation.

We have already made the point that the expression "freedom of the will" can be imprecise and even misleading. The misconception arises from supposing that human freedom flows from and belongs only to the will. The popular view that it does, leads to the imprecise notion that freedom means doing anything one wishes to do. From this misleading notion of human freedom arise many caricatures of freedom in this or that respect, e.g., no restriction in any sense can be put upon "freedom of speech" or "freedom of the press," and so on. There is no doubt about the important moral good of such freedoms and the need to guard them. However, they are not absolute in the sense that they are unlimited and unrestricted; they are relative to a higher good, for example, the common social good. Furthermore, the good in such specific kinds of moral freedom is in proportion to choosing and attaining something *known* to be good. The distinction between license and legitimate freedom reduces to a difference between arbitrary freedom and deliberate freedom, i.e., freedom proceeding from knowledge.

The free act of man must be understood, therefore, as a joint product of intellect and will. Our last wholly interior act prior to the order of execution is the judgment of choice. True enough, the will is dominant here, precisely as influencing the intellect in its very final decision. The will is the moving cause of the intellect's making its final judgment, but the intellect is the determining cause of the will's choosing one object rather than another. Your will motivates you to repay the loan; your intellect specifies what repaying the loan is.

This clarification leads to the distinction between *negative* freedom and *positive* freedom. Negative freedom consists in your being able to reject what you know you should do. You can make a judgment of choice—an act of both intellect and will—contrary to your judgment of conscience—an act only of the intellect. *Positive* freedom consists in your freely choosing to do what you know you should do. You make a judgment of choice in conformity with your judgment of conscience. The relation between negative and positive freedom is thus seen to be a relation between imperfect and perfect freedom.

With this precision, we can see the inadequacy of some notions of freedom currently held; at the same time, we can understand more comprehensively in what freedom properly consists. All views of freedom tending to ascribe it wholly to the will, describing it as doing anything one pleases, exalting it as something absolute and an end in itself, emphasize in varying degrees the negative notion of freedom. The perfection of freedom, contrary to the foregoing views, consists in always choosing what one knows and judges to be right. In this way, one is most free—free as a human being should be free. At the same time, this positive notion of freedom does not imply that all acts of freedom are of obligation, in the strict sense of the term. Many decisions and judgments are such that more than one choice can be made in regard to a given matter, and no obligation need arise as to which choice is finally selected. Often one can only select what appears to be a better choice, not necessarily the best or the only one. Shall I buy a hat today, next week, next month, or not at all this year? The alternatives may be equally good or so little different as not to be of consequence. Serious and important moral issues carry obligation, of course, but even in such cases more than one judgment of choice may be available under the circumstances.

Freedom of Exercise and Freedom of Specification

A final decision should be drawn in order to grasp all that is implied in human freedom from the moral standpoint. The distinction between *freedom of exercise* and *freedom of specification* is one made in terms of the agent as acting or not acting, on the one hand, and in terms of the object as specifying the act done by the agent, on the other. Freedom of exercise refers to the liberty of an agent to act or not to act, not with respect to means, but simply whether to act at all. Freedom of exercise is thus said to concern contradictory alternatives. For example, if you are trying to decide between buying a suit or not buying a suit, you are at that moment not considering a means but an end, and you are free to act or not in this regard. In this sense of the term, we are free with respect to any end or object except happiness itself. This freedom is based on the moral power you have to determine yourself to act or not to act.

Freedom of specification follows upon freedom of exercise. Once you intend to buy a suit, this act must be completed by choosing the means to get this particular suit rather than another, at one store rather than another, and today rather than tomorrow. Freedom thus gets specified concretely in terms of choosing definite means for attaining the desired end.

The importance of this distinction is twofold. First, we recognize through this distinction the sense in which freedom always remains within an agent, unless he is in the presence of a good so absolute and perfect that choice is rendered both futile and impossible—a situation that clearly does not arise in our present life. The freedom an agent always has and which, while normally rational, he can never lose, is freedom of exercise. Freedom of specification, on the other hand, may not always be realizable in certain situations, as, for example, when many alternatives are not presented. It is important to note, then, that a person unable to perform a moral act in the concrete is still free in the sense that he retains freedom of exercise.

The second point is that the type of freedom we treat primarily in ethics is freedom of specification. The reason is that in ethics we presuppose freedom of exercise in a human being and are concerned, rather, with the fulfillment of this freedom in concrete, particular acts, which is the province of the freedom of specification. Our discussion in this chapter, therefore, has centered on freedom of specification, with freedom of exercise presupposed.

When Are Actions Free?

We can now finally answer fully the main question in this chapter by summarizing it as a whole.

All free acts are voluntary, but not all voluntary acts are free. In the broad sense, "voluntary" refers to any tendency toward some good in which the will as a principle is involved, however little. But even in a strict sense not all voluntary acts are free. In the strict sense, a voluntary act is one in which the will is the active principle along with the intellect. Not every act of this kind is a free act.

We began to see the distinction between a voluntary act and a free act by taking some instances of voluntary acts which are not free, e.g. acts of simple willing. We also took an instance of an act admittedly a free one, choice, to contrast it with other voluntary acts not free. This led us to analyze what is called the complete human act, a complex act made up of many smaller acts involving both the intellect and the will.

We saw how the act of choice is not properly concerned with an end as such, but with a means. No one of the first four steps of the complete human act is a free act in the sense of freedom of specification. The free acts of man center on the means and we examined these in steps 5 to 8 in the human act. A refinement of the analysis of them led us to concentrate on judgment as pertaining to the intellect and choice as pertaining to the will. We accordingly saw that a free act does not belong only to the will, but is a joint act belonging to both the intellect and the will; the judgment of choice and the choice of the will are really one act. This clarification led us to the notion of positive freedom, choice in conformity with knowledge.

This chapter has dwelled more on the psychology of the free act than on its morality. The distinction of the various acts of the intellect and will belong to psychology; we have summarized this matter here in order to grasp more fully the moral character of these acts. The moral character arises when we indicate how they are good or evil. For example, we analyzed the acts morally when we related the judgment of conscience to the judgment of choice and to choice as exercised by the will. Now that we know to some extent both the psychological and the moral character of the acts, we can pursue the moral analysis further. Our next step is to see more fully how we evaluate human acts as morally good or evil.

REVIEW QUESTIONS

1. How does an act of desire compare with an act of choice?
2. Is choice connected with pleasure and pain? Why or why not?
3. What is a purely voluntary act? Is it the same as an act of choice?
4. Distinguish between simple willing and choosing.
5. Explain the act of deliberation.
6. What is the relation between deliberation and choice?
7. How closely do you think the outline of the complete human act parallels ordinary experience?
8. Which of the first four steps of the complete human act is most important, and why?
9. Wherein lies the moral importance of the middle four steps of the complete human act?
10. Can human freedom be denied? Explain.
11. What is conscience?
12. Distinguish between subjective and objective conscience.

13. How does judgment of choice differ from the judgment made by conscience?

14. Show how the free act of man is a joint product of the intellect and the will.

15. Distinguish between negative and positive freedom.

16. Indicate some misleading notions of human freedom and contrast them with the precise notion of human freedom.

17. What is the distinction between freedom of exercise and freedom of specification?

18. What is the importance of the distinction between freedom of exercise and freedom of specification?

DISCUSSION

1. A person acts in terms of the ends he seeks; hence the sort of ends he desires characterizes the sort of person he is morally. It is not the case, therefore, that the moral character of a person depends more on what he chooses; it depends equally on the sort of end he intends.

2. A person is judged, not so much by the ends he seeks nor even by the means he chooses, but by the way he fulfills or fails to carry out his intentions and choices. Consequently, the moral order rests primarily on the last steps of the human act concerned with command and execution.

3. Some doctors deliberate about the end of medicine, for they deliberate as to whether or not to allow a patient to die rather than keep him alive in misery. The problem of "mercy killing" generally is a problem about the end of medicine and about which there is much deliberation. Therefore, we deliberate not only about means but about ends.

4. Once a person knowingly wills and chooses to do an evil act, all the moral and physical evil of the act have been accepted by him. Consequently, his actual carrying out of the act neither adds to nor decreases his moral guilt.

5. Choice involves a comparison between things. But to compare things is an act of the intellect. Therefore, choice is an act of the intellect and not of the will.

6. Since conscience is a subjective, particular judgment by a man's intellect, the circumstances surrounding a particular act and the moral standard of the doer cannot be known and judged fully by anyone except the doer. Therefore, conscience is never objective.

7. Moral praise or censure is given to an agent insofar as he is responsible for what he does. But responsibility rests upon a person's choosing what he has judged as right to do, and therefore the act of choice is the climax of the moral act.

8. We intend an end and consent to means before we make a judgment of conscience, and choose. Intention and consent, then, are prior to judgment of conscience and choice. Therefore, our moral life is determined primarily by intention and consent rather than by judgment of conscience and choice.

9. Human freedom is largely illusory. Whatever we do is determined either physically by forces beyond our control or psychologically by knowledge which leaves us no choice. Properly speaking, therefore, there is no freedom of the will.

10. Comment on the following paragraph.

The parents of a kidnapped baby received a message from the kidnapper saying that if the news of the kidnapping was kept from the press for two days, during which time the ransom was to be paid, the baby would be returned alive. A reporter of a large newspaper heard this item of information given by the parents to the police. His paper published the message of the kidnapper in the evening edition. The publisher defended his action by saying that freedom of the press would be violated if the news were kept from the public.

SUGGESTED READINGS

Aristotle, *Ethics*, Book III, chaps. 2-4.
St. Thomas, *Commentary*, Book III, Lessons V-X.
St. Thomas, *Summa Theologiae*, I-II, Questions 11-17.

Bourke, *Ethics*, chap. III, pp. 78-85.
Cronin, *The Science of Ethics*, Vol. I, chap. VII, pp. 196-210.
Gilson, *Moral Values and the Moral Life*, chap. II, pp. 70-78.
Johnston, H., *Business Ethics*. New York: Pitman Corporation, 1956, chap. II, pp. 17-40.
Kant, *Foundation of the Metaphysics of Morals*, third sec. Consult Melden, *Ethical Theories*, pp. 329-334.
Newell-Smith, *Ethics*, chaps. 19-20, pp. 270-314.
Renard, *The Philosophy of Morality*, chap. II, pp. 130-143.
Tsanoff, *Ethics*, chap. 8, pp. 144-168.
Wheelwright, *A Critical Introduction to Ethics*, chap. 13, sec. 2, pp. 383-394.

VII

How do acts become good or bad?

*H*ow human acts become good or bad reduces to a question of the morality of human action. Consequently, before we consider specifically what makes an action good or bad in the moral sense, we should have a precise notion of morality itself. The term *morality* signifies primarily a certain relation human acts have to some end, as to a standard or principle of action. *Morality* is, therefore, an abstract term signifying the moral order of human acts, and we shall understand it more clearly if we contrast the moral order with other kinds of order we can distinguish.

We may speak first of the order of existing things, that is, of reality itself as we experience it. There is an order in the movement of the planets, in the alternation of seasons, and in the growth and development of living things. We simply discover this order, observe it, and seek to understand it, for in no way are we the cause of this order. This is the *real* order.

We may speak also of the order of which we are the sole efficient cause. It is the order made by human reason in its own operations. In this order, we form definitions, propositions, and syllogisms; we establish relations between the objects of the various operations of our intellect. This is the *logical* order.

Distinct from both the real order of existing things and the logical order formed by human reason is the *moral* order. The moral order and the logical order agree in one respect: both orders are caused by reason, although the causality is of a different kind. In the logical order reason is the efficient cause; reason constructs the logical order that it introduces into its own operations. In the moral order, reason is the formal cause; it specifies those human operations which are produced by the will in seeking an end. In studying the moral order, therefore, we examine the order which reason introduces into the operations of the will, especially those operations ordered to an end.

It is in this context that we introduce the term *morality*, understanding it to consist formally in that order which reason establishes in human acts, i.e., the voluntary acts ordered to an end and to means proportioned to an end. This understanding of morality remains general. In this chapter we shall find out specifically how morality is realized concretely, that is, how human acts become morally good or evil. In answering this question, we shall consider first the *sources* of morality and secondly the *norm* or *measure* of morality. By sources of morality we mean the elements of the human act which specify this or that human act as good or evil. The sources of morality can be summarized under two headings: (1) the object of the act, and (2) the circumstances of the act. After this consideration of the sources of morality, we shall be able to treat more intelligibly the measure of morality in the human act, right reason.

The Object of the Act

What primarily *specifies* an act as morally good or bad? It is whatever makes an act the *kind* of act that it is, and in the moral order the *object* of the act specifies what the act is. The moral object of the act, in other words, is that which the act tends to by its very nature.

Let us suppose that I steal a suitcase from a blind person. Let us presume also that I am fully aware of what I am doing. *What* I am doing in this act is the object of the act, namely, the stealing of the suitcase. It is this aspect of the act—the stealing of the suitcase—that makes such an act morally bad, taking for granted the common view of mankind that it is wrong to take something in this fashion. In a more fundamental way we recognize the wrongness of such an act through "right reason," the measure of morality, which we shall consider later in this chapter. Other aspects of the act will not alter the primary specification of the act as one of stealing. The fact the suitcase is a valuable one increases the gravity of the act, but even if the suitcase were a cheap one, the essential moral character of the act would remain. Similarly, the fact that the owner of the suitcase is blind makes the act particularly perverse but does not alter the primary morality of the act. Such aspects relate to circumstances surrounding the act, which we shall consider shortly.

It is evident, then, that what we are calling the moral object of the act specifies the morality of the act *considered in itself*. No other fact or detail about the act can affect this primary moral specification. The moral object, therefore, is the foundation of all morality affecting the act. Thus we arrive at the first source of morality, which we state in the manner of a principle:

1. *The first and essential morality of a human act is taken from the moral object of the act.*

Circumstances

Granted the primacy of the object of the act, it is nonetheless important to recognize that there is a secondary source of morality in human acts, the circumstances. Whereas the object of the act concerns the nature of the act, the circumstances concern the individuality of the act. We speak, of course, only of *moral* circumstances, excluding circumstances which have only a physical bearing on the act. For example, I may be wearing a white shirt when

I steal something, but such a circumstance is usually only physical, not moral. On the other hand, if I tie a white handkerchief over my face when robbing, this fact becomes a moral circumstance, since I voluntarily use the handkerchief as a means to avoid recognition. A moral circumstance, therefore, is a moral condition which is *added* to the moral substance of the act. A moral circumstance *modifies* the act, but it does not cause the act to be the kind of moral act that it is. Hence, we can state another source of morality in terms of the following principle:

2. *The human act derives additional morality from the moral circumstances surrounding the act.*

A comparison with the economic order may help us to see the effect circumstances have on a human act. A pound of butter, having a certain value in itself, takes on additional value if there is a short supply of butter. The circumstance of shortage affects the economic value of butter. Just as the value of a commodity is increased or decreased by various economic circumstances, so is the morality of a human act increased or decreased by moral circumstances. However, the moral aspect of the circumstance must be known and intended by the one performing the act. If I do not know that the person from whom I am stealing is blind, this circumstance would not add an additional moral quality to this act.

We enumerated the moral circumstances when we discussed the voluntariness of human action in connection with the effect of ignorance upon the voluntary character of an act. We shall merely repeat these circumstances without further explanation: *When? Where? How? Why? Who? By what means? What?*

Do all these circumstances affect a human act in the same way and to the same degree? If we recall only a few of our ordinary experiences, we shall realize that these circumstances affect our moral acts variously. One and the same circumstance will greatly condition an act in one situation and hardly at all in another. Thus, the circumstances of place may matter a great deal one time and very little at another time. Hence, the following principle:

3. *Some circumstances add an essentially different kind of morality; others change only the degree.*

A circumstance will add a different kind of morality and change the morality of the act essentially when it adds a goodness or evil over and beyond what the act already has from its object. Thus, in a murder in a cathedral, the circumstance of place adds an evil over and beyond the evil of murder itself, the profaning of a place of worship. A circumstance will change only the degree of morality when there is no distinct moral good or evil added to an act already morally determined by object. For example, to steal a large amount of money rather than a small amount, a circumstance of quantity, will increase the moral evil already present but will not add an evil distinct from that of stealing.

The Circumstance of End

This circumstance has a special importance which requires particular consideration. The circumstance of end is posed by the question *Why?* It refers to the purpose or motive the agent has in performing the act, and is sometimes called the *subjective end* to distinguish it from the *objective end,* the end to which the act itself tends, which is the same as the object of the act. To clarify this important distinction on the meaning of end, we might use Robin Hood as an example. His acts of taking possessions away from their owners are acts of robbery from the point of view of the end of the act. Robin Hood's motive may have been the laudable one of helping poor persons or of righting certain wrongs, but this subjective end does not alter the fact that the objective end of the act is and remains robbery.

It is not difficult to see that the circumstance of end is the most important of the moral circumstances affecting an act. It is a special source of morality because the end of the agent can change completely the moral quality of the action he is doing. His intention can turn the best of acts into the worst of acts. The reason is that the motive one has in doing the act, when one is sufficiently conscious of it, explains precisely why one *is* doing the act. As every lover of detective stories knows, it is the motive that matters. The *why* of the crime is necessary for the fictional plausibility of the story and, in addition, throws light on other circumstances of the act, especially on the important circumstance of who did it. The good detective story author must be well aware of the relevance of moral circumstances in human action.

Detective stories, like all fiction, mirror life in revealing ways. And so in real life, motives matter. The *why* of the act tells much about all other circumstances and affects considerably the very nature of the act itself. Just how much influence does the circumstance of end have on the morality of the act? Two distinct points need to be made in answering this question, and we shall state them as two final principles and sources of morality.

4. *The end of the agent can turn an act morally good by object into a morally evil act.*

Telling the truth is an act good by object, and this is a moral good that is recognized by everyone. But to tell the truth with the intention of injuring somebody when there is no need or obligation for doing so and when the intention is to slander a person's reputation is to turn an act good by object into an act evil as a whole. It is not enough to suppose that because an act is good in itself it is good in any and all circumstances. In particular, the circumstance of end may make all the difference in the world—the difference between a basically good act and an actually vicious one. In cases like this we see how the right ordering of the will is paramount in the moral order of action.

5. *The circumstance of end can never turn an act evil by object into a morally good act.*

This last source of morality is somewhat the opposite in effect of the preceding one. The preceding one indicates to what extent the circumstance of end can affect the morality of an act; it can turn a morally good act into a morally bad one. We now see that great though the influence of the intention is on the act, it cannot turn a morally bad act into a good one.

This last point can be put in more familiar terms by stating that under *no* circumstances can a good end or motive justify a bad means. In this formulation, we take the object of the act—the moral nature of the act—as a means in relation to the end the agent has in mind. It cannot be stressed too much that if an act is morally bad by object, no end the agent has in mind, regardless of how noble and laudable it may be, can alter the essential badness of the act. It might seem, as we saw just a moment ago, that if a bad intention can corrupt a morally good act, then a good intention ought to make an act otherwise bad a good one. But this argument is moral sophistry. The argument is sophistic because it deliberately confuses what is essentially evil with a good extrinsic to the nature of the act, the intention. It may be doubted, furthermore, whether the intention can remain wholly good when a person knowingly tries to use an evil means for a good end.

This is a point in ethics easily misunderstood and a principle too frequently violated in action. We are all tempted to try to justify a bad act by a good intention. Indeed, times and occasions arise when we find it difficult to avoid doing what we know is bad but which we should like to justify by supposing that a good intention will "make things all right." The temptation may be strong, for example, to tell a lie because you do not wish to hurt a person's feelings. Such situations admittedly can be difficult, and we shall see later how we can deal prudently with them. Our point now, however, is only to state the moral principle involved and to see what it means and why it is absolute.

The last two principles of morality show in opposite ways the moral influence the circumstance of end has upon the morality of the act. The end can affect the morality of an act in lesser ways also. Thus, if an act is bad by object, a bad intention can aggravate the evil, while a good intention might lessen the evil without making the act morally good, as we have just seen. Similarly, if an act is morally good by object, a good intention adds to the goodness of the act, while an intention that is not good renders an act defective to that extent.

"Circumstance" Ethics

It is evident that circumstances of all kinds greatly affect our actions in the moral order. The fact that every moral act is modified by the particular circumstances accompanying it sufficiently indicates the moral importance of circumstances, and moral theory would be greatly in error in not taking into account the full effect of circumstances on the morality of human action. Nevertheless, the role of circumstances in human action can be exaggerated, and, in fact, has been by some adherents of a moral doctrine known as "circumstance" ethics or "situational" ethics. The exaggeration consists in trying to eliminate all general principles of morality by making morality wholly dependent on the circumstances of the unique situation. In other words, since each human act is unique, no general principle holds; moral decisions of what is right or wrong to do can be made entirely and only at the time one confronts each unique situation; and every situation is unique. In such a view, the only source of morality is circumstances; the other source of morality we have discussed in this chapter, the moral object of the act, is denied altogether, along with any general principle of morality.

The truth in this extreme view is the important one that no moral act can be rightly evaluated apart from the circumstances surrounding the act. This truth, far from being in opposition to the recognition of a moral object of the act independent of circumstances, necessarily presupposes the object of an act. Moral circumstances are significant only if there are determinate kinds of acts which they can modify. We must know, for example, that telling the truth *as such*, i.e. by its object, is a certain *kind* of act before we can evaluate how the various circumstances affect performing this act here and now. The role of circumstances in human actions does make every act unique, and this is why, in the completely practical order of action here and now, knowledge alone is not sufficient, the rectitude of the appetite presupposed by the virtue of prudence being necessary to act here and now in these circumstances. But the uniqueness of each act in no way denies the nature of an act as determined by its object any more than the uniqueness of each human being denies the human nature found in each individual. A "circumstance" ethics is right in affirming the necessary and important role circumstances play in every act; it is wrong in making circumstances the *only* source of morality in human acts.

Indifference of Acts

Are all acts either morally good or morally evil, or are there also acts which are morally indifferent? This question cannot be answered as simply and directly as might be supposed.

The meaning of "indifference" needs to be clarified first. As we shall see in a moment, moral good and evil is determined by the relation of the object of the act to a measure of morality, right reason. It is in this way we see that some acts are morally good as such, for example, helping a person in distress, and others are morally evil as such, for example, committing murder. In the same way we can see that some acts by object imply neither agreement with nor opposition to right reason, for example, walking. Such acts we designate as "morally indifferent."

This consideration of moral indifference is abstract, however; it is based on the nature of a human act and its general relation to a standard of morality. In the concrete singular order, no human act is morally indifferent. *Circumstances* alter cases. What is done here and now is done when it should be done, where it should be done, or as it should be done. As we have seen, the moral circumstances surrounding singular human acts necessarily qualify morally any individual act when it is actually done.

The circumstance of end, the intention of the agent, is alone enough to eliminate moral indifference from individual human acts. Particular human acts always proceed from some motive of the agent, and this motive will exhibit at least agreement or disagreement with the rule of reason. Walking, *abstractly* considered, is morally indifferent, but no one walks in the abstract. When you actually walk, you walk under certain circumstances and especially with some purpose in mind, however implicit or vague this purpose may be.

There are two points, then, to note about the moral indifference of human acts. First, a distinction must be made between an abstract and a concrete consideration of human acts. In the first consideration there is meaning to the phrase "morally indifferent acts." In the second consideration there is no meaning to "morally indifferent acts," i.e., there is no such human act in the existential order. This distinction helps us to understand more precisely the meaning of a morally indifferent act; it is an act which, as such, is neither good nor evil. It becomes one and not the other through circumstances affecting it when it is done here and now. Moral indifference, consequently, extends to the object of the act but not to the circumstances.

The second point is that moral indifference must be understood in the context of *human* acts, not in the wider context of any act that a human being can perform. In discussing moral indifference, we presuppose that we are considering only voluntary and conscious acts. Many acts we perform are below the level of distinctively human acts; these belong to the subconscious and unconscious levels. Such acts might be thought of as "indifferent," but they are not indifferent in the sense we mean by moral indifference. They lie outside the moral order altogether.

The Measure of Morality: Right Reason

In discussing the sources of morality, we have spoken of *right reason*. In a sense, we can also say that right reason is a source of morality, but it is more precise to speak of it as the measure of morality or, as it is sometimes called, the norm of morality. In addition, then, to the sources of morality as an answer to the question of how human acts become good or evil, we must consider right reason as the measure of morality.

Let us recall that it is proper to a human being to live according to reason, the power by which man grasps what is true. It is this characteristic which distinguishes the human being from other living things. We know, also, that human acts are human insofar as they are voluntary acts, i.e. inasmuch as we *will* them. The rational and the voluntary both characterize human action in such a way that we will our actions according to what we know. To be *moral* is, first of all, to be subject to reason.

But we must reason rightly. The measure of morality is not just reason, but *right* reason. What precisely does "right" mean here? It does not mean right reasoning in the sense that logical thinking is "right." Such reasoning belongs to the purely speculative order and to theoretical knowledge, whereas we are dealing with the practical order and specifically with the moral order. In the practical order we know that the end is primary and that we must be concerned with action as ordered to some end. We reason rightly in this order when we judge rightly of the end with the intention to will accordingly. Human reason, therefore, is the measure of morality in the sense that it is a rule for the human will by which the goodness of the will is measured.

This observation, however, is a very general one, and presumably too general for an effective measure of morality. Let us try to make the role of human reason as the norm of morality more specific. We know, as we have mentioned, that in the practical order we must consider action as ordered to an end. Is it enough to judge rightly in relation to the absolutely ultimate end? True enough, all action is finally ordered to such an end, and if we do know what the ultimate end is and can see that because of such an end this or that action is to be done or avoided, such knowledge measures the morality of the action. For example, we can know through right reason that to murder someone turns us away from the ultimate end, even if we only know somewhat vaguely the ultimate end as happiness.

But often the ultimate end seems to be remote for an action here and now. Our experience tells us that usually we seek a more proximate end by this or that means. In the previous chapter, we summarized the complex human act in terms of twelve steps which carry out the act. The first four steps concerning the end and, particularly, the judgment about the end and the intention of the end, locate where and how right reason operates as the measure of morality. It is through reason we judge the end sought; the rightness of the reason comes from our true judgment and from our intending the end we judge as truly good. As the measure of morality, then, right reason is true knowledge of moral principles, that is, of the ends of human action by virtue of which we know what is right to do.

However, we cannot ignore altogether the order of means. As we know from the previous chapter, once we intend an end seriously we then deliberate, consent, make a practical judgment, and finally choose the means leading to the attainment of the end sought. This is the completely practical order, the realm of prudence. This order of prudent action presupposes and follows upon the judgment of right reason in such a way that we can say right reason extends secondarily to the judgment of prudence in the completely practical order. The judgment of prudence, consequently, is directed by the right desire of a good end proposed by the intellect, that is, by right reason in its primary and essential function.

As we go through the different virtues in the following chapters we shall see in another way how right reason is realized concretely. The virtuous life—that good moral life which is the indispensable means to happiness—is the life of right reason in action. Knowing what the virtues are, we can seek to realize the good of the different virtues in our action. The good of justice, for example, will be judged as something we should will to possess in this action; similarly, with the good of temperance, fortitude, prudence, and so on. When we say, then, that right reason is concerned with judging action as related to some end we mean especially the good of virtue, for the good of virtue is an end constantly proposed through reason. This good of virtue is not the absolutely ultimate end, nor the most immediate end, but a relatively ultimate end—the sort of end that is indispensable for leading us to the absolutely ultimate end. We shall see, in the chapter on intellectual virtues, how right reason is a good of the intellect and, especially, how it operates fully and perfectly in the prudent man.

Two final points remain with respect to right reason. The first concerns the development of right reason in us: how do we come to reason rightly in the moral order? It may be presumed that ethics will be helpful, but the study of ethics is auxiliary at best. We need to turn to experience for a complete answer. We begin developing and forming right reason when we are very young, with our parents or guardians providing help and examples. As we grow older, we learn from the guidance and examples of teachers, friends and others, as well as from our own knowledge and experience. The laws of the community in which we live, both religious and political, give us further determinations of right reason as it is to operate in us. We come to know in time that what political laws express are to be obeyed not merely because law-givers say so but because they reflect, in varying ways, what we might call the law to which the state itself is bound, the universal or natural moral law. No state does and no state can make a law, for example, that murder must be done, because if it did it would violate a more fundamental law at once universal and natural. Right reason, then, is generated in us by external sources as well as by the natural development of reason within us.

The second point follows directly from the first. Right reason, as far as it extends, operates effectively as a measure of morality. But right reason itself has a measure; it is subordinate to a more ultimate rule of morality beyond even that of the natural moral law. This more ultimate rule of morality is, again, reason—not human but divine. Recognizing through human reason as we can that God exists, we recognize also that divine reason is a more ultimate measure of the morality of our action than our own reason. Human right reason, in fact, is the bridge between divine reason and our action. Apart from what we can know through human reason, divine reason is made manifest to us through revelation and becomes our supreme measure of morality.

REVIEW QUESTIONS

1. Distinguish the real, logical, and moral orders.

2. What is the general meaning of "morality"?

3. What is the moral object of an act?

4. Contrast the circumstances of an act with the moral object of an act.

5. How can a circumstance add an essentially different kind of morality to the act?

6. What is the distinction between subjective and objective end?

7. Why is the circumstance of end the most important one?

8. Can a person's motive turn a morally good act into a morally bad one? Explain.

9. Explain the statement "a good end never justifies a bad means." How universal and binding is it?

10. To what extent do circumstances affect the morality of actions? Are they the only source of morality?

11. What is a morally indifferent act? In what sense are human acts never morally indifferent?

12. In general, how is human reason the measure of morality?

13. When is human reason "right" in the practical order?

14. How is right reason formed and developed?

15. Is right reason the absolute measure of morality? Explain.

DISCUSSION

1. Most of the actions we do day by day are insignificant and unimportant. We eat, go to work, talk to friends, look at television, and sleep. Such acts are not morally significant. If they are morally insignificant, they are morally indifferent. Most of our acts, therefore, are morally indifferent acts.

2. Every moral decision has to be based on a unique situation with circumstances peculiar to the situation. But no general principle can be formulated for situations which are unique. The whole moral domain, therefore, is circumstantial and utterly opposed to any application of objective, universal moral principles.

3. A moral circumstance is a singular condition affecting the goodness or badness of an action. But in order for a circumstance to affect the morality of an action, the action itself must be of a certain moral kind. Moral circumstances, therefore, cannot constitute the morality of the action itself, but can only alter the morality the action has of itself.

4. The object of an action is related to the action as effect to cause. The goodness of an effect depends on its cause. It seems, consequently, that the essential morality of an act is derived from the act itself and not from the object of the act, which is its effect.

5. In the moral order, a person's intention primarily determines the morality of his action. As long as a person intends a good end, any sort of action he performs will be morally good. A good end will make the means good because the end is the cause of the goodness of the act as a whole. Therefore, a good end justifies any means.

6. A norm of morality is effective only if it supplies a sufficient sanction. Only when we know through revelation from God that we are to act in certain ways will we have a sufficient sanction for acting. Right reason is therefore not a norm of morality.

7. Toward the end of the World War II, the American Air Force dropped atom bombs on the Japanese cities of Hiroshima and Nagasaki. The object of this act was mass destruction. The motive for the act was to force the Japanese to surrender and thus save countless American lives which would have been lost in capturing the Japanese mainland by assault. However, the object of the act, the hideous destruction of two cities and their population, was evil in itself. Therefore, such an act cannot be justified as a morally good

one, for the circumstance of end can never turn an act evil by object into a morally good act.

8. The principle of double effect, a moral principle, states that when an action results in two consequences, one good and the other evil, the act is morally justified if (1) the good is reasonably proportionate to the evil, (2) if the good cannot be attained without the evil, and (3) if the good is directly intended while the evil is only permitted. The dropping of the atom bombs on the two Japanese cities is a case falling under the application of the principle of the double effect. Therefore, the dropping of the bombs was morally justified.

SUGGESTED READINGS

Aristotle, *Ethics*, Book III. chap. 5.
St. Thomas, *Commentary*, Book III, Lessons XI-XIII.
St. Thomas, *Summa Theologiae*, I-II, Questions 18-21.

Bourke, *Ethics*, chap. IV, pp. 121-160.
Gilson, *Moral Values and the Moral Life*, chap. III, pp. 79-90.
Milner, *The Elements of Ethics*, chap. VIII-X, pp. 88-115.
Renard, *The Philosophy of Morality*, chap. II, pp. 96-127.
Ward, *Christian Ethics*, chap. 6, pp. 71-87.

VIII

Virtues related to the passions

We can now consider the virtues specifically. We have already treated virtue generally in Chapter IV in the context of seeing it as the means of attaining the ultimate end of happiness. We have also investigated the voluntary and free act of man, since a virtuous act is an act of deliberate choice. We shall now treat some of the virtues specifically, for knowing the different virtues will help us to seek to acquire them. We need to have such an end in view because, as we have already insisted, ethics is a practical science whose ultimate end is to guide human beings to moral action. The fact that ethics as a science cannot embrace the completely practical order of singular acts and must deal primarily with-speculative truths about the practical order is not at all opposed to our ordering this knowledge ultimately

116

to action as far as possible. Without this practical ordering the knowledge of ethics is not of much value.

Let us begin by indicating the order of procedure we shall follow in the next three chapters, in which we shall consider the more important virtues.

The Cardinal Virtues

Our mode of procedure will consist in examining primarily the most important virtues, that is, those virtues which have come to be known as the *cardinal* virtues. The cardinal virtues are the virtues upon which the moral life of a human being principally depends and which especially cause the good human life. The etymology of the word *cardinal—cardines,* in Latin, signifies the support a door receives from its *hinges*—suggests that man's moral character "hinges" particularly on these principal virtues.

How many cardinal virtues are there? Throughout the tradition of western thought the number of these virtues has been consistently put at four. This persistent view is based upon an analysis showing why there are just four cardinal virtues, no more and no less. The analysis rests primarily on the recognition of the moral good as that which is in conformity with and determined by right reason. If we note the different ways in which this good of reason can be considered, we shall have as many cardinal virtues as there are ways of realizing the good conformed to reason.

When we speak of "reason," whether in the practical order of morality or in the theoretical order of speculative knowledge, it is necessary to emphasize time and again that "reason" merely refers to the power we have to know reality for what it is. This emphasis is necessary because of a modern distrust, somewhat justified, of an abstract signification attached to "reason" by various idealist and rationalistic philosophers. In an idealistic context "reason" becomes separated from and even opposed to the real order with which we are in contact during every conscious moment of our experience. In using the term "reason," then, we disavow any meaning of the term which suggests the imposition of "abstract thought" on reality. The reverse is rather the case: reason is the human power by which we discover, not manufacture, the real order. We speak of "reason,"

therefore, simply as meaning the power we have for grasping whatever truth we can know about reality.

When we speak of the "good of reason" in a moral context, we
mean the good achieved by reason's *directing* either its own acts or
the acts of other powers. This good of reason can be considered,
first of all, as it is realized in the very act of reason itself, which
gives us the cardinal virtue of *prudence:* reason well ordered in relation to human actions. The good of reason can also be realized by
putting order, the infallible sign of reason, into other acts or operations. If the order of reason is realized in external operations—operations directed to what is due to other persons—we have the cardinal
virtue of *justice.* The order of reason can also be realized in the
passions. As we have seen, there is a fundamental division of sense
appetite into two main kinds. Since the order of reason is realized
diversely in these two divisions of sense appetite, there will be two
cardinal virtues in relation to the sense appetite. If the passions
arouse us to something against reason and therefore need checking,
the good of reason in such passions is realized in the virtue of *temperance,* which orders the concupiscible appetite. But if the passions
seek to lead us away from a good which reason dictates should be
present, then we need to be strengthened to realize this good by the
cardinal virtue of *fortitude,* which deals with the irascible appetite.

Perhaps it is easier to see why there are four cardinal virtues if we
consider the *subject* of each virtue, that is, the power in which each
virtue is located. The general point is that any power in which the
good of reason can be realized becomes the subject of a cardinal
virtue. Clearly, reason itself can be such a subject, and thus prudence perfects the power of reason itself. Any power which can be
rational by participation can be a subject of virtue. The will, which
is intellectual appetite, is certainly rational by participation, and we
find it to be the subject of the virtue of justice. However, the will
does not need virtue in relation to its own object, that is, for the
good of reason proportioned to the will. Hence, man by his will
loves his own good, the common good, and even the divine good in
the natural order without the need of virtue. But for loving the
good of one's neighbor, the will needs the virtue of justice.

The sense appetite, too, can be rational by participation, though
not so fully as the intellectual appetite. Hence, the concupiscible

appetite is the subject of temperance and the irascible power is the subject of fortitude. Since there are no other powers in man which are either rational themselves or rational by participation, there are only four cardinal virtues.

The Cardinal Virtue of Fortitude

There are at least two reasons why it is appropriate to begin with the virtue of fortitude. First, fortitude is clearly an admirable quality to have, and since virtue is often misconceived as narrow, negative, and even weak, it is desirable to take as the first instance of a major virtue one which is admittedly a strong, positive quality that immediately arouses admiration. Such precisely is fortitude; a brave man is admirable. The second reason is that among the cardinal virtues, fortitude seems to be the one best known and most readily intelligible. Even in childhood we become familiar with the virtue of fortitude from many stories and motion pictures we experience and in which we are led to admire the bravery of human beings.

We use the name "fortitude" for the cardinal virtue rather than "courage," even though the latter word may be more familiar. "Fortitude" brings out more formally the perfection of the virtue whereas "courage" is sometimes applied to an emotion not necessarily ordered by reason. Thus, we might speak of the courage of a lion, but never the fortitude of a lion.

When considering virtue in general, we defined it as a mean between extremes. As we take up the virtues specifically, it will be necessary to establish more definitely just how each virtue is a mean between what precise extremes. We already know that the subject of fortitude is the irascible appetite and that the good of reason which will be realized will be that of the emotions of the irascible appetite. The irascible appetite is that division of sense appetite concerned with avoiding what is sensibly unpleasant. There are specific emotions related to what is sensibly unpleasant. Fear is perhaps the emotion which comes to mind most readily, for we fear what is unpleasant and threatening and, consequently, tend to flee from these evils. Sometimes, however, we react in a contrary manner in the presence of an evil confronting us by seeking to vanquish the evil rather than to flee from it. We then have the contrary emotion of boldness; we face the evil threatening us and seek to overcome it.

It is evident, then, that fear and boldness are opposite emotions, for we react in contrary ways when we act out of fear or boldness. It is evident, too, that we think of the brave man, the man with fortitude, as one who withstands fear in a "manly" way or as one who deals boldly with some threatening evil. Keeping in mind that a virtue is a mean between extremes, we thus come to see how fortitude is a mean between two extremes of emotional states, fear and boldness. We wish to emphasize the point that we must say between the *extremes* of these emotions rather than between the emotions themselves. The virtue of fortitude does not utterly subdue the emotions or in any way suppress their activity. Quite the contrary, in fact; otherwise fortitude could not be the realization of the good of reason *in* the emotions. Fortitude, therefore, orders the activity of the emotions; the emotions of fear and boldness blend into a superior mode of action, superior precisely as elevated by reason as a directing principle. The emotions participate in an activity which they are incapable of effecting by themselves. A lion can be bold in an animal sort of way, but only a human being can be bold in a rational sort of way.

We see this situation realized in experience. What characterizes the truly brave man, the one with the virtue of fortitude? He is not one who simply gives way in fright before some evil. The one who fears excessively any and all evils threatening him is a coward, the opposite of the brave man. On the other hand, the truly brave man is not one who has no fear at all, although bravery is often associated popularly and erroneously with the utterly fearless person. Such a person is simply rash, excessively bold, and overconfident. He, too, is opposed to the brave man. We thus see the two extremes which the brave man is not: the coward and the rash man, both excessively emotional in opposite ways.

How Fortitude Is a Perfection

The mean of the virtue of fortitude soars above these two defective conditions of excessive fear and rashness. The brave man does experience fear, for it is perfectly natural to have fear in the presence of danger. In fact, without at least some arousing of fear there could be no activity of the virtue of fortitude. The brave soldier, perhaps the most obvious example of a person with fortitude, is the first to admit he experiences fear in battle. But he masters it, controls it, and directs it. The primary and immediate act of the virtue of fortitude, accordingly, is to *moderate* fear. But the brave man does not stop with this moderation of fear. He must, if possible, also vanquish the evil or danger threatening him, that is, attack it with boldness. Hence the man with fortitude, though experiencing fear, rationally controls it in order to act boldly in the face of danger. Let us illustrate this perfection of fortitude in the manner we illustrated the perfection of virtue generally, by using a triangle.

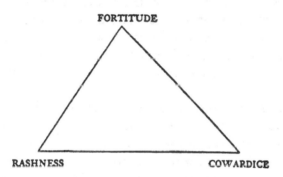

We use the shape of a triangle, it will be remembered, to illustrate graphically how a virtue rises as a mean of perfection above two contrary defects—in the present instance above the vices of rashness and cowardice. The virtue of fortitude is a perfection because it realizes the good of reason in the irascible emotions of man, and by this very fact is opposed to two different vices, each of which goes directly against the good of reason. The one extreme, rashness, is a vice by excess; the other, cowardice, is a vice by defect. At the same time, the peak of the triangle reminds us that virtue is in another sense an extreme, but an extreme of perfection. The virtue of fortitude, as is the case with any other virtue, is not just a mediocre compromise between too much and too little. A virtue is the mean between too much and too little movement of the appetite in the sense that it is a psychological mean between extremes. As a moral mean it is, to reiterate the point, the extreme which is perfection. Thus we see how a virtue brings out the best in man, whereas vice brings out the worst.

It will be noticed that the peak of the triangle is closer to the extreme of rashness than to the extreme of cowardice. We already know that virtue in general is a mean of reason rather than a quantitative mean lying in the exact center. In the case of fortitude, the mean is closer to the excess than to the defect because the primary act of the virtue of fortitude is to withstand and moderate fear, since fear is the natural reaction to a threatening danger. Our first inclination with regard to danger, in other words, is to experience fear, and the first step of the brave man consists in moderating any tendency to let fear become excessive. But in order to moderate such fear, the brave man must incline first toward boldness, and thus the mean of the virtue of fortitude is realized closer to the bold extreme than to the fear extreme. The practical point to note is that we need to counteract the natural inclination to be fearful in the presence of danger by striking the mean more on the side of boldness than on the side of fear.

Yet, a qualification must be added to this point. The mean of perfection is closer to the bold extreme for *most* persons, but not for all. There are some persons who by temperament tend to be bold rather than fearful, and for such persons the mean of fortitude may be closer to the fear extreme than to the bold extreme; they have to moderate their natural inclination to act rashly in the face of danger. So it is that each of us has to take into account his own temperament and inclination in order to act well in the practical order. For you the actual mean of fortitude will be realized somewhat differently than for me. For both of us the mean may be closer to the bold extreme, but more so for you than for me. A third person may find the mean closer to the other extreme. Nevertheless, we are safe in stating generally that the mean of fortitude is closer to the bold extreme than to the fear extreme.

The Definition of Fortitude

By gathering together what we have said so far we can formulate the definition of the virtue of fortitude. Fortitude is *a virtue in the mean moderating the emotions of fear and boldness to achieve the good of reason in the irascible appetite.*

Some further clarification may be desirable. We have already noted that fear and boldness are concerned with evils, particularly those involving dangers. The question naturally arises whether every kind of danger requires the activity of fortitude. We can answer this by recognizing that the emotions of fear and boldness are aroused only if the danger is at least somewhat grave and connected with some event we should describe as terrible. Now it is evident that the greatest danger threatening us is death, since, humanly speaking, death is the most terrible of all things. And it is precisely concerning the threat of death that the most typical acts of fortitude are in fact exercised.

Indeed, the *readiness* to give up one's life is the fundamental disposition necessary for fortitude to develop and blossom into its full perfection. It is enough that this readiness be formed in us; we may never be called upon actually to risk our life. By successfully moderating fear and attacking evil we acquire this readiness to give up even our life, not, of course, rashly or for the sake of suffering injury or death for its own sake but for the sake of a proportionate good, a good established by reason. This point leads us to see that the full development of fortitude requires direction from a higher good attained through prudence and justice, e.g., man is brave in order to achieve what is just.

A precise understanding of the cardinal virtue of fortitude prevents us from confusing acts of apparent bravery with acts of the virtue itself. For example, a person may seem to be facing danger bravely when actually he is only acting primarily out of anger, another irascible emotion which, as a *principle* of action, cannot realize the good of reason. Anger may be helpful in overcoming a danger, but anger alone is not a distinctively human way of facing danger. We achieve the good of fortitude through being directed not by anger but by reason which, in directing anger, makes anger also humanly good. There is also such a thing as stupid courage: a person may appear to be acting bravely when actually he is simply ignorant that danger is present. Finally, to face danger merely because of force or coercion is not to act bravely. True enough, coercion may be present when one does really act bravely, but if one

acts bravely it will never be solely because of coercion. Not everyone who is drafted into military service acts bravely; still, nothing
prevents his acting bravely even if coercion is present. Nor does it
follow that everyone who volunteers for military service acts
bravely; a person may be only avoiding domestic or personal problems. The virtue has to consist in voluntary, habitual acts which, at
least implicitly, are intended for the appropriate good end.

In terms of the definition of fortitude we can state the proximate
and remote objects of the virtue of fortitude. The *proximate* object
of fortitude is the irascible emotion, specifically fear and boldness.
The *remote* object is the thing or event which arouses fear or boldness, primarily an event involving the possibility of death or some
form of injury. This distinction reminds us that a virtue is related
most immediately to interior states and activities. It is true that
events outside us usually produce the beginnings, at least, of our
interior states, but what characterizes virtue formally is the perfecting of these states by realizing the good of reason in them. Fortitude, then, primarily and immediately ennobles our irascible emotions. In a word, it "humanizes" them.

Virtues Connected with Fortitude

The virtues associated with the cardinal virtue of fortitude are
concerned with dangers less than death. Since fortitude has a distinct object, namely dangers relating to death, the other virtues of
the irascible appetite cannot be related to fortitude as various species under a genus in the manner in which we would say that red
and yellow are species under the genus of color. This latter kind of
division is technically known as a division of a whole into *subjective*
parts, each of which would be a distinct virtue sharing the essence
of fortitude. But since no other virtue of the irascible appetite bears
formally on dangers relating to death, no other such virtue is a subjective part of the cardinal virtue of fortitude.

The relation of the other virtues of the irascible appetite to fortitude is of another kind, one known as a relation of *potential* parts
to a whole. In this type of relation or division the parts do not share
in the essence and perfection of the whole but are parts *like* the
whole without realizing the perfection of the whole. They are parts

which are related as distinct powers of a whole, in the manner in which we speak of the executive, legislative, and judicial parts of a government. Fortitude is related to the virtues associated with it in this manner, and this clarification is necessary to understand the nature and role of these other virtues of the irascible appetite. These associated virtues, therefore, are concerned with great projects or events, difficulties or dangers, but not in a way directly involving the evil of death.

Magnanimity

Unfortunately, the word "magnanimity" has lost its vigor of meaning in English: current usage of the word reduces it more or less to a somewhat vague state of being generous. From the etymological point of view, the word "magnanimity" is made up of two Latin words: *magna*, signifying "great" and *anima*, signifying "soul." Thus the nominal meaning of the word is a greatness of soul or mind. What tends to make greatness of mind? This occurs when our mind values great things, aspires to great things, and does not become engrossed with what is trivial and insignificant. From this common description one can see how such a virtue will be connected with the irascible appetite in man, for the irascible appetite concerns sense goods difficult to attain or evils difficult to overcome and it is only greatness of mind that will overcome difficulties for the sake of some great good.

The virtue of magnanimity is therefore defined as the virtue *which inclines and strengthens the irascible appetite to do great acts worthy of honor.* The specific characteristic of magnanimity is that it realizes the good of reason in the irascible appetite by facing and overcoming obstacles and dangers for the sake of achieving what is great and honorable. You are magnanimous to the extent that, believing you can accomplish what is difficult, you do not give way before obstacles in your firm desire and hope to achieve a worthy good that is difficult to possess. For example, you are magnanimous if you sacrifice personal wealth or great effort for the security of your country. If you are led to a point where you would expose yourself to danger of death for the sake of a worthy good, you pass from magnanimity to fortitude, from the lesser virtue to the cardinal virtue. .

The person who acts against the good of reason realized by magnanimity acquires sooner or later the vices opposed to this virtue. We can specify four vices opposed to magnanimity. Three of them occur by failing to curb excessive tendencies in the irascible appetite.

The first of these is *presumption*, which causes one consistently to attempt to accomplish what is beyond his ability. The second is *excessive ambition*; the excessively ambitious person constantly strives in one way or another for honor or recognition not due him and for which he has an inordinate desire. It was in this sense of the term that Mark Antony seemed to say that Caesar was ambitious. The third vice, *vainglory*, is the inordinate desire for fame and praise. These three vices are the same to the extent that all involve the failure to moderate by reason excessive desires in the irascible appetite. They differ in that each is concerned with different objects of desire: presumption with great works, excessive ambition with honor, and vainglory with fame or praise. The person who has these bad habits or is inclining toward them and wishes to rid himself of them must, first of all, restrain and curb these excessive movements of the irascible appetite.

Opposed to these three vices and opposed in another way to the virtue of magnanimity itself is the vice of *pusillanimity*, a term combining two words meaning "very little" and "mind." This defect is a kind of faint-heartedness characterizing a person who avoids doing what great things he is really capable of doing, often because of servile fear. More precisely, he does not regard himself as worthy when in fact he is. Hence, there is an element of ignorance involved to the extent that such a person does not know his own qualifications. But this ignorance stems from laziness and the accompanying refusal to undertake ventures having any magnitude.

It is useful to know the vices opposed to any virtue for at least two reasons. First, by understanding what a particular vice precisely is we come to know, by contrast, just what the perfection of the virtue is. We know more clearly and comprehensively how the good of reason gets realized in various ways in the different virtues by seeing how each vice in some specific way goes against the good of reason. We must always keep in mind, however, that virtue and vice are *voluntary* and *rational* states of moral life. We should not confuse a mere inclination or sentimental desire to do something good with virtue, or a psychological disorder or a physiological disease with vice. The latter conditions, particularly, are not really moral states which we deliberately will to form and develop. A sign of this distinction is that we blame a person for a vice but not for a mental or a physical illness.

The second reason is a wholly practical one. Knowing what the different vices are helps us to check tendencies toward such bad habits. We can take measures in time to prevent the growing of disordered tendencies into settled dispositions. The more we know what to avoid as well as what to do positively, the more likely we are to act in a mature and humanly good way.

Magnificence

We are again faced with a word that has largely lost the force of its original meaning and is now used in a derived, weakened sense. We tend to think of magnificence in terms of splendor of surroundings and sumptuous adornment, and it is thus one speaks of Lorenzo, the Magnificent. The primary and original meaning of the word, however, can be grasped from its etymology: it comes from the Latin words meaning "great" (*magnus*) and "making" (*facere*). Hence the virtue of magnificence refers to the making or doing of great things.

It is easy to confuse magnificence with magnanimity, since both seem to be concerned with great action springing from strong promptings of the irascible appetite. Nevertheless, the difference is significant. Magnanimity is concerned with great deeds precisely as they are worthy of honor. Magnificence has for its special object the production of great works or the accomplishment of some great project; honor need not be involved.

Magnificence is thus defined as the virtue *which inclines one through the irascible appetite to achieve the good of reason by doing great works regardless of cost and effort*. The phrase "regardless of cost and effort" brings out the fact that usually the accomplishment of great projects involves expenditure of money. Hence, magnificence is concerned in a special way with moderating the love of money and wealth so as to use it for great projects demanded by reason. It is a magnificent act, for example, to donate a large amount of money for the erection of an art museum or a building on a college campus.

Noting the vices opposed to magnificence will help us understand the virtue more precisely. *Extravagance* is a vice which causes a person to spend more than is necessary to accomplish some project. *Stinginess* or *niggardliness* is the opposite extreme by which a person, not curbing his love of money, refuses to spend what is necessary to achieve the realization of the work. The niggardly person might spend some money to accomplish a small project; he will shrink from doing a great work because of the appropriate amount of money required, even though he could readily afford it.

It must not be presumed that the virtue of magnificence is realizable only by a person of wealth. It is true that the greatest works usually require large sums of money, and in this respect magnificence is found especially in persons of wealth. Nevertheless, the virtue can be proportionately realized even by someone in modest circumstances, for a virtue is always concerned primarily with realizing the good of reason interiorly in the different powers of man. Consequently, a poor man's small contribution toward the accomplishment of a great work is magnificent for him.

Patience

Patience is, to some extent, a misunderstood virtue. It is often taken to be more passive than it is, and in this context one might expect to find it in the concupiscible appetite. If we realize at once that it is a virtue associated with fortitude and is a good of reason realized in the irascible appetite, we shall estimate patience accurately as the strong virtue it really is.

Patience is the virtue *which moderates sadness arising from various evils other than that of death by strengthening one against succumbing to such evils.* The first part of the definition emphasizes forebearance and endurance, both of which might suggest passivity rather than activity. The last part of the definition brings out the virile quality of patience; the forebearance is for the sake of withstanding the threat of an evil so that the good of reason is preserved. A patient man is not simply one who does not flee from evil; he is one who will not permit himself to be unduly sad in the presence of evil. At the same time, patience promotes cheerfulness and a fundamentally tranquil state of mind despite great injuries and other evils preventing the realization of some good. It is related to greatness of soul, as all virtues of the irascible appetite are, by preventing the breaking down of the soul through inordinate grief and sorrow. A man owns his own soul when he is patient.

Impatience is the vice of succumbing to sadness or irritability in the presence of evil to the extent that one gives up attaining whatever good the evil thwarts. The opposite extreme and vice is a kind of apathy, a lack of concern one should experience in the face of evil. It is perhaps best described as the vice of *impassivity*, an unreasonable lack of concern and feeling that should characterize the operation of the irascible appetite formed by reason. It is the defect of not being sufficiently moved by sorrows or evils affecting oneself or others.

Perhaps the greatness of patience as a virtue would be more appreciated and cultivated if the two vices of impatience and impassivity were taken more seriously. Both of these vices, or even the tendencies toward them, disrupt the basic well-ordered tranquillity of spirit that should underlie our activities in dealing with the many annoyances, dangers, and evils of various kinds which constantly beset us.

Impatience and impassivity often accompany selfish motives of action. The relation of parents to children is often affected in this way. It is no easy task, of course, to deal rightly with children, and perhaps no virtue is needed more than the virtue of patience. A sign that this virtue is especially needed is the fact that parents so easily tend toward the extremes opposed to patience in their relations with their children. It is especially confusing for children when parents are impatient one moment at what their children are doing and quite impassive about the same activity at a later time. Selfishness on the part of the parents is usually the immediate cause of this manner of reacting. Impatience, for example, is often merely the reaction to having one's own life disturbed. Impassivity, on the other hand, is the disinclination to help direct children positively and concretely because of the bother and trouble such a course of action involves. Consequently children grow up molded by undesirable influences which the parents have made no effort to control or modify. The good parent can almost be identified with the truly patient parent.

Perseverance

Perseverance is a virtue *which inclines one to persist firmly in the pursuit of a difficult good regardless of obstacles and annoyances in completing the act.* Perseverance differs from patience in the length of time involved. You persevere, in a virtuous sense, if you persist reasonably in accomplishing a difficult good, even though the length of time in doing the deed is long and laborious. You are patient in moderating the sadness occasioned by the presence of evil; you persevere in seeking the good despite the presence of evil.

Pertinacity or stubbornness is the vice causing one to persist unreasonably in seeking to attain some good. A stubborn person is not inclined to recognize that certain difficulties are too great to be overcome or that the good sought is not worth the effort that would be required. *Softness* is the opposite extreme, which inclines one to give up too easily because of difficulties standing in the way of a good, even though one could reasonably expect to overcome them.

The Cardinal Virtue of Temperance

Temperance, the other cardinal virtue of the sense appetite, seems to be the most misunderstood virtue of all. On the one hand, it is sometimes taken so widely that it is equated with all virtue. For many persons, to be virtuous is the same as to be temperate, and hence all virtue is temperance and all vice is intemperance. On the other hand, some persons take a very narrow meaning of temperance. They understand one part of temperance as though it were the whole of temperance. A familiar example is the meaning associated with "temperance" societies; in this context, the name "temperance" means only abstinence from alcoholic drink. There is, in fact, a double confusion in this usage of the name "temperance."

First of all, as we have mentioned, the name is restricted to only one kind of moral matter covered by temperance, alcoholic drink. Secondly, the name "temperance" is used somewhat imprecisely even in this restricted sense, for the act of abstinence is not so much an act of the cardinal virtue of temperance as it is the act of a specific type of temperance, namely of the virtue of sobriety. Furthermore, total abstinence from alcoholic drink is not the whole of the virtue of sobriety. As we shall see, the virtue of sobriety aims primarily at moderating the enjoyment of pleasurable taste connected with alcoholic drink, not necessarily at the total elimination of alcoholic drink.

In order to arrive at a precise and comprehensive notion of the cardinal virtue of temperance, let us begin by contrasting it with fortitude. Temperance is related to the concupiscible appetite as fortitude is to the irascible appetite. Fortitude is concerned especially with the irascible emotions of fear and boldness. The concupiscible appetite is the division of the sense appetite concerned with desiring what is sensibly pleasant. Temperance, consequently, will be concerned with sense pleasure, particularly with the emotion of enjoyment at experiencing sense pleasures or of sorrow at being denied them. What are the pleasures toward which we are most inclined by nature and with which the concupiscible is chiefly concerned? They are the pleasures attached to the most natural and basic operations we have, the pleasures connected with the use of food, drink, and sex.

Accordingly, temperance will realize the good of reason in the enjoyment of sense pleasure, specifically in the delight accompanying the sensation of touch primarily and taste secondarily. The first and immediate act of temperance is to moderate and regulate such sense delight and enjoyment. Secondarily, the virtue of temperance moderates sorrow at the absence of such sense enjoyment. The mean of perfection found in temperance soars above the two defective conditions of a brutish and excessive seeking of sense enjoyment, on the one hand, and an excessive sorrow when sense enjoyment is absent, on the other hand. The first extreme is *indulgence*, i.e., self-indulgence, a vice which causes one to seek the pleasure of sense to an extent and in a manner wholly opposed to the good of reason. The other extreme is *insensibility*, a vice which impels one to avoid in an extreme manner such pleasures of sense as are desirable from the standpoint of the good of reason. We shall illustrate again by means of a triangle the perfection of the virtue of temperance.

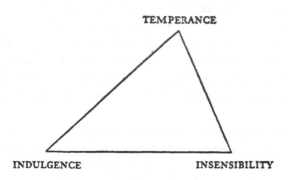

As with the triangle illustrating fortitude, so here the placing of the virtue at the top of the triangle brings out graphically that temperance is a mean of perfection between two defective extremes. The one extreme, indulgence, is a vice by excess; the other, insensibility, a vice by defect.

Contrary to the shape of the triangle for fortitude, the peak of the triangle for temperance inclines toward the defect rather than toward the excess. Moreover, the peak is more off center for the mean of temperance than for the mean of fortitude. The reason for this is not far to seek; temperance is concerned primarily with the pleasures of touch and secondarily with other pleasures of sense. These pleasures are at once basic and vehement. They are basic and strong because they are pleasures connected with the natural operations in a human being which are ordered to producing human life by means of sexual union and to preserving human life by means of food and drink.

Consequently, almost without exception human beings have a strong natural inclination to such pleasure, an inclination that easily becomes excessive. In the case of fortitude it is *likely* that the majority of men find the mean of perfection closer to the bold side than to the fear side of the triangle. In the case of temperance it is *certain* that the vast majority must seek the mean of perfection away from the excess of indulgence. Very few need to seek greater enjoyment in such pleasures of sense in order to establish the good of reason in the concupiscible emotions.

The Definition of Temperance

Temperance is a virtue *in the mean moderating the emotions of enjoyment and sorrow and especially the pleasures of touch and taste in order to achieve the good of reason in the concupiscible appetite.* The *proximate* object of the virtue of temperance is the concupiscible emotions, pleasure generally, and enjoyment and sorrow specifically. The *remote* object is whatever produces pleasures of touch and taste in a human being, namely food, drink, and sex.

Our understanding of temperance in terms of this definition should prevent us from equating temperance with all virtue and from restricting temperance to only one part of the virtue, the part concerning moderation in the use of drink. These misconceptions of temperance have obscured the accurate and positive meaning of temperance, making it appear in a quite different light from the truly admirable virtue it is.

There is a reason, however, why some have been led to regard temperance as equivalent to all virtue. This reason is based on the fact that although temperance is not the greatest cardinal virtue— the other cardinal virtues are greater and more perfect as virtues— it nevertheless is the cardinal virtue most immediately necessary for moral development and maturity. In the order of acquiring moral virtue and leading a happy moral life, temperance is first. Being the lowest cardinal virtue, lowest in the sense that it deals with the lowest part of a human being still amenable to the influence and direction of reason, it is the virtue upon which the others initially depend. Without some progress toward temperance one cannot be truly brave, just, and prudent, for without order in the concupiscible appetite one will be swayed away from the mean of reason in other respects. It is true that no single cardinal virtue can be properly and fully developed as a virtue without the others, yet from the standpoint of time, temperance has a priority. It is for this reason that it is easy to identify virtue with temperance, since at the outset virtue *is* temperance; yet, the unqualified identification of virtue with temperance is not accurate.

The good of reason established through temperance is realized in terms of the necessities of life. What is necessary for life, as determined by reason, gauges the amount of pleasure we should seek and enjoy in the sense appetite. The phrase "necessities of life" should not be taken only in the sense of *absolutely* necessary, that is, in order simply to exist. True enough, this meaning of "necessary" determines considerably how and in what way we realize the good of reason in the concupiscible appetite. For example, you should not become so intemperate in enjoying the taste of food that your health suffers. Good health, insofar as it can be realized, is absolutely necessary for the existence of a human being. On the other hand, this meaning of "absolutely necessary" in no way prevents your enjoying the taste of food, the enjoyment being moderated by ordering it to health. Food cooked in a mediocre way is not of itself more productive of health.

But there is another meaning to "necessities of life." It may also mean what is necessary in a fitting and becoming way to human existence. In this sense, enjoyment of pleasure at its best, i.e. rationally, is necessary for a full human life. Neither the seasoning of food nor air conditioning are absolutely necessary for human life, but they are necessary for a fitting and humanly enjoyable mode of life under certain conditions.

Summarizing in general terms, temperance is a well-ordered self-love. So contrary is this to the usual notion of temperance that it deserves a passing emphasis. First of all, temperance refers exclusively to the individual person himself, contrary to justice, which refers to the good of many, and to prudence, which extends in a sense to all practical affairs. This concern for the immediate good of man himself is the basis for speaking of temperance as a love of self. But, of course, there are two ways of loving oneself: selfishly to a point of destruction, and selflessly to a point of fitting preservation. It is the latter self-love that temperance attains when the good of reason is realized in the movement of the concupiscible appetite. In the last analysis, each person must mold his love of self in this ordered way. He will do so not in a spirit of barren denial but by the positive quality of a serenity of spirit, which temperance realizes by establishing a unified order within one's being. Each person must so temper himself.

The Virtues under Temperance

By the phrase "virtues under temperance" we mean those virtues which are species or subjective parts of the cardinal virtue of temperance. When we discussed fortitude, we pointed out that there were no subjective parts of that virtue since the virtues associated with fortitude do not share in the nature of fortitude itself. With temperance, however, there are three distinct objects which especially arouse pleasure in the concupiscible appetite: food, drink, and sex. Hence, there are three distinct virtues, each of which is a type of temperance concerned with a specific pleasure-arousing object and thus sharing in the nature of temperance itself.

Abstinence is a virtue moderating the enjoyment of the taste of food in order to realize the good of reason. This meaning of abstinence as a virtue is not that of total abstinence, the total denial of food, a condition which evidently cannot last long. To be sure, there can be a total abstinence from one kind of food if there is some ordering to the good of reason or for some religious motive. A vegetarian, however, is not necessarily practicing the virtue of abstinence; he may simply dislike meat. If such is the motive, he is no more virtuous in this regard than you in abstaining from spinach because of dislike of it. The *virtue* of abstinence, as a specific kind of temperance, must moderate the sense desire for something, and if there is no sense desire for some particular object there can be no moderation in this respect, and without such moderation there is no virtuous activity. Nor does it follow that the vegetarian is virtuous because he thinks meat is bad for human health; he would simply be in speculative error. The vegetarian can be virtuous in his total abstinence from meat if he would enjoy the taste of meat but is totally abstaining from it for some proportionate good of reason realizable in his case.

Fasting is not the same as abstinence. Fasting implies a temporary total abstinence from food and sometimes from drink as well. Fasting can be a special act of the virtue of abstinence if it is practiced for some good of reason or for some religious motive and is not carried to the extreme of seriously affecting one's health.

The vice opposed to abstinence is *gluttony*, the inordinate desire for the taste of food sought only for pleasure and not for the good of reason. The opposite extreme from gluttony is a vice not frequently found, as is the case with all the defects of insensibility in the concupiscible appetite. Such a vice would consist in an unreasonable denial of enjoyment of the taste of food. It is quite evident that the mean of abstinence, like the cardinal virtue of temperance, is realized much closer toward the denial of enjoyment of the taste of food than toward the opposite extreme of gluttony.

Sobriety is a virtue observing the rule of moderation in the enjoyment and use of intoxicating drink. As a species of temperance, sobriety is that kind of temperance concerned with intoxicating drink in particular. We have already referred to the popular understanding of temperance, restricting it to mean moderation and even total abstinence from the enjoyment of the taste of alcoholic beverage. Such a restriction reduces temperance wholly to sobriety, whereas the moderation in the enjoyment of drink should be regarded as one virtue under temperance, and not the whole of temperance.

The name "sobriety" sometimes conveys the meaning of total abstinence from drink. This meaning of the term can be justified in the sense that for some persons sobriety has to mean a total abstinence. The only mean for such persons is not to drink at all. But even though they do not drink at all, there can still be moderation of the *desire* for drink, and to the extent this occurs they can be acting virtuously. This situation is possible because, as we have already remarked, virtue consists primarily in the good order realized in an *interior* state. Sobriety is *primarily* concerned with a right ordering of the appetite toward drink, secondarily with the drink itself. Hence, one person who drinks and another person who does not can both be exercising the virtue of sobriety if a reasonable moderation of sense appetite is being realized.

The evil of *drunkenness*, the vice opposed to sobriety, is a particularly grave one, both individually and socially. There is a physiological and psychological side to drunkenness as well as a moral side. As a vice of the moral order, drunkenness has to be voluntary excess in the use of intoxicating drink to a point where not only the good of reason is lost, but even the use of reason itself. Drunkenness, consequently, is a particularly degrading vice. When drunkenness becomes a physiological as well as a moral problem, the remedy has to be medicinal as well as moral. Furthermore, since drunkenness is often a condition produced by complex psychological factors, the attention of experts in psychology and psychiatry may also be required. Often, the basis of the disorder is a spiritual one which only religion can fully resolve. It is, therefore, necessary to recognize that a variety of factors may be present in the evil of drunkenness. It is an unwarranted simplification to regard the evil as only moral, just as it is an unwarranted simplification to regard the evil as only physiological or only psychological.

Related to drunkenness, though distinct from it and less extreme, is *alcoholism*. Alcoholism is constant indulgence in the drinking of intoxicating beverage. Alcoholism is to drunkenness as a bad disposition is to a thoroughgoing vice. The many dangers and evils resulting from alcoholism are almost as serious and lasting as those of drunkenness. Among all the moral virtues, therefore, the mean of sobriety is perhaps the farthest away from the exact center. A sign that this is the case is that there is hardly any need to try to determine the vice contrary to drunkenness. Perhaps only theoretically can one speak of an opposite extreme—of an unreasonable denial of the enjoyment of intoxicating drink—but, practically speaking, such an extreme is hardly ever realized. We are not taking into account, of course, the simple dislike of the taste of intoxicating beverages. This situation is not so infrequent, but it is not moral matter for the virtue of sobriety.

Chastity is a virtue in the mean observing the rule of moderation in venereal pleasure; it seeks the good of reason in the use of the power of sexual reproduction. The term "chastity" is often taken in the sense of total abstinence from the use of the reproductive power, and, as with other virtues under temperance, this restricted meaning is mistakenly applied to chastity generally. There are, rather, two distinct kinds of chastity: *conjugal* chastity and *virginal* chastity. It is to this second kind of chastity that the meaning of total abstinence from all venereal pleasure applies.

Conjugal chastity pertains to moderation in the use and enjoyment of the reproductive act in the married state. Hence, this meaning of chastity presupposes the use of the reproductive power but subjects it to the judgment of reason and choice of the will. Married persons, therefore, can and should practice the virtue of chastity in this meaning of the term. Virginal chastity, on the other hand, is practiced by a person who wholly abstains, for some good motive, from the use and enjoyment of the reproductive act. The moderation of passion is sufficient for the possession of this virtue, just as a person can have the virtue of sobriety by moderating his desire for drink even though he never drinks alcoholic beverage. Consequently, total abstinence from pleasures of the flesh is virtuous activity provided it is ordered to the good of reason or an even higher motive, as befitting a person in a certain state of life, such as the religious. For an unmarried person, it is, of course, a good of reason.

The vice opposed to chastity is *lust*, the immoderate desire for venereal pleasure. Just as chastity has a generic meaning and is divisible into the species of conjugal and virginal chastity, so lust is divisible into different kinds. *Fornication* is the specific vice of illicit sexual relations between two persons who are unmarried; its special evil is that it is directly contrary to the welfare of the child to be reared. *Adultery* is the specific vice of illicit sexual relations between two persons of whom at least one is married to someone else. *Incest* is the specific vice of illicit sexual relations between two persons closely related by blood. *Seduction* is the vice of illicit sexual relations between two persons of whom one is under the authority of parents who are guardians of the person's chastity. *Rape* adds the element of violence to seduction. Most of the foregoing vices and others which follow also contain elements of injustice. Too often only the subjective side of these various forms of unchastity is considered, whereas the objective side of the matter relating to serious injustices is entirely overlooked.

The foregoing kinds of lust are determined in relation to the kind of persons involved, such as married or unmarried, blood-related, and so on. Other types of lust are determined from the standpoint of being morally evil by object. *Artificial contraception* is an example of such a vice. It is intrinsically wrong on moral grounds —on the basis of reason and moral law—and not solely on religious grounds. The intrinsic evil of artificial contraception consists in the voluntary employment of a physical impediment preventing the ordering of the power of reproduction to its natural end. This vice and the following ones are sometimes designated as "vices contrary to nature" because they seek the pleasure while preventing the purpose to which the act is ordered by nature.

Other such vices are *sodomy*, carnal intercourse in any of a number of unnatural ways, including persons of the same sex, and *onanism*, the vice of seeking venereal pleasure in a solitary manner. By the very fact that the sexual power in a human being, though basically good and wholly adaptable to the life of virtue, is the lowest power, the vices related to it are the most bestial and the most degrading. At the same time it is important to recognize, contrary to those who think that all moral evil is reducible to illicit sexual pleasure, that there are more serious moral vices. The different vices of lust tend to arise out of weakness of human nature. Other moral vices, unbridled pride, for instance, can be more deadly as far as the ultimate and permanent moral good of a human being is concerned.

Outline of Virtues Concerning the Passions

I. Fortitude (Division into potential parts)

    A. Magnanimity

        1. Vices by excess: presumption, excessive ambition, vainglory

        2. Vice by defect: pusillanimity

    B. Magnificence

        1. Vice by excess: extravagance

        2. Vice by defect: stinginess

    C. Patience

        1. Vice by excess: impatience

        2. Vice by defect: impassivity

    D. Perseverance

        1. Vice by excess: pertinacity

        2. Vice by defect: softness

II. Temperance (Division into subjective parts)

    A. Abstinence (partial); Fasting (total)

        Principal Vice: gluttony

B. Sobriety
   1. Principal Vice: Drunkenness
   2. Less extreme: Alcoholism

C. Chastity (Conjugal and Virginal)
   1. Principal Vice: Lust
      a) In relation to persons involved: fornication, adultery, incest, seduction, rape
      b) By object: artificial contraception, sodomy, onanism

REVIEW QUESTIONS

1. What makes a virtue a cardinal virtue?

2. Why does the meaning of "reason" have to be clarified, especially in relation to the practical order?

3. Show why, from the standpoint of the good of reason, there are four cardinal virtues.

4. Why is it appropriate to begin with the cardinal virtue of fortitude?

5. With what specific emotions is fortitude concerned, and why these emotions rather than others?

6. Between what extremes is fortitude the mean?

7. What is the immediate act of fortitude, and why must this act be the immediate and primary one?

8. Is the mean of fortitude closer to one extreme than the other? Explain fully.

9. What is the definition of fortitude?

10. What are the proximate and remote objects of the virtue of fortitude?

11. In general, how are other virtues of the irascible appetite related to fortitude?

12. What is magnanimity? What are the vices opposed to it?

13. Is there any value in knowing what different vices are opposed to a specific virtue?

14. What is magnificence? What are the vices opposed to it?

15. What is patience? What are the vices opposed to it?

16. What is perseverance? What are the vices opposed to it?

17. What popular misunderstandings exist about the cardinal virtue of temperance? Why such misunderstandings?

18. With what emotions is temperance concerned?

19. Between what extremes is temperance the mean?

20. Why is the mean of temperance so much closer to one extreme than the other?

21. What is the definition of temperance?

22. What are the proximate and remote objects of temperance?

23. Explain the phrase "necessities of life" in relation to temperance.

24. Explain how temperance is well-ordered self-love.

25. How are other virtues of the concupiscible appetite related to the cardinal virtue of temperance?

26. What is abstinence? How does it differ from fasting?

27. What is sobriety? With what is it primarily concerned?

28. Distinguish between drunkenness and alcoholism.

29. What is chastity? Distinguish between conjugal and virginal chastity.

30. What is the basis for dividing the vice of lust into its various kinds?

DISCUSSION

1. There are as many cardinal virtues as there are ways of realizing the good of reason. In addition to realizing the good of reason in the intellectual, voluntary, irascible, and concupiscible powers of man there is the good of reason realizable in the vegetative power of man, for one should eat according to the rule of reason. Consequently, there should be five cardinal virtues and not only four.

2. It is more natural to experience fear in the presence of danger than boldness. To achieve fortitude one must control fear. Therefore, a man achieves the virtue of fortitude by moderating fear and in this very moderation achieves boldness.

3. It is natural and right for every human being to preserve his life, for self-preservation is the first law of human nature. Readiness to give up one's life is therefore contrary to human nature, and so also is the virtue of fortitude.

4. Fortitude is synonymous with boldness, and to be bold is not to waver because of fear. To moderate fear is to experience fear and, hence, be fearful. Fortitude therefore is to be identified with boldness, and is wholly opposed to fear.

5. Many persons act bravely even when the danger of death and its accompanying fear are not present. For example, a politician who does what he knows to be right regardless of what may happen to him acts bravely. Therefore, the virtue of fortitude is not restricted to moderating fear in the face of death.

6. The emotions by their very nature move in a way that is contrary to reason, as we witness in the emotional behavior of animals. It is necessary, therefore, for a human being to curb the emotions, but it is even more necessary and more desirable to rise above the turbulent effect of the emotions altogether by being indifferent to them. The perfection of fortitude or of temperance therefore consists in a state of rational calm, a mean of perfection rising above all agitation of the passions.

7. The desire and need to preserve one's own life is greater than the need and desire to reproduce. Therefore, the virtue of temperance should be concerned primarily with taste as related to food and drink, which are necessary in order to live, rather than with touch as related to reproduction, which is not necessary in order to live.

8. The ultimate end of man is said to be happiness because only in the realization of the state of happiness do we find complete satisfaction and enjoyment. Temperance moderates our enjoyment and prevents our having full satisfaction of all desires. Temperance, therefore, cannot be a virtue because it prevents our attaining complete happiness.

9. The perfection of chastity consists in refraining from all enjoyment and use of the power of reproduction. This quality can be attained only by persons not married. But no virtue is limited to a certain class of persons. Therefore, chastity is not a virtue.

10. Alcoholic drink by its very object is ordered to intoxication, and a state of intoxication is contrary to the good of reason. Since alcoholic drinks are ordered to an evil end, there can be no moderation in the enjoyment of them. Therefore, the only virtue possible in relation to alcoholic drink is the virtue of complete temperance, that is, abstinence.

11. It is inhuman to endanger one's health for the enjoyment of a sense good. There are times when the health of a wife may not permit the bearing of children. At such times, because of the higher good of health, artificial contraception is both justifiable and desirable.

12. The sexual power in human beings is lowest in the sense that enjoyment in the use of it is least amenable to the direction of reason. Therefore, the vices arising from excesses in this order are the greatest and most serious of all moral vices.

SUGGESTED READINGS

Aristotle, *Ethics*, Book III, chaps. 6-12; Book IV, complete.
St. Thomas, *Commentary*, Book III, Lessons XIV-XXII; Book IV, complete.
St. Thomas, *Summa Theologiae*, I-II, Questions 59-61.
Plato, *Charmides* and *Laches*.

Bourke, *Ethics*, chap. IX, pp. 304-323.
Gilson, *Moral Values and the Moral Life*, chaps. X-XI, pp. 276-308.
Pieper, J., *Fortitude and Temperance*. New York: Pantheon Books, Inc., 1954.
Tsanoff, *Ethics*, chap. 7, pp. 125-143.
Wild, *Introduction to Realistic Philosophy*, chap. 6, pp. 116-131; chap. 7, pp. 132-153.

IX

Virtues related to the will

*E*veryone is familiar to some extent with the virtue of justice, but this very familiarity easily conceals a certain ambiguity in the signification of the name. We speak of a just price, a just wage, a just war, and sometimes even of a just man without qualification, and while all of these meanings are closely related, nevertheless they are not wholly the same. The closeness of the different meanings, in fact, may be the very reason that we fail to discern the differences, which are important to note if we wish to understand justice fully, and the other virtues in the will which are related to it.

Let us begin, therefore, with the broadest meaning of justice and then take up the more specific meanings. And we shall find it advantageous also to take as our starting point what we mean by an unjust man. By noticing first, as more obvious, what a just man is not, we can arrive more readily at what a just man is.

At least two characteristics are always found in a man whom everyone would regard as unjust. One of these characteristics is a refusal to obey laws; we mean by this characteristic that a man is so disposed that he regularly and intentionally violates laws. The purpose of any law, properly speaking, is to advance the common good, for a law specifies concretely how human beings as citizens can act for the common good. A man who deliberately seeks to go against the common good by violating laws—in a word, by being lawless—is certainly an unjust man. Lawlessness is thus one characteristic of the unjust man.

The other characteristic of the unjust man is the desire to attain more than he has coming to him. He seeks gain for himself at the expense of others in any and all ways possible. He grasps at whatever will benefit himself and is quick to leave whatever is evil and disadvantageous for the other fellow. He is simply unfair.

The lawless man and the unfair man both would be considered by everyone to be unjust. And with double reason would a man be unjust who has both characteristics. Such a man would be unjust without qualification. This person has the vice of general injustice, and from this understanding of general injustice we can readily understand its contrary, the virtue of general justice.

The Virtue of General Justice

The man who is wholly just, by contrast with the man who is wholly unjust, is both law-abiding and fair. He is just in all respects, and from this notion of the wholly just man we can gather what the virtue of general justice is. By the phrase *general justice* we mean perfect or complete virtue, the quality by which a man is virtuous in all respects. General justice is equivalent to moral righteousness and ranges over the whole area of moral actions. Hence, general justice is the perfect and universal virtue which contains all virtues, just as, in an entirely opposed way, general injustice is general or complete vice, containing all vices.

General justice is also known as *legal justice*. This latter name adds a precision in meaning, for by the name "legal justice" we understand this virtue to contain the acts of all virtues in the sense that through law they are ordered to the common good. Therefore, we may define legal justice as *the virtue by which we exercise the acts of all virtues in relation to the common good*. This definition makes evident why it is a perfect virtue, and why it is universal and not particular. It is perfect because it concerns not only ourselves but the common good. It is universal because it contains all virtues and exercises all of them in relation to the common good. This precision also brings out the sense in which legal justice, though the same as general justice, is also a special virtue insofar as it has the common good as its proper object. Indeed, there is a preference for the name "legal justice," since the virtue is both general and special: *general* insofar as it has no determinate and particular matter, but relates to the acts of all virtues; *special* insofar as it does have as a proper object the common good to which it orders the acts of all virtues.

In the sense in which it is a virtue having a special object, legal justice is not realized in the same way in all human beings. Since it is the virtue inclining the will to give to the common good the legally required exercise of virtue and whatever disposition of external goods is necessary to promote the common good, the virtue will operate differently in the rulers and citizens of a country.

Legal justice is found primarily in the rulers of a country and secondarily in the citizens. It is found primarily in the ruler because he has the obligation to preserve the due order of justice by maintaining law and order within society. The citizen has the obligation to carry out the due order of justice in his civil and social acts, and to observe the common good in such acts. Hence, in a representative form of government we should look especially for the possession and exercise of the virtue of legal justice in persons who aspire to rule. In the last analysis, however, excellence of representative government depends on the citizens making up the state, for only by being just themselves are they likely to elect persons characterized by the virtue of legal justice.

Legal justice is not to be identified with law; rather, it presupposes law as already existing. The politically just man loves and respects law as a directing principle of his action for the common good. However, law does presuppose the object of justice—that which is just or right. And, just as law is in part natural and in part positive—for we recognize that some actions are universally right or wrong and others are right or wrong only in a qualified way—so is what is just in part natural and in part legal. Some things are naturally just, for example, that children be nurtured and morally developed. Some things are just by human enactment, for example, observing the right of way of traffic when entering a major highway. Before considering particular justice, therefore, we shall examine the object of justice.

The Notion of Right

The proper object of justice is *right*, i.e., that which is "just." The Latin word for "right" is *jus*, and hence "right" is only another name for "the just." The immediate meaning of "right" implies a relation, specifically a relation of equality between persons. To illustrate with an obvious example: if I borrow ten dollars from you, I am bound to return the equivalent to you because what I have borrowed from you is now due you. It is right—it is the "just thing"—for you to receive back what you lent.

Two meanings of the word "right" should be distinguished: *objective* and *subjective* right. Objective right signifies a thing or action due another, and it is in this sense of the term that we speak of right as the object of justice. Subjective right is the moral, as distinct from a physical, power you or I possess for doing or acquiring something. In this sense of the term I can speak of having the right to vote as a qualified citizen in a democratic form of government.

From this clarification of the term "right," two important points arise. The first is that the source of both objective and subjective right is law—not positive law, but natural law. Law, as an extrinsic principle of human action inclining us toward what is good, is treated fully in political philosophy, another part of moral philosophy. In a later chapter we shall summarize the meaning and division of law to the extent that it is needed in a beginning course in moral philosophy.

The second point is that subjective right is dependent upon objective right both for its meaning and its existence. We acquire a subjective right only because objective right exists first; hence this moral power we have is called a "right" in relation to and consequent upon objective right. The contrary view might be supposed to be the case, that objective right depends upon subjective right, a view held by some moral philosophers both in the past and at the present time. But if subjective right is the primary kind of right, it follows that the order of law and justice is subordinated to the liberty of each individual; if "right" primarily means whatever I have the power of doing in any manner whatsoever, then whatever I am free to do I have a "right" to do. As a consequence, instead of the common good being the end and measure of what is right, individual liberty becomes the end. And individual liberty, erected into an absolute end, necessarily makes the moral order, and in particular the order of rights, subjective and wholly relative to each individual. If individual liberty is an end beyond the common good, then freedom of speech, for example, would have no justifiable limitation. Nothing could prevent anyone from saying anything about anyone at any time and under any condition. The state might set limitations to such individual liberty, but, without an objective moral foundation and objective right, any limitation would be arbitrary.

Such a view cannot be reasonably justified and defended. To quote a familiar instance against such a position, no one has the right to cry "Fire!" in a crowded theater merely because he has freedom of speech. Individual liberty, therefore, though an important moral good that must be zealously safeguarded, cannot be considered apart from its ordering to the common good of the social and political order. In other words, subjective right cannot be the primary meaning of right; it is dependent upon and measured by objective right.

Division of Right

Objective right is *natural* or *positive*. As the name suggests, a natural right is anything due to another which is based ultimately on the natural moral law. Such a right cannot be abolished any more than the natural law can be abolished; consequently, the existence of such a right is not dependent upon the power of the rulers of a state. A natural right so understood is immediate or mediate. An immediate natural right is one constituted by the natural order of things in an absolute way. For example, a male human being by nature is related to a female for the engendering of offspring; the male and female therefore have a natural right to marriage and procreation. A mediate natural right is one depending upon a certain qualification. It is in this sense of the term that private property —ownership of land, for example—is a natural right. Such a right is not absolute in the sense that an immediate natural right is, but only under certain conditions and for some significant use.

Positive objective right is a right determined by the legislative power of a particular state, e.g., various rights of citizens as constituted under a certain form of government.

Subjective right is natural or positive, corresponding to the division of objective right. A natural subjective right is the power or claim, as determined by what is objectively just, to exact something in regard to someone or something else. The inalienable rights of man spoken of by the founders of the United States are natural subjective rights, and they are inalienable because they belong to men as possessing a rational nature. A positive subjective right is one a person has which is determined by the form of government under which he lives. In a democratic form of government, a person can claim the right to vote as laid down by the constitution under which he is a citizen and which entitles him to make such a claim.

Particular Justice

Now that we have seen what the object of justice is, we can define particular justice. First, however, let us indicate how general or legal justice and particular justice are alike, and how they differ. They are alike in that each is a virtue dealing with what is due another, but they differ by reason of the matter with which each is concerned. Legal justice, as we have seen, relates to all moral matter and is a universal cause of the acts of all virtues. Particular justice, as the name suggests, deals with particular moral matter, that is, with what is owed by one person to another with regard to a particular good, such as money or honor or truthfulness.

Consequently, particular justice is defined as *the virtue by which one with constant and perpetual will gives what is due, i.e., what is objectively right, to another with respect to a particular good.* Particular justice is the cardinal virtue of justice, for like any cardinal virtue it has a specific matter which it treats. For this reason, the cardinal virtue of justice is distinct from general or legal justice.

Two distinct acts belong to the cardinal virtue of justice. One of these is explicitly mentioned in the definition, the act of giving what is due to another. This act refers to the external execution of justice. The second act, the internal act, is the act of determining what is just, that is, a judging of what is equal or proportionate between the things and persons involved. Strictly speaking, this act of judging is an act of the intellect and is not a proper act of justice insofar as justice is a virtue located in the will. Nevertheless, it can be designated as an act of justice in the sense that through the virtue of justice, the will disposes the intellect to judge correctly.

From the definition of justice, and from our consideration of right as the object of justice, we can see that the mean of particular justice differs from the mean of the other moral virtues. In the other moral virtues, the mean is one of reason as distinct from the objective or quantitative mean. The mean of particular justice is at once a mean of reason and an objective mean. Although the mean of justice is one established by reason, it is determined entirely by the object as it exists in reality. There is an identity of the mean of reason and the mean of the object because justice is concerned with operations related to external objects which are the measure of the acts of justice. At the same time, as we shall see when we consider the different kinds of particular justice, this objective mean is not to be identified with absolute equality, for sometimes the willing of what is due consists in only a proportional equality.

The definition points out that there must be a perpetual and constant will to do what is just to others. Isolated acts of doing what is just are not enough to constitute the cardinal virtue of justice. Like all virtue, justice centers primarily on a constant disposition within us. Unlike other moral virtues, however, it focuses on our relations with other persons. Justice, therefore, perfects our will by inclining us to be rightly ordered to other human beings.

The Kinds of Particular Justice

Particular justice is divided into two subjective parts, *commutative* and *distributive* justice. This division occurs because of different relations affecting the individual person. Commutative justice concerns the relation between private individuals. Distributive justice concerns the relation of society to a private person.

Commutative justice is the virtue *which inclines the will of one individual to give to another what is his due according to absolute equality*. It is the virtue which directs and regulates mutual dealings between private persons, particularly commercial dealings of one kind or another. It is the kind of justice we tend to think of first when the name "justice" is mentioned, because it is more obvious and familiar. We recognize at once that it is a matter of justice that I give the equivalent in money for groceries I buy at the store, and likewise that it is a matter of justice for the grocer to give me the equivalent in groceries for the sum of money I pay. Commutative justice also has the sort of mean we tend to associate with justice, an exact or arithmetical mean. In the definition of commutative justice we referred to this characteristic by stating that "absolute equality" is due. This absolute equality may be realized either in identical form, as when I return ten dollars which I have borrowed, or in equivalent form, when I buy ten dollars' worth of groceries.

Distributive justice is the virtue *which inclines the will of public officials in a state to apportion to a part of the state—a private citizen —what is due him by proportional equality*. The name "distributive" is applied to this virtue because it is a form of justice by which society, through its rulers or agents, *distributes* rewards, honors, and also burdens, to its members. It might be supposed that distributive justice resembles legal justice more than particular justice. The contrary is the case, however, for distributive justice is concerned with the private good of each member of society, whereas in legal justice the members of society are ordered to the common good of society itself.

Commutative justice and distributive justice, therefore, are two species of particular justice. They differ in two respects: (1) commutative justice is a relation of part to part, while distributive justice is a relation of whole to part; (2) they differ in kind of equality. Commutative justice, as we have seen, is based upon absolute equality. Distributive justice, as the definition states, is based upon proportional equality. This latter kind of equality can be understood by noting that in distributive justice something is given to a private person insofar as that which belongs to the whole is due to a part. Now, whatever is distributed to the part, the private citizen, depends on the position of the part in relation to the whole. Hence, the mean realized in distributive justice will have to be a proportional equality, not the absolute equality between private persons, but an equality obtaining between the rank the private person holds in society and society as a whole.

Taxation on income is a familiar illustration of distributive justice. In *proportion* as a person has more income, he is taxed more; a person with few or no dependents is taxed more proportionately than a person with more dependents. To take another example, one person may be given more honor or more protection in society than others because of a difference in position or rank. Society owes more protection to the ruler of a country than to an ordinary private citizen.

This proportional equality in distributive justice is a geometric proportion, whereas the absolute equality in commutative justice is an arithmetic proportion. Three is the arithmetic mean between two and four because it is one greater and one less than the extremes. The geometric equality depends upon a proportion, for instance, six is to four as three is to two. In this case the equality is not the same by which one exceeds the other, for six is two more than four while three is only one more than two. The equality lies in a proportion, the proportion of one and a half by which six exceeds four and three exceeds two. There is an equality, therefore, but a proportioning of it between two sets of extremes which are not equal. Thus in distributive justice, as one person is more excellent than another in a given respect, so what is given to one is proportionally greater than what is given to another, or what one owes is proportionally greater than what another owes. The working out concretely of both the proportional equality of distributive justice and the absolute equality of commutative justice is sometimes difficult and complicated. Some of the many problems connected with attaining what is just will be indicated in connection with the treatment of the vices opposed to the different kinds of justice.

Injustice

Injustice can be considered in two ways, either as a vice against general, i.e., legal justice, or as a vice against particular justice. We shall consider it first as a vice against legal justice, which we have already mentioned at the beginning of this chapter.

Insofar as legal justice is concerned with a special object, the common good, the vice opposed to legal justice is a special vice. It is the set disposition to will and do what is contrary to the common good of society. But this vice may become a general one when, by intention, one has contempt for the common good to such a degree that all evil acts flow from this contempt as from a principle. In this latter way, one is simply and unqualifiedly unjust. The vice of injustice against legal justice, therefore, is understood either as a *specific* vice, one directed against the common good of society itself, or as a *general* vice, one which, because of a thorough contempt of the common good, leads to evil acts against all virtues.

To be unjust in either way, however, the acts must proceed by intention and choice. This point deserves emphasis, because it is quite possible to perform an act that is unjust without intending it to be so. For example, you may be led out of ignorance or passion to commit an injustice without any intention on your part to be unjust in your relation with others.

There is a difference, consequently, between *being* unjust and *acting* unjustly, even though the two are usually closely related. You can do an unjust act without being unjust, and you can perform a just act without being just. You *are* just only if you choose to be just and possess the virtue. Thus, you might return a loan, not because you will the good of the just act, but only because you fear the consequences. You act unjustly without really being unjust if you take what does not belong to you, not by full intention, but out of passion. Such an act would be wrong, at least to some extent, but not vicious. When we speak of the vice of legal injustice, then, we are referring to an abiding fundamental disposition not to will the common good and, in fact, to hold it in contempt.

In addition to the vice against legal justice, there are vices against particular justice. We shall take these up according to the division of particular justice into distributive and commutative.

With respect to distributive justice, the specific vice opposed to it is *respect for persons*. This vice consists in giving honor or position to a person, not because he is worthy of it and deserves it, but because of extrinsic and irrelevant circumstances. Disorders of this kind frequently occur when politicians in office give appointments and privileges to persons not entitled to them. *Nepotism* is a particular instance of this vice, a favoritism shown by someone in power to his relatives. Unmerited advancement in rank or position, as in military, business, academic and other circles, is another instance of the vice opposed to distributive justice.

Vices Against Commutative Justice

The vices against commutative justice are numerous and frequent, and hence they deserve a special and more extended consideration. Knowledge of such vices will at least help us to be aware of them and, being aware of them, dispose us to avoid them. In general, the vice opposed to commutative justice is the willing of inequality with respect to what is due another. However, since there are many ways of willing inequality in relation to another individual, we shall summarize these ways as particular vices under two main headings: involuntary and voluntary injustices.

First, we shall consider vices against commutative justice which consist in one person's committing some wrong against another in some affair to which the other person in no way consents. Such dealings between persons are called *involuntary* in this special sense of the term, that the action done is against the will of *one* of the two persons involved—the one against whose good the action is directed. *Murder* is an injustice of this kind, since by such an action one person unjustly takes the life of another person. One person can also injure the life of another by *physical assault* or by *false imprisonment*. Further, one person can injure another by injuring someone related to that person. *Adultery* is an example, and in this way adultery is a vice against justice as well as a vice against temperance. Other vices against temperance are also forms of injustice to the extent that others are wronged. Finally, one may injure another person with respect to his possessions; for example, *stealing* is the vice of taking unjustly what belongs to another.

The above injustices are all committed by *deed*. Other injustices of this same kind are committed by *word*. Many of these injustices are concerned with trials in the courtroom. The prosecutor may make *false accusations* or the opposing attorney may make *false statements*. The witness himself may give *false testimony*. Apart from lawsuits, injustices committed by word of mouth are so numerous that we can mention only the principal ones. *Detraction* is the vice of attacking the good name of another person. It has a cowardly aspect as well as being unjust, for it is committed when the person concerned is absent. Closely related to detraction is *contumely*, which consists in speaking in a manner derogatory to the honor and reputation of another. *Gossiping* is the vice of secretly talking about the defects of another with the intention of destroying friendship. *Cursing* is the vice of willing injury to another by invoking evil upon him. *Mockery* is the vice by which a person laughs contemptuously at another or intends to cause shame in another by making known, in a jesting manner, his vices.

Secondly, we shall consider *voluntary* dealings between persons, that is, transactions in which, though one morally injures another, both nevertheless are dealing willingly with each other. The principal vice here is *fraud*, the deliberate use of deception to cause the loss of some value to one of the two individuals. In any case of buying and selling there is an obligation on the part of both buyer and seller to take reasonable care that the exchange is one of equal value. The seller practices fraud if he knows that the article to be sold is defective and does not discount the price accordingly or let the buyer know the fact. The seller may cheat also by selling short in number or in weight. On the other hand, the buyer practices fraud if, aware that the seller is ignorant of the true value of the article, he takes advantage of the fact and does not pay the seller anything approaching the true value. The buyer also cheats if he takes advantage of an error in calculation on the part of the seller or if the seller inadvertently gives back more change to the buyer than is due him. Injustices, consequently, are by no means practiced only on the part of the seller. Allied with forms of fraud in buying and selling is *deceptive advertising*, by which excessive or false claims on the part of an advertiser lead a person to buy a product under false pretenses.

Usury is the vice of charging excessive interest on a loan of money. This meaning of usury is a modern one. In ancient and medieval times, usury meant the charging of *any* interest on money borrowed. Such interest was considered to be unjust because money was conceived to have only one essential use, to be spent. A person would make a loan when he had no use for the money involved, that is, no need to spend it for something and when he wished to accommodate someone else who needed the money. Consequently, to charge interest for such a loan amounted to making a charge for being denied a use of money when in fact one was not denied any use. Hence, it was considered an act of *usury* and unjust. In modern times, money is also employed for investment to develop capital. A loan is now considered to be a subtraction from one's capital and with it a loss of interest one would otherwise receive. Hence, the lender may without injustice charge interest on money he lends; he may also, of course, out of more than simple justice lend money without interest. At the present time, therefore, usury is understood to consist in charging a rate of interest that is excessive, i.e., beyond a rate usually determined by law.

The complications of modern commercial life are so vast that few of the many problems arising with respect to just and unjust action in this area can be covered in a general text or course in ethics. The importance of the problems in this area of justice can hardly be overstressed, and there is great need to counteract a widespread tendency to drive a wedge between the business life and the moral life as though the two domains had no connection. Hence the importance and need, especially for those entering business as a profession, to have a special course in *business ethics* in which there is time to give this development of modern life the attention it deserves. Just action between individuals in any commercial dealing is the indispensable prerequisite for the very life of business activity. It should be no more surprising to find a virtuous businessman than a virtuous clergyman.

Virtues Allied with Justice

These virtues are connected with the cardinal virtue of justice insofar as they realize a certain element of justice in our action in relation to others. They do not attain the complete perfection of justice but realize only a certain aspect of it, and for this reason they are understood as virtues which are annexed to justice. Consequently, they are not subjective parts, as distributive and commutative justice are subjective parts of particular justice, but potential parts.

Any form of justice is a rendering of what is due to another. These allied virtues, therefore, will also be related to some sort of debt, i.e., to whatever is due in some respect to another. Until now, we have been considering what is due out of legal obligation. This is *legal* debt, which is most properly the object of justice. There is also *moral* debt, that which is due out of rectitude of virtue. It is this kind of debt that we must take into account when treating the allied virtues of justice. We shall consider only the more significant allied virtues and the distinctive vices which are opposed to them.

Veracity is the virtue of speaking and acting in accord with truth. It is a virtue allied with justice, because we have a moral debt to express ourselves truthfully to others in speaking, writing and in other modes of communication. The vice opposed to veracity is *lying,* the deliberate intention to say or manifest as true what is known to be false. The malice of lying is sometimes not sufficiently recognized. An attempt is often made to justify a lie on the grounds that, unless a lie is told, someone will be offended or hurt; it is in this context that the so-called "white lie" is defended. The fact remains, however that a lie is always morally wrong. It is evil by object, and can never be morally justified no matter how serious the situation. The reason for this apparently severe moral position is that a lie formally consists in an intrinsic disorder between what we know to be true and the falsity that we will to express to someone else. In expressing falsity to another, an act of injustice is committed since we morally owe to others the expression of what we truthfully think, if they have any legitimate claim to know from us what is true. And even if they have no legitimate claim, we are not justified in replying with a lie.

There is no doubt about the fact that frequently situations arise in which it is awkward, embarrassing, or difficult to say what is true. One's own life or the life of another may be involved. Nevertheless, the lie is still unjustifiable, from the point of view of moral rectitude. However, there are alternatives other than simply telling the truth and simply lying. One may, for example, be able to escape the situation by saying nothing, by changing the subject, or by using a mental reservation. *Mental reservation,* the use of some expression which, without formally conveying falsity, nevertheless does not convey the whole truth or the relevant truth, is justifiable when reasonable protection is warranted. When, how, and under what circumstances to employ a mental reservation belongs more to the virtue of prudence than to justice.

Gratitude is the virtue by which one acknowledges some benefit or favor done by someone else. It is enough for this virtue that you recognize your indebtedness and be thankful for the benefit, but whenever possible this acknowledgment should be made manifest to the one who has conferred a favor upon you. *Ingratitude* is the vice of refusing, in one way or another, to acknowledge and manifest thankfulness to some benefactor.

Vindication is the virtue by which one, in conformity with relevant circumstances, observes due measure in meting out punishment to one who has committed some moral offense. Vindication is justifiable vengeance, that is, the willing of punishment for the sake of preserving justice and restraining evildoers. It is easy to slip from vindication to unwarranted vengeance or simple revenge. *Revenge* is the vice opposed to vindication, for the revengeful person seeks to punish merely to satisfy his own feelings and without the motive of preserving justice.

The virtues of veracity, gratitude and vindication are all concerned with moral obligations and are needed in order to have moral rectitude. There are two other allied virtues of justice which, though not necessary for having moral rectitude, nevertheless increase moral rectitude in us.

Liberality is the virtue which moderates one's love of wealth in such a way that he wills to part with it readily according to a good which reason dictates. Liberality differs from the virtue of magnificence, which we treated under fortitude. The liberal person gives money readily for the good of others, whereas the magnanimous person, when he spends large sums of money, does so not for the sake of giving but for the sake of achieving some difficult and worthy deed. The proper meaning of liberality has been lost in modern times by a confusion of it with charity, or perhaps it is more accurate to say that the meaning of charity has been confused with that of liberality. In any case, charity, as we know from moral theology, is the virtue of loving God in a supernatural way, but the word is commonly used now to signify merely the giving of money for the help and benefit of others. "Charity drives" really should be "liberality drives." When we give money freely to persons and organizations for worthwhile purposes, we are acting in a liberal way, a manner of acting most immediately allied with justice. If we explicitly will to give money out of love of God, the act is then also allied with the virtue of charity.

Avarice is the vice of inordinate love of money for the sake of acquiring more material goods than are desirable or even necessary. This vice is produced by a particularly strong form of hard-heartedness, a refusal to consider the need and good of anything else because of greediness for wealth. It is connected with miserliness, that vicious quality by which a person lives miserably simply to increase his material state and wealth.

Affability is the second allied virtue contributing to an increase of moral rectitude in us. It is the virtue by which one promotes and maintains agreeable relations in social life. It is more than politeness and good manners, although both of these flow from affability. It is a friendliness, an establishment of cordial relations with others in the usual circumstances of social life. It is not the same, however, as friendship, a special kind of love between two persons which we shall consider later.

Adulation, the vice opposed to affability, is the obsequious and servile praise of someone else. *Flattery* is the more familiar term for this defect. A flatterer is one who seeks to gratify another's vanity in order to ingratiate himself; by so doing he destroys the desirable social quality of friendliness.

Religion

The most important virtue allied with justice is religion; consequently, it deserves treatment apart from the other virtues associated with justice. It may seem surprising to speak of religion in connection with justice, and a word or two of explanation is necessary not only to clarify this connection but to explain the meaning of religion as a moral virtue.

In ethics we do not speak of religion as it signifies the profession and practice of religious beliefs. This meaning of the term would refer, for example, to the Christian religion, particularly in the sense that the Christian religion contains supernatural truths revealed by God. Our concern in ethics is with religion as a natural moral virtue and as a good habit of rendering in some way what is due to God. It is true, of course, that religion in its supernatural meaning and religion as a natural moral virtue are closely connected, for Christianity presupposes and makes use of the natural moral virtue of religion. Indeed, to practice the moral virtue of religion fully, it is necessary to possess the supernatural truths God has revealed and to accept His grace in order to carry out the precepts and duties He has revealed as necessary for man's salvation. At the same time, however, the impression must not be gathered that religion is entirely supernatural, entirely separated from any natural foundation.

The task in ethics is to show how all human beings have an obligation in justice to give what is due to God by way of reverence and worship. This debt is incumbent on man naturally as well as supernaturally. A human being who fails to acknowledge and give what is due to God is acting unjustly. This general point, that all human beings have an obligation to recognize their indebtedness to God, can be shown on grounds of reason as well as through revelation. A book on ethics, however, is not the place to develop the reasons showing the existence of God and the dependence of man upon God. Other branches of philosophy, particularly metaphysics, demonstrate the existence of a supreme being that is the first cause of everything that comes into existence, of an ultimate final cause to which everything tends, of an absolutely necessary being upon which everything depends. In ethics, we accept the truth, as known through reason, that God exists, and with this knowledge the indebtedness of man to God follows.

The very language we have been using when speaking of our indebtedness to God shows that the virtue of religion must be allied with justice, since justice is the cardinal virtue concerned with what is due another. It may seem strange, however, to speak of something owed to God as though God stood in need of anything from human beings. He does not, of course, and we do not imply that He does when we say we owe something to Him. Likewise, the moral virtue of religion cannot be understood to imply that there is any sort of real equality between God and man. Nor, finally, in acknowledging our indebtedness to God do we suppose that we are realizing justice in the ordinary sense of the term, particularly as we find it in commutative or distributive justice. To understand how we can speak of religion as an allied virtue of justice it will be helpful, first, to consider two other virtues allied with justice which bear a certain likeness to religion as a virtue. These two virtues and religion have the following in common: by means of them, one renders what is due to another without attaining equality, either absolute or proportional. These three virtues thus differ from all other virtues associated with justice.

Veneration is the virtue by which we show honor and respect to persons who, in a variety of ways, are in a position of dignity and authority. For example, we esteem a good and outstanding civil official, a great military hero, a notable scholar, and so on, without seeking to establish any form of equality between those we honor and ourselves. Such persons are owed a certain respect and veneration.

Piety is the virtue by which we manifest the respect and honor we owe to our relatives, particularly our parents, and our country. As a distinct moral virtue, piety is to be distinguished from the religious meaning of piety; in the latter sense, piety is the same as the virtue of religion. With respect to members of our family, we speak of this virtue as *filial piety*, while the familiar name of *patriotism* applies to piety as it concerns the honor and respect we have for our country. It is clear that with both filial piety and patriotism a debt is involved. To our parents we owe our individual existence. To our country, we are indebted for our right to live as a citizen and to participate in the common good. Yet, in neither case do we achieve an equality in the acknowledgment of our debt.

Definition and Acts of Religion

It should not be difficult now to understand religion as a moral virtue associated with justice. Even more than is the case with veneration and piety, religion does not realize an equality, for there can be no equality in any sense of the term between God and man. Nonetheless, it is evident enough that we have an obligation to the ultimate cause of our existence; it is, indeed, the most fundamental and serious obligation of all.

Religion is defined as the virtue *perfecting man's will and his action so that he gives to God the reverence and worship due Him.* Religion perfects the *will*, contrary to a widespread tendency to identify religion with stimulation of the emotions, perhaps because some religious movements have been highly emotional in origin and practice. But, as the definition reveals and because religion is associated with justice, the virtue of religion is located in the will; and while the will has an influence on the activity of the emotions and vice versa, the connection is not a necessary one. A person may be deeply religious with or without strong emotional response.

The virtue of religion centers on a special relation we have with God, specifically one acknowledging our indebtedness to God. Even this qualification does not fully designate religion as a moral virtue. What specifically characterizes the moral virtue of religion is the acts of reverence, honor and worship we make to God. It is in these specific ways we acknowledge our indebtedness to God. Aside from the element of justice, the benefit of the virtue of religion is all on our part, since by it we are rightly ordered to the primary cause of our existence, and as a consequence live a more complete, more orderly, and better life. Just as a child lives a better life by being subjected to a good parent, and a citizen by being ordered to the rule of a good state, so a human being lives a fuller and better life by being rightly ordered to God.

The acts of the virtue of religion are primarily interior acts though directed to God as a term. These interior acts come from the will and the intellect. The primary act of the will in the moral virtue of religion is *devotion*, the promptness to do whatever pertains to the worship of God and a readiness to serve God through worship. An act of devotion is the most important of the acts of the virtue of religion. On the part of the intellect, the primary act of religion is *prayer*. Prayer is an act of the practical intellect asking something of God for some worthy motive. In so petitioning God we praise, honor, and respect Him, for petitioning is an acknowledgement of our complete dependence. Since man is not a solitary but a social being, devotion and prayer are public as well as private. Public devotion consists in worshipping socially through the church as an organization. Public or common prayer is prayer said aloud by many or by one for many.

There are exterior acts of religion as well as interior ones. The exterior acts are secondary acts because they follow upon and depend upon the interior acts. Without true devotion and prayer, the exterior acts of religion have little value. *Adoration* is the act of bodily humility, for example, kneeling, through which is signified an interior act of devotion toward God. Because of the intimate relation between soul and body, it is fitting that the body participate in the worship of God in this and other ways. *Sacrifice* is the act of using some sensible or corporeal thing as an offering to God in testimony of God's dominion over us.

As with other virtues, there is a vice opposed to the virtue of religion. It is *superstition*. Superstition consists in offering divine worship to something other than God or in offering worship and devotion to God in an improper manner. It is a vice by excess, not in the sense that too much worship can be given to God, but that the manner of worship can be excessive in any of a number of ways. There is also a vice by defect, the vice of being *irreligious* or irreverent. This vice occurs in a number of ways, from outright negligence and indifference to contempt and sacrilege.

In discussing religion as a moral virtue, we have stressed: (1) that it is a perfection of man to have such a virtue and (2) that there is a real obligation on the part of every human being to perform acts of religion. Contrary to a popular misconception, religion is not merely a matter of subjective inclination. It is objectively incumbent on all human beings to acknowledge their indebtedness to

God. Hence the importance of seeing that religion is a natural moral virtue, necessary and desirable for all men. Of course, religion is much more than a natural moral virtue; it is also a supernatural moral virtue in that God has revealed how He is to be served and worshipped. But reason alone can establish that each human being is indebted to God, and should perform acts of worship. We can understand also that religion is the most excellent of all moral virtues because it relates man to a higher object than any other virtue, God.

Equity

The understanding of equity as a special virtue depends upon an understanding of how laws are related to singular acts. If we consider the number of singular acts a human being performs during a lifetime and then reflect on the number of human beings performing singular acts throughout their lifetime, we realize that human acts attain a certain infinity in number and variety. Given this infinity of human acts, it is not possible for a law to be drawn up which will not fail to apply in some cases. But a legislator cannot take into account all of the individual cases to which a given law is to apply. He can consider only what usually happens or what happens for the most part. For example, a law may state that possessions should be returned to their owner. In a particular case, however, this law may not hold according to the letter. Thus, you may have Paul's pistol, but it would be evil to follow this law literally and return the pistol if Paul had become insane. It would be evil because it would be an act against the common good, which a law intends to observe.

Therefore, in particular cases a law may not apply, in the sense that understood literally it would fail to obtain the good to which the law is actually ordered. The law needs correction in its application in this particular case in order to achieve the good the legislator is actually intending. This correction is supplied by the virtue of equity, and therefore equity is defined as the virtue *inclining the will to correct law when law fails to apply in particular instances*.

The exercising of this virtue is not limited to any particular matter, i.e., it is not limited to only certain moral situations. Equity extends to any moral matter to which law is in any way applicable, and for this reason it corresponds to legal justice. However, the relation of equity to legal justice depends upon the understanding of legal justice. If legal justice is taken in the sense of ordering acts of virtue to the common good according to the ordinary and literal interpretation of law, then equity actually exceeds legal justice and is superior to it. If legal justice is understood as ordering acts of virtue to the common good according to the intention of the legislator as well as the letter of the law, then equity is part of legal justice, and moreover the principal part. It is interesting to note that this distinction has been observed from early times in the English court system, which provides for two kinds of court, the court of law and the court of equity. This division of the court recognized the difference between the ordinary case of justice and the exceptional case of justice. In the United States, on the other hand, these two distinct functions are supposed to be exercised by one court.

As far as the individual man is concerned, the equitable man is a just man in a superior way. Disposed by this virtue, he seeks the realization of the common good in all of his virtuous acts. This does not mean that he will deprive himself of his proper good, but it does mean that he will refrain from taking advantage of the letter of the law when it would benefit him at the expense of the common good. The man of equity, in other words, wills what is just simply and without qualification.

OUTLINE OF JUSTICE

I. General Justice and Injustice
   A. The virtue of general or legal justice
   B. The vice of general injustice

II. The Object of Justice: Right
   A. Natural
   B. Positive

III. Particular Justice: The Cardinal Virtue
   A. Commutative justice
   B. Distributive justice

IV. Vices against Particular Justice
  A. Vices against commutative justice
    1. Involuntary
      a) By deed: murder, physical assault, false imprison-
                    ment, adultery, stealing
      b) By word: detraction, contumely, gossiping, curs-
                    ing, mockery
    2. Voluntary: fraud, usury
  B. Principal vice against distributive justice: respect for per-
     sons, e.g., nepotism

V. Virtues Allied with Justice and Their Principal Vices
  A. Veracity—Lying
  B. Gratitude—Ingratitude
  C. Vindication—Revenge
  D. Liberality—Avarice
  E. Affability—Adulation

VI. Virtues Associated in a Special Way with Justice
  A. Veneration
  B. Piety
    1. Filial piety
    2. Patriotism
  C. Religion
    1. Interior acts: devotion, prayer
    2. Exterior acts: adoration, sacrifice
    3. Vices
      a) By excess: superstition
      b) By defect: irreverence

VII. Equity: The Perfection of Justice

REVIEW QUESTIONS

1. What kind of person is unjust without qualification?
2. What is meant by "general justice?"
3. What is the definition of legal justice?

4. What clarification in meaning does legal justice add to general justice?

5. Distinguish between objective and subjective right.

6. What is the relation between objective and subjective right?

7. Distinguish between natural and positive right.

8. Define particular justice.

9. Why is the cardinal virtue of justice identified with particular justice?

10. How does the mean of particular justice differ from the mean of other moral virtues?

11. Define commutative justice.

12. Define distributive justice.

13. How do commutative and distributive justice differ?

14. Explain why and how the mean of distributive justice is one of proportional equality.

15. What is the difference between *being* unjust and *acting* unjustly?

16. What is the specific vice opposed to distributive justice?

17. Summarize the vices against commutative justice which are involuntary.

18. Summarize the vices against commutative justice which are voluntary.

19. Compare the old and modern meaning of usury. Is the modern meaning justified?

20. Distinguish between legal debt and moral debt.

21. What is lying? Discuss whether lying can be justified in any circumstances.

22. What is liberality? With what is it often confused, and why?

23. Do all human beings have an obligation to practice the virtue of religion? Why or why not?

24. What is veneration?

25. What is piety?

26. What is the definition of religion as a moral virtue?

27. What are the interior and exterior acts of religion?

28. What problem arises with respect to the relation of law to singular acts?

29. What is the definition of equity and how does it solve the problem about law and singular acts?

30. How is the equitable person just in a superior way?

DISCUSSION

1. General justice is perfect or complete virtue. But legal justice, as the name suggests, is specifically concerned with the relation of law to virtuous acts. Therefore, general justice and legal justice differ from each other insofar as general justice is a general virtue and legal justice is a specific virtue.

2. Right, in any objective sense of the term, must be determined in an objective and concrete fashion. This determination can be made only by the legislative power of a particular state. Therefore, rights of human beings are necessarily dependent for their determination and for their concrete existence upon the legislative powers of states.

3. A right is an inviolable power by which I vindicate my doing or acquiring something. The function of this power is to protect my possessions and my liberty of action. Since right is also the object of justice, my right to life, liberty, and the pursuit of happiness is guaranteed by the order of justice itself.

4. Any form of justice is a rendering of what is due to another; consequently, justice is related to our exterior acts. The moral order, however, is concerned with our interior acts. Hence, justice is to exterior acts as morality is to interior acts. But rights belong to the order of justice. Therefore, rights are distinct from the moral order.

5. Individual liberty, it is claimed, cannot be considered apart from its ordering to the common good of the social and political order. However, individual liberty derives from the autonomy of the human person. Hence, individual liberty is prior to the common good and cannot be limited in behalf of the common good without destroying the person's essential autonomy. Therefore, individual liberty is the primary and fundamental right of man.

6. The individual cannot develop as a human being without the social and political order, for the preservation of order is necessary for the development of good human life. Consequently, if the very existence of the social and political order is threatened, the state is dispensed from its obligations under distributive justice. In such a situation, the state may act unjustly toward its citizens as long as such action is necessary to preserve the social order. Therefore, the

rulers of a state are justified in taking any action necessary to preserve the social and political order.

7. Installment buying has greatly increased in this century. This method of buying is equivalent to a bank loan, and just as interest may be charged on a bank loan, so may it be charged on installment purchases. Mr. Jones, who had formerly only borrowed from banks, bought a product on the installment plan. After paying on it for six months, he unexpectedly received some extra money and wished to settle his account at once instead of making the payments over a period of three years. He discovered, however, that paying up his amount in full brought no rebate on the interest charge for the three year period. Mr. Jones regarded this as usury. Is he right?

8. A business man, in an attempt to put his competitor out of business, undercuts his prices to a point at which neither he nor his competitor can make a profit. He is successful and is soon in complete control of the sale of a particular product. He justified his action on the grounds that in lowering his prices to the point where he drove his competitor out of business he enabled people to buy the product who could not otherwise afford it. He was also justified, he argued, in raising the price later to compensate for his loss. Has he acted justly?

9. George has two tickets for an important college football game. He paid five dollars for each of them. His friend, Bill, is very anxious to see this game, but is unable to get two tickets because the game is sold out. George tells him that for ten dollars each he can get two tickets for Bill, and when Bill agrees, George sells him his own tickets. George claims there is nothing unjust about his action, since he deserves special compensation for being deprived of seeing this important game. Is George right?

10. I am an officer in the army and we are at war in a foreign country. I am captured by the enemy and am asked whether my troops are on a certain hill. I know that the troops are at this location. If I answer in the affirmative, or remain silent, the enemy will bomb the site and kill all the men. To prevent this massacre from happening, I can only answer that the troops are not at this location. In such a case and under such circumstances, is telling a lie morally wrong?

SUGGESTED READINGS

Aristotle, *Ethics*, Book V.
St. Thomas, *Commentary*, Book V.
Plato, *Crito*, *Euthyphro*, and *The Republic*.

Bourke, *Ethics*, chap. X, pp. 325-350.
Gilson, *Moral Values and the Moral Life*, chaps. IX-X, pp. 246-275.
Hume, D., *An Enquiry Concerning the Principles of Morals*, Sec. III.
    Consult Melden, A., *Ethical Theories*, pp. 252-264.
Johnston, *Business Ethics*, chap. IV, pp. 78-100.
Mill, J. S., *Utilitarianism*, chap. V. Consult *The English Philosophers
    from Bacon to Mill*, edited by E. Burtt. New York: Modern Library,
    1939, pp. 928-948.
Pieper, J., *Justice*. New York: Pantheon Books, 1955.
Wheelwright, *A Critical Introduction to Ethics*, chap. 10, pp. 251-286.
Wild, *Introduction to Realistic Philosophy*, chap. 8, pp. 154-175.

X

The intellectual virtues

Virtue is usually understood to mean moral perfection. There is good reason for this view, for moral virtue is the primary meaning of virtue and we generally use a word in its primary meaning. The word "brother" is an example. It has a primary meaning, namely that of a male person related to another person having the same parents. We do not hesitate, however, to use the same word to signify some male person not so closely related or not related in the same way, for example, a person in a religious community; similarly, persons refer to each other as "brothers" in a fraternal association. The word "brother," then, signifies in an analogical manner. The word "virtue" is also analogous.

If we see at the outset that "virtue" signifies both moral and intellectual virtue analogously and not univocally, we shall not find it strange to speak about intellectual virtue. We have now completed our treatment of moral virtue, and we have seen how virtue, as a good habit, is found in fortitude, temperance, and justice. As we now begin to treat intellectual virtue, we must keep in mind that "good habit" will not signify wholly in the same way as it did when we analyzed moral virtue.

The Good of the Intellect

Let us begin to understand intellectual virtue by considering what we mean by the "good" of the intellect. In order that there be intellectual virtue there must be some good realizable in the intellect, for virtue always implies a perfection of human power, which is to say, it attains whatever is the good of a power. This excellence is realized in the proper operation that the power has. Our immediate point is to make clear what the good is in which intellectual operation consists.

We have sufficiently considered in previous chapters how the intellect differs from the power of willing and from the power of sense desiring. Both of these latter powers are appetitive powers, whereas the intellectual power is a cognitive power. We are also sufficiently aware of the difference between intellectual knowing and sense knowing, even though both of these are cognitive powers. The intellectual power of a human being consists in grasping things in a rational mode of knowing. Consequently, the good of the human intellect will be, first of all, to know objects well through reason. To know something well through reason is to know something as true, for it is precisely through knowing what is true that the intellect is perfected. Truth, therefore, is the *good* of the intellect.

Speculative and Practical Reason

Human reason, however, does not know what is true about various things in the same way. It is one thing to know the truth of a mathematical conclusion but quite another to know whether doing this action here and now is true or, as we often say, "right." The difference between these two kinds of knowing—the truth of knowledge itself and the truth of action—is fundamental. When things known by reason differ in kind, the functions of reason also differ. While we are thus led to recognize two such different kinds of knowing, we should not be led to assume there are two distinct powers of reason. It is one and the same intellectual power which knows in two diverse ways. It is in this fashion we understand *speculative* and *practical* reason, distinguished because of two different ends in knowing, the end of knowledge and the end of action.

Presuming this basic distinction between speculative and practical reason, we must next see that speculative reason differs from practical reason as the *unchanging* differs from the *changing*. What we know through speculative reason is something which always is what it is; it is invariable and therefore cannot be otherwise than what it is. In this way we know, for example, that a triangle cannot be otherwise than having its angles equal to two right angles. What we know through practical reason is variable, for in seeking to know how to act we are dealing with what is in itself changeable and subject to alteration. But, to avoid a possible misunderstanding here, let us note that what is variable can be known in two ways: in general and in particular.

General statements about what is variable are themselves unchanging. For example, the statement that every twenty-four hours the earth turns completely on its axis is a general statement about something changing. Such knowledge is still speculative even though it is concerned about something changing. We are not now concerned with knowing what is variable in this fashion, i.e., generally, but with knowing variable things individually, this change or that action now going on. We are referring principally to the vast area of single events and actions about which we must deliberate in order to know what to do about them. No one deliberates about the rotation of the earth, but you can deliberate about going around the world yourself. This is the domain in which practical reason operates.

Speculative reason, then, embraces the necessary and the invariable, and also the general knowledge of the variable. Practical reason is directed only to the changing, singular action. From this distinction arises another that will further differentiate these two ways of knowing. It will permit us also to state more fully what the "good" of speculative reason is and what the "good" of practical reason is. We shall then be ready to examine intellectual virtue, reason operating at its peak of perfection.

The good state of speculative reason is simply knowing truth, and speculative reason is operating well when it knows what is true. The bad state of speculative reason is knowing falsity, and speculative reason is operating badly when it is knowing falsely. Allowing for the analogous meaning of "virtue" and "vice" we can now make sense out of speaking about speculative intellectual virtue and speculative intellectual vice.

The good state of practical reason does not consist simply in knowing truth. Because practical reason is connected with singular action involving desire on the part of both the will and emotion, the virtue of practical reason, though an intellectual virtue itself, will be necessarily connected with moral virtue. We can see the distinction of practical intellectual virtue—specifically, prudence—from moral virtue, and the intimate connection of the two in the following way. The intellect alone judges, either by affirming when it assents to what is true, or by negating when it denies what is false. The intellect in its practical knowing judges in the same way as in its speculative knowing. However, proportioned to the two intellectual acts of affirming and denying as they are in the practical intellect are two acts in our appetitive powers, seeking and avoiding. By will and emotion we seek what is good and avoid what is evil. Our practical intellect in its affirming and denying and our appetitive powers in their seeking and avoiding are so intimately connected with each other that we need both in order to know and act in practical affairs.

What precisely, then, is the good state of practical reason? Because of the close association practical reason has with the appetitive powers in which moral virtues are located, let us first recall that we defined moral virtue in Chapter IV as primarily a habit of choice. We stated also in Chapter VI that choice, an act of the will, is guided by deliberation, an act of the practical intellect. Actually both practical reason and appetite concur in choice, which is the special act of moral virtue. In order that the choice be good, i.e., good in the moral sense, the practical reasoning must be sound and the appetite must be good; that is, it must seek what reason affirms to be good.

To answer, then, the question of what the good state of practical reason is, we could say simply *practical truth*, bearing in mind what we have said about the close connection between the practical intellect and the appetitive powers; in other words, the good state of practical reason is *action in agreement with right desire*. It is this agreement of action with right desire that is called "practical truth." We are led accordingly to see how practical intellectual virtue—we are here considering prudence rather than art—differs both from speculative intellectual virtue and from moral virtue of the appetitive order.

Practical Reason and Right Appetite

A difficulty seems to arise from the foregoing remarks. In our attempt to distinguish practical truth from speculative truth, we said that the good state of practical reason is action in agreement with right desire. Suppose that we now ask: What makes practical reason right? Presumably we would answer, conformity with right appetite. But what makes appetite right? Presumably we would answer, conformity with right reason. This seems to be reasoning in a circle, proving X by Y and then Y by X.

The difficulty is only an apparent one. Its solution will help us to see the intimate connection between practical reason and appetite, and how much each affects the other. Let us begin to solve the difficulty by recalling that in the order of appetite we seek both ends and means. There is a difference, however, between the way we seek an end and the way we seek a means. The final end of man, for example, is determined ultimately by his nature. It is because man is what he is by nature that he seeks happiness as his ultimate end. The means, on the other hand, are not determined by nature but must be investigated by reason, for even when an end is given, deliberation and choice must work out the means.

The distinction between seeking an end and seeking a means leads to the full solution to the question of whether appetite makes reason right or reason makes appetite right. Each does make the other right, but in different respects.

Rectitude of the will, or appetite, with respect to the end makes practical reason true, i.e., right. Willing a good end determines the rightness of practical reason. Thus we say that the truth of practical reason is determined according to right appetite, i.e., right appetite of the end. But with respect to willing a means, the truth of practical reason makes the appetite right. The appetite is rightly ordered with respect to means when it seeks what true practical reason indicates.

An example will help to clarify this relationship of appetite and practical reason. When you will to treat your neighbor justly you are willing a good end. Because of this good intention of an end, your reason is disposed to judge accordingly. In willing a particular means by which to achieve a just act in relation to your neighbor, your practical reason, disposed by the willing of the good end, judges what means the will is to choose in order to achieve the good end. The will chooses the means rightly as guided by the intellect.

The answer to the problem may now be summarized simply in the following way. In the order of *ends*, right appetite makes practical reason true or right. In the order of *means*, true practical reason makes the appetite right.

We can now summarize our general consideration of speculative and practical reason. The "good" of both speculative and practical reason is truth. The operation of the speculative intellect, however, concerns truth alone, whereas the operation of the practical intellect relates to action in conformity with right desire. The practical intellect is the intellect operating in view of an end. Its operation is not any sort of knowing but the discovery of how to attain an end; hence, end is essential to the practical intellect. The practical intellect thus operates to attain an end, that is, a good, of another power or of man himself.

Speculative Intellectual Virtues

Let us consider first the intellectual virtues related to speculative reason, the intellect as simply knowing truth. We admire someone who knows not only that something is true but precisely why it is true. Indeed, we ourselves seek to know in just such a way, because we commonly recognize that this kind of knowing character-izes a person who is *well formed* intellectually. The most evident speculative intellectual virtue in this respect is *science*, the good intel-lectual habit of demonstrating conclusions. We use the word "sci-ence" in its original, strict sense, namely, the knowledge of true and certain conclusions following necessarily from premises. In this meaning of the term, science is opposed to *opinion*, the knowing of something as only probably true. In excluding opinion from being a virtue, we in no way deny its importance and utility. Opinion is not merely a subjective guess but an objective, likely estimation of what is true. However, opinion cannot be an intellectual virtue since what we know only as opinion is not necessarily true and certain; it may even be false, and to know something which might be false is not to be as well formed intellectually as possible.

We know in a strictly scientific way when we know not only that something is true but also why it is true. This knowledge is made manifest in a scientific way by a syllogism, that is, by demon-stration or deduction. A syllogism can be expressed in the follow-ing manner:

> Every rational animal is capable of speech.
> Every man is a rational animal.
> Therefore, every man is capable of speech.

Accepting the first two propositions, the premises, as true and necessary, we *know* (1) *that* every man is capable of speech and (2) *why* every man is capable of speech, namely, because of the definition of man as rational animal. To know in this way is to know *well*; to be able to demonstrate in this way is to have the *habit* of demonstrating conclusions, which is to have the intellectual virtue of science.

The principles of demonstration, the premises, are not the same as demonstration itself. Demonstration consists in reasoning from premises to the conclusion. Now the premises are either capable of proof, in which case, they become conclusions with their own premises, or they are not capable of proof. If they are not capable of proof, they must still be true and certain, otherwise scientific conclusions could not be drawn from them. If they are true with-out proof and are not merely assumed hypothetically, they are true as self-evident. It is clear that there must be some self-evident principles of this kind, otherwise there could never be proof in the unqualified sense of the term; and without unqualified proof there would be no virtue of science. We are thus led to see the need and place of another kind of knowing, a knowing by which we grasp something as true without proof. We come to recognize also that strict proof requires the knowing of some propositions that are true without proof. Hence we recognize (1) a kind of knowing other than knowing by proof and (2) the need of another good of the intellect, that is, another virtue.

This second speculative intellectual virtue is called *understanding*. By understanding we mean the distinct habit of knowing by which we grasp indemonstrable principles as true and upon which all demonstration ultimately depends. Such principles are known as soon as the terms of the principles are known. For example, when one knows what is meant by "whole" and by "part," one immediately, i.e., without reasoning, knows that every whole is greater than any of its parts. We thus *understand* such a principle.

The virtue of science is related to the virtue of understanding, as deduction is to induction. By *deduction* we mean reasoning from universal principles to universal conclusions, as is manifested in the syllogism. The ultimate starting points of deduction are self-evident universal principles. We know such principles by induction. By *induction* we mean going from the experience of individuals to the universal principle. The virtue of understanding employs induction, for we induce the universal principle from several instances, as in the case of inducing the principle that a whole is greater than its part from several cases of whole and part. Just as true and certain deduction is distinguished from deduction that yields only a probably true conclusion, so the induction by which first principles are grasped is distinguished from the induction which, from a variety of singulars, yields only a principle which is probably true. This latter type of induction does not constitute an intellectual virtue.

The perfection of the speculative intellect in knowing is not fully achieved by the good habit of demonstrating and by the good habit of grasping indemonstrable principles. A sign that this is the case is that while we call a person "scientific" in the strict sense of the term when he knows in a reasoned way and can prove something as true, we do not necessarily call such a person "wise." Nor do we call a person "wise" who merely grasps the truth of indemonstrable principles. *Wisdom*, therefore, designates an intellectual perfection over and beyond the perfection of science and understanding.

There is practical wisdom as well as speculative wisdom. We are now concerned with speculative wisdom, although practical wisdom gives us a clue to understanding what speculative wisdom is; hence we shall refer to it first. In the order of art, which is practical knowledge, we speak of wisdom in relation to an art which rules and directs the knowledge found in subordinate arts. The architect, for example, by virtue of his knowledge of construction, is a master artist—is "wise"—in relation to the carpenter, the plumber, and to others.

The architect can be called wise in a qualified sense, namely, in the order of planning and constructing buildings. As he is related to other artisans, so a person who is wise in an unqualified sense is related to a man of science. What is such unqualified wisdom? It is speculative wisdom, a knowledge of what is highest in the universe, God, and a knowledge embracing the whole of reality as related to such an ultimate cause. Such speculative wisdom is traditionally known as *metaphysics*. It is also called *First Philosophy*, not in the sense of first known, for one cannot be wise without knowing many things beforehand, but first in the sense of being ultimate in the order of knowledge and as treating the most profound cause of all things. It is knowledge of everything that is insofar as it is—being as being—and in a special way attains knowledge of God as the cause of being.

This virtue of speculative wisdom embraces the other two speculative virtues while reaching beyond them. Wisdom is understanding, not merely in the sense of grasping self-evident principles as true, but inasmuch as it discusses and defends them. Wisdom is science inasmuch as it also demonstrates conclusions from principles. Being concerned with the most ultimate things and their causes, however, it is more eminent than other sciences. It is properly "knowledge come to a head," that is, knowledge terminating in the highest and most intelligible objects knowable by the human intellect.

Some have thought that practical wisdom is the highest kind of knowledge. But practical wisdom could be the highest kind of knowledge only on the supposition that man is the highest being that exists. On the contrary, metaphysics—speculative wisdom—is the highest kind of knowledge because God, not man, is the supreme being. Nevertheless, man needs practical wisdom; indeed, his more immediate need is for practical intellectual virtue rather than speculative intellectual virtue, even though the latter exceeds in nobility. We turn, therefore, to the two practical intellectual virtues, art and prudence, which all men need to possess in varying degrees to live well humanly.

The Virtue of Art

The consideration of practical intellectual virtue brings us to the order of action again. We recognize from experience that, while we perform many actions, they reduce to two main kinds: the *making* of something and the *doing* of something. There is no individual action that is not one or the other. Making is that kind of action which begins in an agent and passes into some external material in such a way as to form something of it. It is in this fashion that a man makes a chair. Doing is that sort of action which begins in the agent but also remains in the agent. Acts of knowing and willing are actions of this kind. This fundamental distinction between making and doing, between transitive and immanent action, is the basis for seeing that there are only two practical intellectual virtues.

The virtue of art, to state the definition most simply, is the right way of making something. The simplicity of this definition, however, hides a certain complexity that characterizes artistic making. Let us amplify the definition to say that art is *the intellectual virtue enabling the practical intellect to direct the making of an object.*

By means of this expanded definition we can distinguish three stages in artistic making, whether we are making a house or a statue. The first is the consideration of how something is to be made, that is, a plan. This is especially the work of practical reason, thinking in terms of the action to be effected; specifically, it is thinking of something to be made and how to make it. The second stage is the actual work on some exterior matter, such as wood. The action here is directed by the practical intellect in terms of the plan conceived.

The third and final stage is the completion of the work, the object made, which is a reflection of the working out of the original idea in the artistic mind. Thus, a well-made table is a finished product effected through the work of the agent as directed by his intellect in its practical operation. It is evident that products of art are necessary and desirable for human living, and that art adds a distinct perfection to human beings and merits being called a virtue.

There are several distinct kinds of art, and many individual ones of each kind. There are, for example, the many manual or servile arts, such as carpentry, cooking, and construction, as well as the many highly developed industrial arts of modern civilization. Some of the fine arts are virtues of the practical intellect, for no one would think of denying the realization of a good of reason in the making of paintings and statues. The liberal arts are also virtues, but because they remain within the limits of the intellect they are virtues of the speculative intellect. It is evident that "art" does not retain the same meaning when signifying servile, fine, or liberal, yet we can apply the definition we have given to all kinds in an analogous manner, for in all of them is realized the notion of art as a discipline that regulates reason in the making of a kind of work.

In understanding the virtue of art as the good habit of practical thinking by which we make things well, we come to see more and more the need and desirability of having the different arts. The servile arts are necessary in order to sustain our very existence, and because we need first to eat, to be clothed, and to have shelter these arts were the first to appear. They have been extensively developed in modern civilization, particularly in the realm of technological and industrial production. The fine arts, on the other hand, are necessary in another sense, namely, to *live well*, that is, beyond the order of material and physical existence. Fine art leads us to enjoy, through a delightful mode of knowing, objects that are aesthetically pleasing. The good achieved through both servile and fine art, however, is not the good of man himself, for the perfection of art is realized primarily in the thing made. The virtue of art, in other words, is not a principle directly affecting good moral action. The proper principle of the good moral act is prudence, the other virtue of the practical order, which is directly concerned with the good of man himself.

Art and Morality

In stating that the virtue of art is not a principle directly affecting good moral action, we touched upon the question of art and morality. Before we examine the virtue of prudence, we should give some consideration to whether, granting a distinction between the order of art and the moral order, there is any connection and relation between them.

The question can be simplified by limiting the meaning of "art" when we speak of it in connection with the moral order. First of all, we are not concerned with servile art. The products of such art are not of themselves morally good or evil. Their *use* is another question, falling under the domain of prudence. Nor are we concerned with liberal art, the art of regulating objects in the mind and in the imagination, such as we find in logic or mathematics. Logical and mathematical objects are clearly not moral objects.

The important question of art and morality arises only when we consider the fine arts, poetic art, musical art, or the art of painting. It is evident from our experience in enjoying and understanding the works of these arts that each in its own way imitates human action and passion. By "imitation" in the artistic sense we mean not mere copying but imaginative representation, in an intelligible and delightful manner, of some aspect of reality more or less familiar to us. The play represents dramatically a human situation, and the symphony represents the subtle movement of human passion through an intelligible ordering of musical tone.

No matter how fanciful an artist may be, he is always interpreting some aspect of reality, for God alone creates absolutely. Thus, given a necessary connection between art and reality, there will also be a necessary connection between art and morality whenever a work of fine art represents something of human action and passion. As we have seen, action and passion humanly experienced is a voluntary act; and, since every human act in the concrete is morally good or bad, any representation of such an act is necessarily connected with the moral order.

To the extent, therefore, that moral matter is present in the representation of the artist, the work of art is moral as well as artistic. Morality in this way enters into the very delight, intelligibility, and beauty of the work of art. By "morality" here we mean the sound knowledge of what constitutes good and bad moral action. This being the case, the artist has an obligation *as an artist* to represent faithfully what is true morally as well as what is plausible artistically. Specifically, as an artist he should seek to represent as morally good what is morally good and as morally evil what is morally evil. To the extent he departs from this ordering, his work suffers as art, for there will be a proportionate lack of the intelligibility and beauty that all art requires.

This is not a question of subordinating art to morality in the sense of trying to teach or propagandize morality through art. Such a procedure is bound to be defective, from the standpoint of both art and morality. Art has its proper end which, as such, is not moral, and the teaching of morality is ill fitted to the mode of artistic representation. Nor are we raising the question of whether the artist himself is a good man; such a question belongs primarily to the order of prudence, which is not to be confused with morality, for morality is the *knowledge* of what is good or evil. It is certainly possible, and it in fact happens, that an immoral artist produces great works of art. But it is not because he is immoral that he does so; rather, it is in spite of it. On the other hand, simply being morally good obviously does not guarantee artistic greatness. Hence, the greatness of works of art rests not upon the private moral life of the artist but upon his skill in making delightful and intelligible representations of *plausible* reality. At the same time, reality is plausibly represented in art only if it is portrayed as morally sound and consistent, and the artist need not be morally good himself to represent what is morally sound. This brief survey of an important and complicated problem can only indicate the general relation between fine art and morality. We shall refer to another aspect of this problem after our consideration of the virtue of prudence.

The Virtue of Prudence

The importance and necessity of prudence can be seen in several ways. First of all, it is a cardinal virtue; it ranks along with fortitude, temperance, and justice as a major virtue upon which other virtues depend for their direction and perfection. Indeed, as we shall see when we define it, it is the most necessary virtue of all, a second reason for its importance. The necessity of prudence derives from its essential role of directing man to his attainment of good moral living for, given the end of happiness, prudence more than any other virtue determines how we shall realize this end in our action.

The importance of prudence is also indicated by the fact that it is the only virtue that is both intellectual and moral. It is an intellectual virtue because the virtue itself is located in the practical intellect; it is a good habit of practical thinking, in which respect it is like art. At the same time prudence is not only an intellectual virtue, for it requires rectitude of the appetite to operate. A good end to which the will is directed must be presupposed for a person to think and act prudently. A burglar may be skillful in planning and carrying out a robbery, but we would be speaking in an equivocal manner if we were to call the burglar "prudent" in his act of robbing. Precisely because prudence presupposes and requires the right intention of a good end, it is also a moral virtue. In this respect it is unlike art, for the virtue of art requires only that the artist act with knowledge, not with a right intention as far as a moral good is concerned.

Finally, the importance of prudence may be indicated by the fact that we generally attribute a kind of wisdom to the man of prudence. We mean, of course, practical wisdom, not the speculative wisdom which constitutes a distinct speculative intellectual virtue. Nevertheless, our speaking of the prudent man as wise testifies to the high regard we have for him, a regard which rests principally on his ability to *deliberate* well with a view to attaining some good end. We take counsel from his deliberation and we seek his advice because of his fruitful experience and rectitude in practical affairs to try and order our own lives in a similar way.

Definition of Prudence

Most simply expressed, prudence is the right way of doing something. This definition, like that of art, needs to be expanded. Prudence is *the intellectual virtue which rightly directs particular human acts, through rectitude of the appetite, toward a good end.*

The special acts we perform through the virtue of prudence give us further understanding of prudence and show us how it operates as a virtue. There are three of these acts, which are to be related to corresponding acts in the will, discussed in Chapter VI. The first is *counsel*, which consists in inquiring into the means and circumstances necessary in order that an act be done well. The second act is *practical judgment*, an assent to good and suitable means. It amounts to a practical decision, which terminates the counsel that precedes it and immediately disposes one to make a choice leading to action. The third act is *command*, the direct application of the counseling and judging to action. It is by virtue of command that we finally do or omit doing an act.

All three acts are necessary for the full exercise of prudence, but command is the most important and the principal act. The reason for the pre-eminence of command is that what matters most in the practical order is the application of knowledge to action. It is precisely by making such an ordering, i.e., by commanding, that good action actually results. Deliberation and counsel of themselves need not lead to action; in fact, one can deliberate too much and never act. Similarly, with judgment one can assent to what should be done, but without effectively commanding the execution, action does not follow.

In stressing command as the most important act of the virtue of prudence, we disassociate the virtue from the narrow meaning of "being cautious," often taken to be its proper meaning. True enough, a prudent person will exercise caution when the circumstances so dictate, but to be prudent in the full sense of the term is, first and foremost, to act in a determinate fashion. A prudent person is more a commanding person than a cautious person.

Divisions of Prudence

We shall divide prudence first according to the two secondary acts of counsel and judgment. This division is one of dividing the virtue into its potential parts, because neither of these acts fully realizes the perfection of prudence. These potential parts are the special virtues needed for performing well the acts of counsel and judgment. The act of command is not included because command is properly the act of the virtue of prudence itself.

The good habit of deliberating well—producing the act of good counsel—is called *eubulia*. This Greek name signifies "good counsel." Hence, we call the act of this habit "counsel," and translate *eubulia* into its literal English equivalent of "good counsel." It is a perfection of the practical intellect by which we rightly deliberate about the available means that will lead to a desired good end.

The other secondary act of prudence, judgment, has two virtues associated with it because we make two different sorts of judgment about what must be done. The first type of judgment concerns good moral judgment about ordinary moral matters. The name of the virtue producing such an act is *synesis*, which we might approximate in meaning by saying that it is good common sense in making judgments about what to do and what not to do in the ordinary run of affairs. The second type of judgment arises when an unusual moral situation requiring an exceptional sort of judgment confronts us. This type of judgment differs from the first as equity differs from justice. It goes beyond the ordinary way of solving a moral problem by judging according to the spirit of law and regulation. The virtue producing such an act is called *gnome*. It is the virtue by which a person, seeking to preserve the spirit of what is just, judges it right to perform an action not required strictly by the letter of the law. It is a virtue belonging particularly to the good judge when he deals with problems not wholly covered by the law.

The essential division of prudence, the division into subjective parts, is into *individual* prudence and *political* prudence. The basis for this division is prudence as it is concerned with what is good or evil for the individual, and as it is concerned with what is good or evil for society. We have been speaking so far of individual prudence and have associated the name "prudence" with this kind. There is reason and custom to justify this usage of the term, for prudence especially seems to be concerned with the attainment of the individual good. In ordinary speech, we use the term in this signification.

Nevertheless, the importance of political prudence can hardly be exaggerated. It is the virtue by which one rules or is ruled in relation to the common good. There is a political prudence proper to the statesman, to the person who governs civil society, whether in a legislative, executive, or judicial manner; and a political prudence proper to the one who is ruled in society, the citizen. Political prudence is necessary for the citizen, not only for his thinking and working well with others toward the common good, but also for his own good in the sense that there is a mutual relation between one's personal good and the common good. We can distinguish also a domestic prudence, the good habit of practical thinking needed by a husband and wife who seek the good of the family as a whole. The success of married life depends in good measure on the amount of domestic prudence exercised: inversely, the difficulties of married life become unresolved largely in proportion to the failure to exercise domestic prudence.

Vices Opposed to Prudence

Along with all moral virtue, prudence is a mean of perfection between extremes. The extremes of defect and excess are various ways in which we act contrary to prudence and so form the opposing vices. We shall consider first, under the general name of *imprudence*, the vices opposed to prudence by defect.

Impetuosity is the name given to the vice of acting too quickly because of failure to consider adequately the available means. It is a failure to take counsel or to deliberate enough about a course of action to pursue. It is a vice directly opposed to eubulia or good counsel. *Thoughtlessness* is a closely related vice; it is distinct from impetuosity in that it is a defect of practical judgment. It is, therefore, directly opposed to the virtues of synesis and of gnome, both of which are perfections of practical judgment. The thoughtless person does not take the care and pains to form a careful judgment.

Inconstancy and *negligence* are two other vices opposed to prudence by defect. They are both directed against the good of the act of command, the principal act of prudence. Inconstancy is the failure to complete a moral act by refusing to command that an act be done. This vice develops in us because of our giving way to inordinate pleasure. Although this inclination of undue appetite is the occasion for the development of the vice in us, the vice itself is directly caused by a defect of reason. Negligence is a defect on the part of the intellect to direct the will in carrying out some good action. Since such a defect in the prompt execution of command directly attacks the principal act of the virtue of prudence, negligence is the most serious vice by defect.

The general name of *false prudence* is given to vices opposed to prudence by excess. The phrase "by excess" does not mean, of course, too much prudence, for there cannot be too much of a virtue. It refers, rather, to excessive thought and concern about attaining various objects of desire. Thus, one may have excessive solicitude about attaining such objects of desire as power, position, wealth, or fame. *Prudence of the flesh* is the vice by which a person is excessively concerned about the good of the body, for example, with physique, beauty, or sensual pleasure. *Astuteness* is a vice when the name is taken to mean the use of improper means to attain a desired end, even though the end may be good.

Ethics and Prudence

Prudence as the virtue of practical reasoning with regard to individual action is quite distinct from the knowledge we attain in a moral science such as ethics. As we have seen, prudence is the reasoned way of acting in conformity with right appetite. It is wholly practical, not concerned with general knowledge, but with acting here and now in particular circumstances. It is what we described in Chapter I as completely practical knowing. Although in ethics we are concerned ultimately with action insofar as ethics is a practical science, we always remain on a general level of knowing about good action, about vice, and about an ultimate end.

The distinction between ethics and prudence needs emphasis because there is a tendency to conceive ethics primarily as casuistry, that is, as a system of dealing with cases of conscience in relation to doing what is right or wrong in particular instances. Ethics is thus often conceived as the detailed application of moral principles to every possible particular situation. It is presumed that because ethics is "practical" it should serve as the proximate principle of individual moral action. This view radically confuses ethics and prudence.

It is not possible to derive, from moral principles alone, what you should do in an individual case. True enough, the moral principles serve as a guide to action. You know, for example, that what belongs to someone else should be restored to him and, for the most part, this principle can be directly realized in action. But can you deduce from it that in any given situation you should restore what belongs to another? Can you, for example, deduce from this principle that you should restore this person's pistol when he has vowed to shoot you? On the contrary, it is *prudent* in this situation not to return the pistol. In stating the matter this way we do not mean to imply that we go *against* a moral principle, but rather that a moral principle tends to be less directly applicable the more we descend into particular conditions and circumstances. There is no purely automatic application of a moral principle to a concrete situation. It is precisely the work of prudence to make the application to the particular situation, and this application is not merely a judgment of moral science but a judgment in conformity with the condition of right desire.

The reasoning of ethics, on the other hand, is a matter of the intellect alone. True enough, we want to know all that we know in ethics in order to act well. But actually acting well goes beyond ethics, and requires right desire as well as knowledge. The practical reasoning of prudence is reasoning in relation to desire. Hence, we see how ethics alone cannot solve the problem of good moral action; at the same time, we are aware that ethics helps the man of prudence to act rightly in each successive act he does. We see, in other words, how ethics and prudence are distinct, but also how they are related.

Art and Prudence

A comparison between art and prudence is desirable for at least two reasons. First, by contrasting them we can understand not only how they differ but also more what each virtue precisely is. Second, their comparison adds an important footnote to the question of art and morality, which we have already discussed in a general way.

We have seen to some extent how art is the virtue of right *making*, and prudence the virtue of right *doing*. The essential difference between art and prudence is based on the essential difference of making and doing. We may, however, contrast the two in another way. Art is concerned with an exterior good, the good of the made object; prudence is concerned with an interior good, the good of human character and personality. This latter difference points up more sharply the contrast of art and prudence.

Since prudence is directed to human good, it is necessarily connected with moral virtue. In order to act prudently, a man must be well disposed with regard to the ends of human action. Prudence presupposes this right ordering in relation to an end, which is nothing other than rectitude of the appetite. Art, however, which is directed not to human good properly, but to the good of the artifact, is not connected necessarily with the moral virtues and does not require rectitude of the appetite. A morally bad man can build a house well, paint a portrait or compose a symphony. Nevertheless, while there can be artistic skill without moral rectitude, the *use* of artistic skill requires moral virtue. A man can have the art of building yet not be willing, because of some moral defect, to put his art to work properly.

The need of moral virtue, and prudence especially, to rectify the use of art has been evident throughout history. For example, the Hippocratic oath, originating in ancient times, binds physicians to a moral code in their practice of medicine; physicians must be men of prudence as well as men of art. In contemporary times, because of the enormous advances of industrial, mechanical and military arts, the need of prudence to regulate the use of art is greater than ever. In the case of making a hydrogen bomb, the distinction between art and the moral use of it is so delicate that a serious question arises not only with respect to using such a weapon of destruction, but even of making it. It is difficult, perhaps even impossible, to justify morally the use of an art and its product if the effect is directly aimed at the mass annihilation of human beings.

There is a further point to note in contrasting art and prudence, a point concerned specifically with fine art. Because fine art represents in a special way human action and passion, a particular problem arises. We have already seen that fine art necessarily involves moral principles in its work of representation, and that the fine artist must represent, when moral matter is present, the morally good as morally good and the morally evil as morally evil. This point does not concern the relation of the virtue of art to the virtue of prudence, for a fine artist can make a work of art without prudence.

However, the use of fine art, more specifically the publication and exhibition of fine art, requires prudence on the part of both the artist and the beholder. It is a matter of prudence that children should not see some motion pictures. It is a matter of prudence that adults—allowing for a legitimate variation of susceptibility among different individuals—should not see a motion picture if it directly aims to represent moral evil as good. It is also a matter of prudence that an artist should not prostitute his art for any of a number of unworthy ends, whether political, moral, or otherwise. Extrinsic circumstances, such as time or place, may make it imprudent to publish a certain novel or produce a certain play. However, the most important point is that if a work of fine art is designed primarily to be destructive of fundamental morality—in which case, it is bad as art as well, even though it may be technically skillful—the good of prudence and morality generally justifies the banning of such a work. The artist's freedom, and the beholder's freedom, important though they are, are not unlimited. The value of a work of art is not as great as the moral good of man himself.

This latter point is the basis for moral control over the use of fine art even to the point of full censorship. To the extent this point is well understood, there is justification for moral control over the exhibition of art. Nevertheless, the difficulty in exercising moral control over art cannot be minimized. The difficulty is at least twofold.

The first difficulty is one of restraining the exercising of the censorship to its strictly moral purpose, for the power of censorship can be easily abused and perverted to ends which are neither artistic nor moral. The second difficulty lies in selecting qualified persons to exercise the censorship, for sometimes those who have such authority are neither morally competent nor artistically critical.

Finally, it is necessary to take into account that sometimes the practical situation is made worse through censorship even when it is exercised with the best of intentions. Nothing stimulates a certain kind of person so much as to be told that he cannot see something. Such a person is one who places an apparent private good above the common good; in addition, he is usually affected by a naive belief that it is good for him to see anything. Consequently, he is often incited by censorship to see something he otherwise would not have the faintest desire to see. In varying degrees, censorship tends to affect many persons in a similar fashion even though they may not be disordered in appetite. Therefore, considerable prudence must be exercised in effecting censorship: the moral evil must be serious enough and the good sought should be reasonably expected to outweigh accidental evils.

The fundamental point remains, however, that inept solutions and abuses in regulation do not deny the legitimate relation between fine art and the prudent use of the art, including if necessary partial or total censorship.

OUTLINE OF INTELLECTUAL VIRTUES

I. Speculative Intellectual Virtue
   A. Science: the habit of demonstrating conclusions
   B. Understanding: the habit of grasping indemonstrable principles
   C. Wisdom: the habit of knowing ultimate principles and causes

II. Practical Intellectual Virtue
   A. Art: the right way of making something
      1. Servile
      2. Fine
   B. Prudence: the right way of doing something
      1. The three acts of prudence
         a) Counsel
         b) Practical judgment
         c) Command
      2. Division into potential parts
         a) The virtue connected with the first act of prudence: eubulia, the habit of good counsel
         b) The virtues connected with the second act of prudence: synesis, the virtue of good common sense; gnome, the virtue of judging according to the spirit of law

3. Division into subjective parts
   a) Individual prudence
   b) Political prudence
4. Vices opposed to prudence
   a) By defect: Imprudence
      (1) Impetuosity: defect of sufficient consideration of means
      (2) Thoughtlessness: defect of practical judgment
      (3) Inconstancy: wavering resulting in refusal to command
      (4) Negligence: defect in prompt execution of command
   b) By excess: False prudence
      (1) Prudence of the flesh: excessive concern about bodily goods
      (2) Astuteness: use of improper means to attain end

REVIEW QUESTIONS

1. Explain the expression "good of the intellect." What is the "good" of the intellect?
2. Distinguish between speculative reason and practical reason.
3. Is everything which is changeable known through practical reason? Explain.
4. What is the good state of speculative reason?
5. What is the good state of practical reason?
6. How does practical reason become "right" reason?
7. Is there any way in which practical reason measures desire or appetite? Explain.
8. Describe the intellectual virtue of science. How is it related to opinion?
9. What is the virtue of understanding? How is it related to the virtue of science?
10. What is the virtue of wisdom? How is it related to the other speculative virtues?
11. What is the distinction between transitive and immanent action, and how does this distinction relate to practical intellectual virtue?

12. What is the virtue of art? What are the stages of artistic making?

13. What are the different kinds of art? Give examples of each kind.

14. Explain how a work of fine art is moral as well as artistic.

15. In what consists the importance and necessity of prudence?

16. What is the definition of the virtue of prudence?

17. Explain the special acts performed by the virtue of prudence.

18. Which is the most important act of prudence, and why?

19. What does "eubulia" mean?

20. What is the difference between "synesis" and "gnome?"

21. Explain the essential division of the virtue of prudence.

22. What is the general name given to vices opposed to prudence by defect? Explain each of the specific vices opposed to prudence by defect.

23. What is the general name given to vices opposed to prudence by excess? Explain each of the specific vices opposed by excess.

24. Distinguish between ethics and prudence. Can one derive from principles of morality what he should do in a particular case? Explain.

25. Contrast art and prudence.

26. How is prudence especially related to fine art?

27. What is the problem of censorship? Is censorship justifiable on both moral and artistic grounds? Explain.

DISCUSSION

1. The meaning of virtue necessarily implies a perfection of a human power. The perfection of a human power is a moral good. Every virtue, therefore, must be a moral perfection, even though the virtue may be located in the intellect.

2. It seems that conformity with right desire makes practical reason right. But we cannot desire what is right or truly good unless reason guides us in our desire. If this is so, then right desire cannot make practical reason right; rather, practical reason makes desire right.

3. The perfection of speculative reason consists not only in knowing that a statement is true, but also in knowing why it is true, which is to prove the statement. If a statement cannot be proved to be true, the intellect is lacking in its perfection of knowing. Therefore, the understanding of indemonstrable principles is not a virtue.

4. Whatever is more necessary is more valuable and desirable. But human beings have a more immediate need for practical intellectual virtue than for speculative intellectual virtue. Therefore, the practical intellectual virtues are more valuable and desirable.

5. The greatness of works of fine art is said to be necessarily connected with principles of morality. But it is a fact that great works of fine art have been made by artists who were immoral. Therefore, there is no necessary connection between fine art and morality.

6. A person with the virtue of prudence is especially characterized by the fact that he exercises caution. Consequently, a prudent person knows when not to act as well as when to act. Command, however, is directly related to action. Therefore, command is not the most important act of prudence.

7. Charles completed a course in ethics at college. The following summer he consulted his father for advice on how to solve a moral problem he was facing. His father refused to give him any advice, saying that since Charles had taken a course in ethics he should be able to solve moral problems himself. What should Charles' reply be to his father?

8. Mr. Black argued strongly against the state censorship board which banned the showing of "Martha's Dying Kiss."
   "It is contrary to the Bill of Rights," he maintained, heatedly. "It is a violation of the inalienable rights of human beings to freedom of speech, the press, and the screen."
   Mr. White thought that the Bill of Rights was not being violated. "It is a question of showing an indecent motion picture," he observed, mildly.
   "Who is to know what is indecent?" demanded Mr. Black. As an afterthought he added, "Hollywood would not make a picture that was intended to be merely indecent. Besides, the artist has a right to say what he thinks, as long as it is art. Art is wholly distinct from morality."
   How would you resolve the issue between Mr. Black and Mr. White?

SUGGESTED READINGS

Aristotle, *Ethics,* Book VI.
St. Thomas, *Commentary,* Book VI.
St. Thomas, *Summa Theologiae,* I-II, Questions 57-58.
Plato, *Thaetetus.*

Gilson, *Moral Values and the Moral Life*, chap. VIII, pp. 233-245.

Maritain, J., *Art and Scholasticism*. New York: Charles Scribner's Sons, 1946, chap. IV, pp. 8-18; chap. IX, pp. 56-67.

Newman, Cardinal, *On the Scope and Nature of University Education*. New York: Dutton, Everyman's Library, 1955, Discourses IV-V, pp. 80-127.

O'Neill, C., *Imprudence in St. Thomas*. Milwaukee: Marquette, 1955.

Wild, *Introduction to Realistic Philosophy*, chap. 5, pp. 97-109.

XI

Law

*V*irtue is the primary means by which we are directed toward the good of human happiness. In the immediately preceding chapters we have investigated the different moral and intellectual virtues. The actual possession and practice of virtue goes beyond the province of ethics. As we have noted before, even though ethics is a practical science it does not immediately and directly apply to action. The knowledge of virtue is distinct from the practice of virtue. Nevertheless, the knowledge we acquire about virtue at least disposes us to seek virtuous living in our human activity.

We shall now consider another means by which we are ordered to leading the good life. Although this means also will not in itself guarantee good moral action, nevertheless it is a directing principle of good moral action about which we should have an adequate understanding. This other means is law.

Virtue and law, both productive of good moral action, are related as intrinsic and extrinsic principles of action. The virtues are interior principles because they are qualitative modifications of the most interior causes of action we have, the powers of reason and desire. Law is an exterior principle of action in the sense that it establishes, in a universal and objective fashion, an order of action to be followed by human beings seeking a common end. It is a measure or rule by which we are induced to act or are restrained from acting. Because it is a regulation with respect to what to do or what not to do, law is something pertaining to reason. It is the expression of what is reasonable to do under universal conditions.

A treatment of law belongs properly to political philosophy, a distinct part of moral philosophy. Only in the context of the science of government can law be analyzed fully and adequately. There is, further, a treatment of law that belongs to moral theology; the law given by God through revelation, for example, the Ten Commandments. In ethics, the introductory part of moral science, we shall give only a general summary of the notion of law and its principal divisions. It is relevant here to the extent that the happiness of the individual is influenced by an extrinsic measure of moral action.

The Notion of Common Good

Before we give a definition of law in general, it is necessary to have a precise notion of what is meant by the common good. It is evident from all our experience with law that the common good is the end and purpose of any law. There is, indeed, no point in formulating a law, or prescribing the doing or omitting of action, unless it leads to the attainment of some end. As we have seen, an end is always viewed as a good, and if a good is attainable by many, the good is common. We all have some such notion of the common good but, unless we understand it more precisely and more comprehensively, we shall not grasp the purpose for which law exists. And, without a grasp of the purpose of law, we shall not appreciate sufficiently the meaning, need, and desirability of law.

Let us begin by contrasting a *private* good with a *common* good.

By a private good we mean the good of one person only; it is his good and no other's good. The possession of a private good by you, whether a spiritual one like your honesty, or a material one like your hat, excludes the possession of this good by any other person. A common good, on the contrary, can be possessed by many persons *simultaneously*. The good aimed at in a properly conducted discussion group is a common good, realizable only by the participation of the members in the discussion.

Nevertheless, the expression "common good" may easily become ambiguous. To some the term may mean a good belonging to a group as a whole, without being shared in wholly by each member of the group. Such a good is not really a common good, but a collective good. This good, though possessed by all as a group, is not really participated in by the members of a group, but is divided up into several *private* goods when apportioned to the different individual members. A dinner, for example, is a collective good for a family. It belongs to the family as a whole and not just to one individual. However, as the dinner is eaten, it disappears as a collective good, for it is divided up into parts for each member of the family. As divided up, the collective good becomes several private goods, for each member of the family consumes, not the whole dinner, but a portion of it. The distinguishing feature of a collective good is that as the number of participants increases each one actually possesses less of that good. Furthermore, as each one actually possesses it, the good in no sense remains common, but becomes private.

A true common good, on the contrary, is properly universal, diffusive of itself, and hence a *distributive* common good. It is not just a collection of singular goods, but is a good communicable to many. It is a good possessed as a whole by each individual *without its becoming anyone's private good*. Moreover, the possession of the common good by one person in no way excludes other persons from possessing this common good, nor does it diminish in any way the extent to which the others possess it, for each person possesses the whole common good, not merely a part of it. We saw how the dinner is really a collective good which, when shared, becomes several private goods for the individual members of a family. However, the sociability of eating together is a common good which can be shared wholly by each and every member of the family without its becoming a private good for any one member. The common good of sociability, in fact, is a particularly clear illustration of how a common good cannot exist except as a good which can be shared by many.

The common good is of necessity spiritual, i.e., an immaterial good. Only an immaterial good can be shared in such a way that there is no limitation in the sharing of it. Any number of persons can share a common good, with each one possessing it wholly. There is a hierarchy of common goods based on the different communities to which a person belongs. Most immediately an individual belongs to a family, and the domestic common good is participated in by each member of the family precisely as he enjoys membership in the family. In civil society the human person participates in the common good of peace and order. In religious society a human person participates in knowing, loving and worshipping God, Who is a common good both naturally and supernaturally.

To the extent that a person is a member of a community the common good of that community is a higher good than any private good he has *as a member* of this community. We see this principle realized in any form of communal activity. The highest good for a member of a football team is the victory of the team and not some private good of one member, such as fame, enjoyment or monetary reward. The *good* football player is one who subordinates his private good to the common good of the team. Similarly, the good member of a family or the good member of a state subordinates his private good to the common good to which the whole community is ordered.

Of course, conflicts may arise between a private good and a common good, and in some instances it is not easy to work out the right relation between the two. In this connection, it is well to note that not every common good is higher than every private good. A common good of a lower order may have to give way to a private good of a higher order. For example, the private good of one's health need not be sacrificed for the common good of victory in an athletic contest, nor can a person's honesty be sacrificed in an attempt to further the common good of the family. But within the same order the common good is a higher good than the private good. The common good of peace and order is higher than any private good human beings have as members of political society.

From all of the foregoing remarks, it is clear that when we speak of the common good as the end of law, we mean the common good in the proper sense of a distributive common good. We mean, further, the political common good to which human beings as members of civil society are ordered. This common good of peace and order belongs wholly to each citizen as long as he does not by misconduct withdraw from participation in it.

The Definition of Law

Having considered the purpose for which law exists, the common good, we can now define law as *a certain ordination of reason for the common good, promulgated by one who has care of the community*.

An *ordination* of reason signifies the establishing of an order such that a given proper end may be attained through the means that are proportioned to such an end. This ordination has to come from practical reason, because it is reason alone that determines means in relation to some given end. Law, therefore, is not formally an act of the will; it presupposes an act of the will, but derives from and is formulated by an act of practical reason.

Not every ordination of reason is a law; hence, the ordination is said to be of a *certain* kind. One kind of ordination gives law, another kind gives a *precept*. A precept is any form of command intended to serve as a rule of conduct that falls short of being formally a law. We have seen that law formally aims at a common good, and thus, the primary difference between a law and a precept is that a law is directed to the social and political common good, whereas a precept is directed to a private good, although it may be extended to the good of a small community such as a family. Another significant difference is that a law tends to be permanent, enduring over and beyond the power and life of this or that legislator. A precept, on the contrary, tends to be transitory and is usually terminated by the death of the one who makes it or by a loss of his authority.

We have already spoken at length of the phrase *for the common good*. Two additional points, however, may be added here. The first is that by designating the common good as the necessary end of every law, we are able to distinguish a true law from a so-called law laid down by a tyrant. A tyrant is a person who, although nominally in control of a state, lays down ordinances that are directed to his private good, or at least in clear opposition to a true social and political common good. Since such ordinances are directed against the common good, they are not true laws and do not, properly speaking, carry an obligation to be obeyed. In individual cases, however, it is a matter of political prudence whether or not to obey what in fact are unjust laws. Failure to obey, open defiance, or, in extreme cases, rebellion, would be prudent only if the good sought could be reasonably expected to be attained and would outweigh accompanying evils.

In mentioning above that the common good is the proper and necessary end of every law, we come to the second point that should be noted. While it is true that the common good is the necessary end of every law, it should be recognized that the common good can be attained directly or indirectly. The common good is attained directly when the actions prescribed by the law benefit immediately the community as a whole. The common good is attained indirectly when some laws cause an advancement of a private good, but do so only as a means of realizing the common good. For example, a law might be designed to protect in a special way the security of a high governmental administrator in order that he may work better in his official capacity to promote the common good.

Promulgation is the act which makes known to the public the terms or contents of a law. It is a necessary condition for the validity of any law, for those who are subject to a law cannot know of its existence unless it is published and made public in some form. The promulgation of a law gives it binding force, for by making a law sufficiently manifest a legislator is able to impose actual obligation on those subject to it.

The phrase *by one who has care of the community* designates the legislator, the one who has competent authority for making law. Fundamentally, establishment of law for the attainment of the common good is the function of the community itself. In practice, however, some person or persons must be charged with the responsibility for exercising the care of the community, and we refer to such persons as legislators. The word "legislator" derives its meaning from its Latin roots: *legis* and *lator*, a proposer of law. By the word "community," we mean a *perfect* community, one complete in itself and having adequate means for reaching its own proper end.

Civil Law

There are different kinds of law, and we shall take up first the kind with which we are most familiar and which is most obvious to us. This is civil law, or human positive law. According to our mode of knowing, it is the kind of law that most immediately realizes the common definition of law given above. By paraphrasing the common definition to particularize it for civil law, we understand civil law as *the ordinance of reason by one who has authority to direct the state and its members to the common political and social good, a happiness consisting primarily in peace and order.*

We are so inclined to take civil law for granted that we rarely reflect on what human life would be without it. It is true that below the level of political communal living, human life could exist without civil law. But any developed form of communal life requires the formulation of explicit laws in order that the community attain the end to which it is ordered, the well being of the community as a whole. The primary need of civil law is for the very preservation of society itself. In addition, we must know in particular what to do to live well, and the alternate name of "positive law" brings out this need of civil law, namely, the *positive* determination of what actions to do and of what actions to avoid. Hence, civil law adds a perfection to human life, directing it concretely and in some detail to the attainment of a higher stage of life than would be possible otherwise. Civil law is not, contrary to the opinion of some, primarily an evil condition restricting man from leading a supposedly freer and happier life; nor is it to be regarded as primarily a coercive force. Penalty and punishment are attached to civil law by way of compelling ill-disposed human beings to observe the law. But law itself is directed to the attainment of a good that would not otherwise be possible.

Civil law directly concerns the *external* acts of human beings, for it is our external acts that are immediately directed to the common good of society. Of course, there is an intimate connection between our interior acts and our exterior acts, and consequently, law affects the interior acts to the extent that they are the immediate cause of our exterior acts. But, as we have seen, the proper causes of our interior acts are the powers themselves—reason, will, and sense desire —and the virtues which are formed in these powers. Civil law does not, then, directly aim to make men virtuous in their action, but it does specify certain actions which will dispose men to become virtuous. It will, in fact, command some acts of virtue to the extent they are necessary for attaining the common good, particularly acts relating to justice. It will forbid some acts of vice, particularly those harmful to others, which would make life in society impossible, such as acts of murder and theft.

Civil law derives permanence and stability from the very fact that it aims primarily at directing man to the natural end of society. Nevertheless, this permanence is not absolute. Civil law is changeable to the extent that it is concerned with variable matter. Specific laws may become less useful for the common good according to changing conditions of time, place, and circumstance. The legislator may see the need of adding laws or of modifying or even abolishing existing laws in order to lead citizens to a greater good. For example, the law prohibiting the sale of liquor in the United States had to be repealed because the good it sought was greatly outweighed by the evil it promoted. The permanence of civil law is thus limited by the varying condition of the citizens themselves, which may require different laws under different sets of circumstances.

The interpretation of civil law is often complicated and difficult. The general principle is clear. Assuming that the legislation is legitimate, every law is judged by the relation it has to the common good. If, in particular circumstances, the letter of the law would go against the common good, the law would not be followed. Such an interpretation must be made by the legislator or by a judge who has the power to declare that the law does not apply in a particular case. Even when it is clear that the letter of the law is to be followed, many problems of interpretation and application of the law remain. Hence, courts of justice have to be maintained by a government to resolve such legal problems as well as possible.

The question of interpretation of law presupposes the more

fundamental question of when civil law is just and when it is unjust. Three general points can be laid down by way of determining whether a law is just. First, and most evidently, a law is just when it is ordered to the common good, at least indirectly. Secondly, a law is just if it does not exceed the authority of the legislator. The legislator, for example, cannot make laws affecting purely domestic matters. Thirdly, it is just to the extent that it imposes burdens on citizens according to a proportional equality. This last point is connected with distributive justice.

In general, it can be said that a law is unjust (in which case, it is law only in name and not in fact) when it violates any one of these three points. Over and beyond these points, a law is clearly unjust if it commands an act that is intrinsically evil, that is, an act that is evil by its very object. For example, no law could command an act of theft, murder, or lying.

Allowing for the points just made, and recognizing that only just laws are really laws, we can say that every law, insofar as it aims at the common good, carries an obligation to be obeyed. In fact, the efficacy of civil law resides in the exercise of moral obligation on the part of those subject to law. At the same time, it must be acknowledged that the obligation to obey civil law rests on more than civil law itself, i.e., on positive, written law. Its force and authority does not arise from the reason and will of the legislator alone, but derives from a more fundamental law than civil law. This more fundamental law—an "unwritten law" that is everywhere acknowledged to be essentially and fundamentally the same for all —is the basis for the authority of civil law. To this other kind of law, we must now give our attention.

Natural Law

The name "natural law" has been given to the unwritten law that is more or less the same for everyone everywhere. The word "natural" may be somewhat misleading here. Natural law is not called "natural" in the sense in which we say that a tree is a natural thing. Since law must always be some dictate of reason, natural law also will be some dictate of reason. Natural law does not have, therefore, an existence independent of reason, as a purely natural thing like a tree has. As a dictate of reason, natural law primarily expresses in universal form the fundamental inclinations of human nature, formulated by reason in a judgment that is *naturally* made, i.e., with little or no discursive process of reasoning. This is the literal basis for such figurative descriptions of natural law as the law "engraven in the heart of man." Hence, natural law is "natural" on two scores. It is natural as expressing the inclinations of human nature toward fundamental goods, which we shall mention shortly. Consequently, it is not law *made* by human reason, but law *discovered* by human reason. Secondly, it is natural in the sense that all men naturally know at least the most universal precepts expressed by natural law.

Our understanding of natural law will be more precise if we consider the principles—usually called "precepts"—of natural law. Since we already know that natural law is more basic than civil law, the primary precept of natural law will be the most basic principle about human action that can be formulated. Just as there is an absolutely first and indemonstrable principle in the speculative order, so is there a similar one in the practical order. The first principle of the speculative order, upon which all other speculative principles of knowing depend, is the principle formulating the impossibility of contradiction. The first principle of the practical order is a principle that directs human acts in all their operations, and it will be concerned with the good, since we act in terms of what at least seems good to us. Hence, the primary principle of the practical order—the primary precept of natural law—is a formulation based upon the notion of the good and is stated in the following way: The good (according to reason) must be done, and evil (what is contrary to reason) must be avoided.

This primary precept of the natural law is usually expressed simply as *do good and avoid evil*. Although we rarely express it explicitly, just as in the speculative order we rarely state the principle of contradiction expressly, nevertheless we always act in terms of such a precept. This fact points to the fundamental truth of such a precept, and indicates how it expresses something *natural* to man. A human being naturally inclines to seek what appears good to reason, and naturally shrinks from what appears to be evil. Hence, the justification of speaking of this basic moral law as natural law.

There is more to natural law, of course, than this primary principle of the practical order. We distinguish, within natural law, primary and secondary precepts. The primary precepts will correspond to the order of natural inclinations in man. In addition to the most fundamental inclination of all, to do good and avoid evil, there are other primary precepts in terms of such natural inclinations as the inclination to self-preservation, to marry and bring up children, to live in society, to avoid harm to others, and to know truths about God and man. The primary precepts of natural law, resting upon these basic tendencies of human nature, are unchangeable to the extent they concern the primary ends of natural inclination in human beings. No civil law can justly change the order of such basic human inclinations. The formulation of civil law, in fact, presumes these precepts of natural law and makes particular determinations of them to the extent they are needed for the good order of society.

Secondary precepts of natural law are related generally to the primary precepts, as derived formulations are to self-evident principles. It is self-evident not only to do good and avoid evil, but to seek self-preservation, the good of marriage, the good of living domestically and socially, and the good of knowledge. All of these concern things to which human nature is immediately inclined. The secondary precepts are concerned with things to which we are not inclined so immediately. Hence, they are called "secondary" not so much in the sense of secondary in importance, but in the sense of not so immediately knowable; they are known secondarily as determinations following from self-evident principles. Thus, a primary precept of the natural law concerns the preservation of one's life; a secondary precept, following as a more particular formulation from the primary precept, is that a person is entitled to protect himself if attacked.

We may now be able to see that, just as secondary precepts of the natural law are related to primary precepts, so civil law is related to the secondary precepts. This is an analogous relation, and not the same in all respects. But it does bring out the truth that secondary precepts are like further determinations of the primary precepts of natural law, and civil laws are like further and more detailed formulations related to the secondary precepts. Civil laws, for example, specify when and how a man is unjustly attacked by another.

Above all, the relationship manifests the necessary dependence of much of civil law upon natural law and emphasizes the point that civil law is not merely an arbitrary formulation made solely on the authority of the will of the legislator.

Natural law is sometimes compared to civil law as the unchanging is to the changing. In this view, natural law is considered to be exactly the same for all men everywhere and equally knowable, but this is an over-simplification. It is true, first of all, that civil law is subject to change to the extent new laws are made and old laws are modified or even abrogated; but in other respects, civil law has a permanence and stability. It is also true that natural law is unchanging and universally knowable so far as its primary precepts are concerned, an obvious point since the primary precepts of natural law merely make manifest the natural inclinations of human nature. Natural law, in other words, is immutable to the extent it is rooted in the ordering of human nature to certain fundamental goods. However, when we consider the secondary precepts of natural law and recall that they are related somewhat in the fashion of particularizing formulations, we have to make allowance for some change in natural law. Such change can take place by way of addition, by proposing more particular formulations because of circumstances and new situations that arise. Some change can also take place by way of subtraction, by removing certain formulations which are not operative, again because of circumstances.

There is another point of comparison to note between natural law and civil law. In the case of civil law, knowledge of such law is possible only by making public in an official manner its content. With regard to natural law, the primary precepts are known by all men in the very exercise of reason. The primary precepts of natural law do not have to be published to be known; their "promulgation" consists in their being implanted in the very operation of reason itself. The same holds true somewhat with respect to the secondary precepts. They are not to be regarded, however, simply as intellectual deductions concluded from the more universal principles of the primary precepts. Rather, as our experience increases, we see the need for a more determinate formulation of the more universal principle, and then, in view of the more particular good to be attained, we formulate a new principle of action more closely and practically related to attaining the particular good. The more particular formulation will be consistent with the prior and more universal principle. Hence, while the "promulgation" of natural law exists in the operation of reason itself and extends to the more particular formulations we make consequent to the primary precepts, nevertheless the more particular formulations lack the evidence and certainty of the primary precepts. Moreover, as we approach a particular good to be attained, such influences as corrupt appetite, bad habits, and insufficient education may prevent our making a particular formulation of a universal precept.

Eternal Law

This is still another kind of law that we must consider, a law even more fundamental than natural law. In understanding natural law, we come to recognize that it is a participation in a still higher law. This higher law is called *eternal* law and it refers to the idea of the government of things which exists in the mind of God. Since God is eternal, so is the plan of the government of the world eternal as existing in His mind. We thus understand eternal law as *the plan of God's wisdom by which all action and motion of the universe are directed.*

Eternal law is properly law. It is, first of all, an act of reason, of God's reason as He is the governor of the whole community which is the universe. Such a law, further, directs this community to a common good, the common good being God Himself. It is promulgated in the sense that it is in God from all eternity and in creatures as they exist in time. Everything in the universe is subject to eternal law: material beings, such as stars, plants, animals; rational and intelligent beings, such as men and angels.

We are not here referring to a revealed and supernatural law, a law declared by revelation, for example as given in the Ten Commandments. True enough, except for the commandment on observing the Sabbath, the Commandments embody principles knowable by reason alone through natural law. However, as revealed, the Ten Commandments are divine positive law and knowledge of divine positive law is beyond the province of moral philosophy. But knowledge of eternal law can be arrived at by reason alone from our knowledge of God as the ultimate cause of the universe. We can see the need and role of eternal law by noting that just as natural law is the basis for civil law in such a way that civil law participates in natural law by particularizing its principles, so eternal law is the basis for natural law in such a way that natural law is a participation in eternal law by which human beings are naturally inclined to the mode of acting toward an end proper to them.

Our knowledge of eternal law, nevertheless, is only indirect. We can know eternal law only through its effects. We know that God's knowledge is the measure of the truth of things, and that every truth has its origin in the eternal law of God. Every man knows something of truth, particularly of the first principles of thought and action. This latter knowledge pertains to knowing natural law as it participates in eternal law. In knowing natural law, therefore, we are aware of the effect of eternal law operating within us, ruling and directing us. Consequently, to say our knowledge of eternal law is indirect is to say that we know it through our knowing natural law. At the same time, we see how eternal law is that in which natural law participates, for without the eternal law of God operating, natural law would be impossible; and, without natural law, civil law would have no objective basis. *Eternal law is thus the ultimate source of all law.* It is the ultimate directive principle of all acts and motions of creatures to their proper ends.

In beginning the treatment of the different kinds of law, we noted the desirability of starting with civil law because it is the most obvious kind of law according to our mode of knowing. Having now gone through the different kinds of law, we can see that "law" signifies analogously when referring to the various kinds of law. Failure to appreciate the analogous signification of the word has led to needless confusion and controversy about the different kinds of law. Natural law, in particular, has been attacked on the erroneous supposition that it is supposed to be "law" in the same sense and in the same way as civil law. The explanations given above indicate how they differ in the signification of such a word as "promulgation," and how civil law is something made by human reason whereas natural law, being implanted in human reason, is discovered. Consequently, it is important to recognize that, on the one hand, according to our mode of knowing the common definition of law is first realized in civil law, and that, on the other hand, natural law is still properly law though less evident and not wholly the same in meaning. The case is similar with eternal law in relation to natural law.

Moral Obligation

It is evident that all law carries some obligation to be obeyed, for, without obligation and proportionate means of enforcement, law would be of little value as an ordering principle of human acts. Let us investigate what is meant by obligation in the moral sense, and how it operates with respect to the different kinds of law.

Obligation clearly implies necessity of some kind. Moral obligation, an obligation imposed in relation to human acts, derives from the first principle of human action, the end. The kind of necessity moral obligation has, therefore, must be a necessity deriving from an end. Hence we understand, in a general way, moral obligation to be the necessity of doing or refraining from doing certain acts, given a certain end. Insofar as the end referred to in law is the common good, we can speak of this necessity as absolute in relation to that end. More precisely, by absolute necessity in relation to an end we mean that the attainment of the end is impossible without doing or omitting certain acts. Since the common good is an end that must be realized in varying degrees, there is an absolute necessity for doing or omitting certain acts.

Moral obligation, therefore, is the result of a double necessity: the necessity of the act in relation to the necessity of the end. The human goal of acts, i.e., the common good, is necessarily given as following from human nature. This act of justice, for example, must be done as necessarily leading to the given end; this refraining from the act of stealing must be done so as not to lead away from the given end. In stating the matter this way, we must not leave the impression that such necessity destroys the liberty of the will. Moral obligation does bind the will in the sense that there is this necessary relation of an act to an end. It does not destroy the liberty of the will, since it still leaves intact the power of the will for acting or not acting. Hence, even though doing or omitting an act is necessary for attaining the end, the will always retains the power of not tending toward the end in particular circumstances. The will, in other words, always retains freedom of exercise. There is not an unqualified "must" about the will, but an "ought."

We are speaking here primarily of moral obligation in relation to eternal law and natural law. The same obligation applies in an analogous manner to civil law to the extent civil law derives from and participates in natural law. With respect to civil law, the question of moral obligation is usually stated by asking whether civil law binds in conscience.

In answering this question specifically, we must recall that civil law is either just or unjust, although the latter is law in name rather than in fact, as we noted earlier. If a civil law is just, i.e., if it is properly a law, then it has the power of binding in conscience, this power deriving from natural law, and, through natural law, from eternal law. A man of equity, described in Chapter IX, would always view observance of law in this manner. Earlier in this chapter, we noted the three conditions a civil law must meet in order to be just. It must aim at the common good, it must not exceed the authority of the legislator, and it must impose burdens on subjects with proportional equality. If a particular law does not meet these conditions, it is not really a law at all and would not, therefore, carry an obligation in conscience. However, particular circumstances may dictate the observance of an unjust law in order to avoid scandal, undue disturbance, and the like.

REVIEW QUESTIONS

1. How are law and virtue related to each other?
2. Contrast the private good with the common good.
3. What is a collective good?
4. What is a common good? Illustrate with an original example.
5. Is there opposition between the private good and the common good? Explain.
6. Give the common definition of law.
7. What is the difference between law and precept?
8. Comment: Every law attains the common good.
9. What is promulgation? How necessary is it for law?

10. Define civil law. How is this definition related to the definition of law in general?

11. Comment: Civil law aims to make men virtuous in their action.

12. How permanent is civil law?

13. How can it be determined when civil law is just and is truly law?

14. Explain the meaning of "natural" in natural law.

15. Explain what is meant by the primary principles or precepts of natural law, and illustrate.

16. What are the secondary principles or precepts of natural law. How are they related to the primary ones?

17. How are civil laws related to the secondary precepts of natural law?

18. Comment: Natural law is unchanging and universally knowable.

19. Does promulgation apply to natural law? Explain.

20. What is eternal law?

21. What is the relation of eternal law to natural law?

22. How do we come to know eternal law?

23. Indicate how and why "law" is an analogous name.

24. What kind of necessity does moral obligation have?

25. Does every civil law carry a moral obligation to be obeyed? Explain.

DISCUSSION

1. No passion of man is in itself morally evil. No action following from human passion is morally bad unless some law forbids the action. But a law cannot be known until it is made, and it can be made only by some human person. Therefore, no action can be declared to be against any law until human beings give authority to some person to make a law.

2. The common good, as the name suggests, is a good common to many. The good of one person is that which is proper to that person alone and is the good of this person as a substance. It is therefore a substantial good. But a common good is an accidental good because it is not a good for any one substance. Therefore, there is a clear distinction between the common good and the private good; and, when there is a conflict, the private good takes precedence over the common good, since a substantial good is higher than an accidental good.

3. The essential characteristic of all government, in the last analysis, is authority and force. In some cases, force depends upon the power of the ruler, while in other cases force rests upon the consent of those who are ruled. But in either case, there is coercive force, which has to be used sooner or later. All law, therefore, is based on force.

4. The Declaration of Independence speaks of certain self-evident truths, such as all men are created equal, and are endowed with inalienable rights, among which are life, liberty, and pursuit of happiness. The Declaration of Independence can only be speaking of rights following from the natural law. Hence, there is a natural law distinct from, and the basis for, civil law.

5. The Declaration of Independence is a product of the eighteenth century. In the twentieth century, we do not accept any truth as self-evident, nor do we make any such connection between the political order and the plans of the Creator as that document suggests. Consequently, no argument based on the Declaration of Independence is valid, for the doctrine of natural rights and natural law referred to there is now outmoded and only of historical interest.

6. If nature prescribes a certain order of social organization for man, this order should be manifested over and over again in primitive societies as well as in advanced societies, just as every falling body moves exactly according to the law of falling bodies. But no such strict uniformity of action is observed in human social activity and organization. Therefore, there is no reality to natural law.

7. Natural law is related to civil law as a principle is to a conclusion. But a conclusion is already contained in a principle. Consequently, if one understands the precepts or principles of natural law thoroughly, one can deduce all conclusions, i.e., all civil laws, from it. Therefore, civil law is a part of natural law and not distinct from it.

8. Natural law, as the name suggests, is based on nature itself. But nature is universally the same everywhere and knowable to the same degree. Therefore, natural law is universally the same for men everywhere and knowable to the same extent.

9. Eternal law is the plan of God's knowledge directing all action and motion of the universe. But no human being can know the plan of God's knowledge, at least by reason alone. Therefore, either eternal law is not knowable by man, or, if it is revealed to man by God, it is not within the province of a philosophical treatment of law.

10. Some philosophers of law maintain that certain civil laws do not

carry an obligation to be obeyed and are, therefore, purely penal laws. In regard to such laws, one need be willing only to pay the penalties which are attached, as in tax laws. Moreover, there is no explicit appeal to conscience made by the legislator in such laws. Therefore, it seems that not all laws made by the state carry an obligation in conscience to be obeyed.

SUGGESTED READINGS

St. Thomas, *Summa Theologiae*, I-II, Questions 90-97.
Plato, *Republic*, Book IV. *Laws*.

Bourke, *Ethics*, chap. V, pp. 162-195.
Cronin, *The Science of Ethics*, Vol. I, chap. XIX, pp. 633-659.
D'Entrèves, A., *Natural Law*. London: Hutchinson's University Library, 1951, chap. IV-V, pp. 64-94.
Gilson, *Moral Values and the Moral Life*, chap. VI, pp. 103-212.
Maritain, *Man and the State*. Chicago: University of Chicago Press, Phoenix Books, 1951, chap. IV, pp. 76-107.
Messner, J., *Social Ethics*. St. Louis: Herder, 1949, Book I, Part III, pp. 147-245.
Miltner, *The Elements of Ethics*, chaps. IV-V, pp. 36-62.
Renard, *The Philosophy of Morality*, chap. III, pp. 194-241.
Rommen, H., *The Natural Law*. St. Louis: Herder, 1947, chap. XI, pp. 191-201; chaps. XIII-XIV, pp. 215-263.
Wild, *Introduction to Realistic Philosophy*, chap. 9, pp. 176-192.

XII

Continence and incontinence

*H*uman action in its most perfect form is virtuous activity. Because virtue is the best means of attaining the end of happiness to which moral life is ordered, we have considered both moral and intellectual virtue at great length. We have also considered law because of the need and desirability of an extrinsic principle directing us to good human action. It might seem as though we have investigated sufficiently the means of attaining the end of happiness, but in reality our account of the moral order would be significantly deficient were we not to consider, however briefly, the role of continence and its opposite, incontinence, in human action.

We shall understand fully the relevance of considering continence and incontinence if we recall, first of all, that virtue and vice are extremes of moral life in the sense that virtue is an extreme of perfection and vice an extreme of imperfection. The best kind of human life is the life of virtue and, conversely, the worst kind is one of vice. But it is important also to take into account that relatively few persons are fully developed in virtue, and on the other hand, relatively few persons are wholly vicious. Most human beings are between these extremes; either they tend more and more toward the perfection of virtue or they fall increasingly into vice. Consequently, we may first understand, although only in a general way, continence as the tendency toward virtue and incontinence as the tendency toward vice.

It is evident, therefore, that the role of continence and incontinence deserves to be considered in ethics, since most persons in fact are continent rather than virtuous, and incontinent rather than vicious. We speak here of both continence and incontinence in the broadest possible meaning; we shall shortly restrict this meaning. A second reason for considering continence is that most of us acquire virtue by first being continent. It is helpful, therefore, to know about continence, not primarily for the sake of itself, but rather to see how it can lead to virtue. Somewhat negatively, but nonetheless significantly, knowing about incontinence helps us to see how this tendency, if unchecked, leads to moral defeat, the acquiring of vice.

The Objects of Pleasure

We shall have a more precise understanding of continence and incontinence if we begin with a consideration of pleasure. The role of pleasure is the starting point because continence is specifically a resistance to vehement passion in relation to sense pleasure, and incontinence is a giving way to vehement passion. In beginning with pleasure, we shall appreciate more readily the practical importance of continence and incontinence, for we first begin to master pleasure by being continent, just as we first begin to be overcome by pleasure by being incontinent.

It has already been noted that continence leads to virtue, in particular to the virtue of temperance. Just as temperance is usually the first virtue we begin to acquire, so our start in moral life will be through continence, the disposition leading to temperance. We are aware, from experience, that we must first order ourselves well in regard to sense pleasure, otherwise we shall be seriously handicapped in living well morally in all other respects. The reason for this is evident: pleasure is the most obvious aspect of our experience and the one which most immediately attracts us. We begin to order ourselves well in relation to pleasure by being continent.

Normally, this development in us should be fostered and guided by our parents or guardians. Indeed, unless we have some early, good training in this regard, our moral life is almost sure to get off to a bad start. It is for this reason we can assign parental delinquency as the primary cause of juvenile delinquency. The most immediate and serious obligation parents have with regard to bringing up children is to foster in them good dispositions in the moral order, dispositions that will lead readily to the formation of good habits, the moral virtues. The initial aim parents should have, then, is to make their children continent; it would not be reasonable to presume that children could become virtuous rapidly. On the other hand, bad dispositions not only tend to develop more rapidly than good dispositions, but, if unchecked, quickly become bad habits. Hence, the imperative need of guiding children early through continence to virtue.

Objects of pleasure can be divided into those which are *necessary* and those which are *desirable*. Those which are desirable concern such things as honor, wealth, and victory. They are not strictly pleasurable objects in themselves, but they become pleasurable in proportion as they are objects of desire. For that reason, we can speak of being continent and incontinent with respect to them, even though the meaning of continence or of incontinence is not strictly realized.

More properly, continence and incontinence are concerned with necessary objects of pleasure, namely, the pleasures concerned with bodily needs, particularly those pertaining to food, drink, and sex. These are the same objects, as we already know, with which temperance and intemperance are concerned. The difference is a matter of degree; continence will deal with them not as well as temperance, incontinence not as badly as intemperance.

Let us consider first the incontinent person. He pursues an excess of pleasure and shuns what is painful. He is not, however, intemperate. One who is intemperate acts in such a way, too, but by choice and deliberation. The incontinent person pursues the excess of pleasure, not strictly out of deliberation and choice, but contrary to his choice and judgment. He knows that the excess is wrong, but he succumbs to the strong impulse of passion. He is "soft" with regard to pleasure, and it is moral softness and weakness that characterizes the incontinent person. The most striking difference between the intemperate person and the incontinent person can be phrased in the following way. The intemperate person deliberately *chooses* the excess and becomes confirmed in evil. The incontinent person *succumbs* to his desire and passion for excessive pleasure, but with a measure of unwillingness; after the subsiding of the passion that aroused him, he is repentant. The intemperate person experiences no repentance.

The Incontinent Person and Knowledge

Since the state of the incontinent person is somewhat paradoxical —he knows what he should do and in a sense wills to do what he knows, but still does otherwise—it is important to investigate just how the incontinent person acts in relation to what he knows. To clarify this matter, let us distinguish, in the context of this problem, two meanings of the word "know." In one sense, we say a man knows who has knowledge and exercises it, that is, goes on to act in conformity with what he knows. In another sense, we say a man knows who has knowledge but does not exercise it, that is, he does not act in conformity with what he knows and may even act contrary to what he knows. To put the same point in slightly different terms, the incontinent man becomes subject in his knowledge and action to a disordered influence and direction of his sense appetite.

We can see more clearly and fully how both types of knowing occur, especially the latter type, if we consider the mode of practical thinking exemplified in what is called the *operative syllogism*, i.e., the practical syllogism. The ordinary meaning of a syllogism, treated in logic, is the laying down of two propositions as antecedent to a third proposition, which, as the conclusion, is the necessary consequent. Such a syllogism is productive of scientific knowledge that is true, certain, and necessary; it is composed of universal propositions, sometimes in combination with particular propositions. The operative syllogism, on the other hand, whose end is action and not knowledge, and is therefore a derived meaning of "syllogism," has singular propositions for the minor premise and the conclusion.

The incontinent man reasons, that is, uses an operative syllogism, in the following way. He knows from common moral knowledge that:

> Nothing alcoholic should be drunk to excess.

At the same time, he is impelled through concupiscence, the movement of sense appetite in pursuit of a good, to consider another universal proposition contrary to the foregoing one:

> All alcoholic drink is pleasurable and desirable.

The two universal propositions both stand as major premises in his practical reasoning. The incontinent person yields to the drive of concupiscence and departs from the first universal proposition, realizing, at the same time, that it is true and the one he should follow. Because his concupiscence binds his reason, a singular minor premise is taken, not in relation to the universal of reason, but to the second universal proposition formed through concupiscence. His singular minor premise therefore becomes:

> This alcoholic drink is desirable.

Once this singular minor premise is stated and adhered to, the singular conclusion, actually a command and already issuing into action, follows:

> I will have this drink.

The person thus acts incontinently against reason by taking a drink to excess, and he goes against the universal judgment formed by reason relevant to this situation. Hence, he knows in one sense: he knows a truth of moral knowledge. But he does not exercise this knowledge by acting in accordance with it, or, it might be said, he goes on to know in another fashion, namely, as subject to the influence of concupiscence.

There is a contrariety, therefore, in the incontinent person, a contrariety between his universal moral knowledge and his knowledge as subject to inordinate desire. The case of the wholly intemperate person is different. He simply lives to enjoy excessively the things of sense desire; his vice precludes any consideration of thinking and acting in relation to judgments of moral knowledge. There is no contrariety in him. He has only one major premise, a proposition formed through concupiscence: *All pleasure should be enjoyed*—without qualification. His minor premise and conclusion follow at once: *This is an act of pleasure; therefore, I will do it.*

Let us now consider the case of the continent man. It is clear that, like the incontinent man, he uses a syllogism with four propositions. There is also contrariety in him. However, in balancing the first major premise against the second, he acknowledges the truth of the judgment formed through moral knowledge even though inclined by concupiscence to entertain the contrary proposition that every pleasure should be sought. Accordingly, the judgment of reason wins out, and he draws his minor premise and conclusion from the first major premise.

With the temperate man, finally, there is a syllogism with only three propositions, for he is moved only by reasoned judgment and, since the virtue is located in the concupiscible appetite under the direction of reason, there is no contrary tendency on the part of the appetite to form an opposition. Through this latter example we see how thoroughly well-formed the truly virtuous person is.

Definition of Continence and Incontinence

In view of the foregoing remarks, we can now define precisely both continence and incontinence.

Continence is *a disposition in the will by which one resists vehement evil desires of the concupiscible appetite, especially those pertaining to objects of taste and touch.* The word "disposition" indicates that continence is not as well developed as virtue or, on the other hand, as isolated as a single act. The sense appetite, in other words, is not completely subject to the rule of reason, although there is at least a strengthening of the will to provide resistance to succumbing to the passions. The subject of continence, accordingly, is the will, not the sense appetite. The good which moves the continent man, therefore, does not seem to be the good of temperance—a good proportioned to the concupiscible appetite—but a more universal good toward which the will tends. Consequently, the will influences the concupiscible appetite to act in such a way as not to oppose the movement of the will toward its good. In locating continence in the will, we distinguish it from the virtue of temperance, which, being located in the concupiscible appetite, brings the good of reason to the appetite itself. The man who is temperate has won the battle, whereas the continent man must still continue to fight. The temperate man has realized good order in the very movement of sense appetite; the continent man is still struggling to attain it.

Incontinence is *a disposition in the will by which one is disinclined to overcome the strong impulse of passion and abandons himself to the concupiscible appetite.* As continence is contrasted to temperance, so incontinence is contrasted to intemperance. The vice of intemperance introduces disorder into the very movement of the concupiscible appetite. The incontinent man gives way to disordered movement of the appetite, but with a certain reluctance. A sign of this is that the incontinent man is regretful later, while the intemperate man is in no way repulsed by the disorder.

The Role of Continence and Incontinence

In the beginning of this chapter, we spoke of the importance of understanding continence and incontinence and of seeing the part each plays in human life. Let us conclude by expanding this point with a few additional observations.

Continence, of course, is not a virtue and should not be confused with it. At the same time, it is important to recognize that it is, within its limits, a favorable disposition toward good moral life. The significance of the point lies in the fact that more persons are continent than temperate. Although, as we have said, continence is not to be confused with temperance, nevertheless it is helpful and encouraging to recognize that to be in a continent state is to be on the way to becoming truly temperate. The possession of the virtue of temperance is no easy matter, although when possessed it makes life not only more enjoyable but easier as well. Given the difficulty of acquiring temperance, a person easily might be discouraged in working toward it unless he realized that to the extent he is continent he is on the right track. To be continent is not so hard to accomplish as to be temperate; at the same time, to achieve continence is no small accomplishment.

A similar observation can be made about incontinence. True enough, it is an unfavorable disposition. The incontinent man is defective with respect to resisting what a person ought to resist successfully. Yet he is not rooted in evil as the intemperate man is. As long as he is still incontinent and not intemperate, the tendency is in him to check himself and move in the other direction. He need only begin choosing the universal formed by reason rather than the universal formed through concupiscence. For such a person, the role of continence may have practical importance in the fact that continence is more readily attainable than the life of temperance, which, from his point of view, may seem too remote and too difficult to attain. He has every chance of turning from incontinence to continence, and, once he is continent, he has every chance of advancing to virtue. Incontinence may thus be taken as the warning signal of disaster, but not as the disaster itself.

Extrinsic influences contribute considerably toward making a person either continent or incontinent. We have already mentioned one such influence, the family, which inclines a person so much toward either continence or incontinence. Friendship is another important influence. The persons we associate with as friends do much to move us along toward continence and virtue or, conversely, toward incontinence and vice. Hence, the importance of forming and keeping good friendships which aid us in leading a good moral life. The importance of friendship and the effect friends have on us is not sufficiently recognized. For this reason and others, our next chapter will be devoted to friendship. Social restraints, or the lack of them, also contribute to continence or incontinence in a person. The wise regulation of indecent literature can save a young person from developing a degree of incontinence he otherwise would develop, and the positive direction toward good literature can help to form continence. It seems not to be sufficiently appreciated how much a lack of sufficient social restraint directly produces incontinence. For example, a young man entering military service may do things he would not do under the wise restraining influence of the home. Unless sufficient care is taken by military authorities, he may simply give in to influences tending to produce incontinence and, in time, vice. Finally, and most important of all, the role of the church has enormous influence in these respects. Reception of the sacraments and acts of fasting and abstinence powerfully aid a person in a supernatural way to move him through continence to virtue, and, negatively, to restrain movements of concupiscence leading to incontinence and intemperance.

As a concluding observation, we may note that if we are inclined to suspect that many persons are not as good as they could be, that is, they are not virtuous, they still may be good in a qualified sense by being at least continent. If, on the other hand, we are inclined to suspect that many persons are evil, it may be well to recognize that they are not altogether evil, that is, vicious, but rather incontinent. The incontinent man has not yet confused good with evil; moreover, he remains acutely aware that he is turning from what is a true good. In the incontinent man, therefore, the best thing is still preserved—the recognition of the rule of reason—even though he is not abiding by it. The basis is still there for his truly human development.

REVIEW QUESTIONS

1. How, in general, are continence and incontinence related to virtue and vice?

2. Why is it necessary to consider the role of pleasure in treating continence and incontinence?

3. With what sort of pleasurable objects are continence and incontinence concerned, and why?

4. How does the incontinent person differ from the intemperate person?

5. Distinguish two meanings of "knowing" relevant to the problem of the incontinent person and knowledge.

6. Explain the operative syllogism.

7. Give an original example of an operative syllogism which an incontinent person might employ.

8. Explain how the continent person, the temperate person, and the intemperate person would proceed in an operative syllogism.

9. Define continence. Explain how it differs from temperance.

10. Define incontinence.

11. How much importance do you think the roles of continence and incontinence have in human life?

12. What extrinsic influences affect you most toward being continent or incontinent? Why these rather than others?

SUGGESTED READINGS

Aristotle, *Ethics*, Book VII.
St. Thomas, *Commentary*, Book VII.

XIII

Friendship

*A*t first glance, it may not be evident why and how friendship should be included in a book on ethics. We do not usually discuss friendship in a moral context, nor is the topic often included in a book on moral philosophy. Yet, the omission is surprising when one reflects that friendship is clearly a moral quality and that it concerns human acts directed toward the immediate good of a certain kind of love between human beings. Such a good is certainly connected with human happiness. There is even reason for thinking that friendship may be classified as a virtue, since it appears to be a special quality acquired by regular, deliberate acts. Even if friendship is not, strictly speaking, a virtue, it would seem to be closely related to virtue as somehow presupposing virtue in human beings. Whether friendship is

226

strictly a virtue, as is justice, which friendship especially seems to resemble, or whether it is altogether distinct from virtue, cannot be decided without investigating just what friendship consists in and how it is realized.

Let us begin by recognizing the human need of friendship, a necessity deriving principally from the end of happiness. We shall presume, at the outset, the common understanding of friendship we have through the ordinary experience of having friends.

The Necessity of Friendship

Friendship is necessary for all human beings at practically all ages of life. Young persons, for example, are prone to go to excess in pleasure, and, if they form good friendships early, they may be kept more readily from evils encountered in seeking pleasure in an excessive way. True enough, the wrong kind of friend may only aggravate the tendency of youth toward excess in pleasure, but such association is not genuinely friendship, as we shall see shortly. For example, the members of a gang, bound together by the common aim of some form of destruction or robbery, are not rightly regarded as "friends" in the proper meaning of the term. And if associates of this kind in effect mock the name of friendship by injuring their real personal and common good, we may presume, with some reason, that those who are truly friends—who seek a true personal and common good—will mutually benefit by their association with each other. Young persons especially profit from friendship of this kind.

Old persons likewise need friends, though for a different reason. Because of age, needs are greater and often more numerous, and friendship is especially characterized by willingness to help another in need. Persons in the prime of life need friends as well, for, in most affairs, two or more united together can accomplish more good than one alone. Furthermore, in the prime of life, persons may be expected to profit most from the benefits and advantages of well-developed friendships. Thus, at any age of life, friendship is not only desirable but necessary in order to avoid certain evils and to achieve greater good than would be possible otherwise. Moreover, friendships which endure a long time, even for a lifetime, seem necessary by way of achieving the degree of happiness proper to human beings, for the sociable nature of human beings demands the sort of relationships found only in enduring friendships.

Families also seem to thrive on friendship. We tend to restrict the term "friendship" to associations formed with persons not related to us by blood. There is some reason, of course, for this restriction of the term, since we presuppose a close relationship to blood relatives that is somehow more fundamental than what we usually mean by friendship. Nevertheless, blood relationship should not preclude friendship; it should be the basis, rather, for what we might call *natural* friendship as distinct from *acquired* friendship. Hence, we can speak of a kind of natural friendship parents have for their children as well as a friendship children can have for their parents and for each other. The healthy development of a family would seem to rest upon natural friendships developing in the same fashion as acquired friendships do. We shall refer to this type of friendship later in the chapter.

Other reasons and considerations could be given for the necessity of friendship in good human life. Perhaps it is sufficient to give, finally, a reason touching primarily on the perfection of friendship itself. The primary value of friendship lies in the fact that in itself it is praiseworthy as a moral perfection of human beings. It is a moral good without qualification, and, as we have already indicated, indispensable for the achievement of human happiness. Our concern in the remainder of this chapter will be to make clear in what this moral perfection of friendship consists.

The Definition of Friendship

All of us have some common notion of what friendship is, but the common notion we have is usually not very precise, nor is it likely to take into account the degrees or kinds of friendship. Let us approach the definition of friendship by considering the various elements necessary for friendship of any kind. Once we have reached a satisfactory general definition, we can then profitably consider the different kinds of friendship.

It is evident, first of all, that friendship is a kind of love. In this way we distinguish one who is merely an acquaintance from one who is a friend. We do not bear any special love toward an acquaintance; such a person is simply one we know from passing him occasionally in the street or seeing him at various social or business meetings. There may well be some liking of an acquaintance, but it is never the kind of love we experience for a friend. We share nothing beyond chance meetings and casual bits of conversation with an acquaintance. Nothing really in common binds mere acquaintances; if neither ever met again, it would matter little. To call such associations friendship is a travesty on the name.

The situation is quite otherwise with respect to the love of friendship. It is common to any form of love to tend toward something apprehended as good and desirable. The love of friendship is clearly a tending toward another human being in this fashion; still, not every instance of so loving another person is necessarily a love of friendship. The distinguishing mark of love of friendship is to love another more for his own sake than for one's own private good or gain. The latter kind of love is a selfish one that is contrary to a genuine love of friendship.

One must will the other's good, then, to love him as a friend. Yet, even this added qualification may not be enough to insure the state of friendship. The one so loved must likewise return the same kind of love. It is quite possible for a person to will the good of another without any return of love on the part of the other. Love of this kind is a love of *benevolence*—the willing of good to another—but it is not a love of friendship. The love of friendship, therefore, has to be mutual. Each loves the other in the sense of willing the other's good; hence, friendship may be understood as the love of *mutual benevolence*.

A final clarification must be made before we can define friendship. What is the "good" that each loves in the other? We can answer this question by listing the three types of good that human beings love. One kind is the pleasurable good, the good appealing primarily to the senses. Another kind is the useful good, the good serving as a means of attaining something else. The third kind, a good loved simply for itself, appeals directly to the will, whose proper object is the good. This type of good may also be called the good of reason in the sense that the will loves what reason proposes to it as good. A person's character, known and loved, is a good in this sense of the term.

We can now define friendship as *the love of mutual benevolence between two or more persons, a love by which each recognizes and wills the good of the other*. Since the good is divided into the useful, pleasurable, and proper good, friendship is also divided into useful, pleasurable, and proper or true friendship. These are three distinct kinds of friendship, though not in the sense that they are three equal kinds of friendship. They stand, rather, in a relationship of greater and lesser realization of friendship. At the same time, it is true that in each kind of friendship there is a mutual return of love and willing of the other's good, and this is the basic element in any friendship. The difference lies, as we have indicated, in the kind of good both love: it may be the useful good, the pleasurable good, or the proper good, the latter consisting in the love of virtue principally.

The Friendship of Utility

As the name suggests, persons who are friends in this way love each other primarily not because of what each one is in himself but for what each can do for the other, that is, the usefulness each can receive from the other. Commercial associations frequently are friendships of this kind. It is advantageous and useful to be in contact with someone who can aid you in some business transaction. Similarly, it is useful to have a doctor for a friend who, in turn, may find you useful as a lawyer or a salesman. The number of ways in which persons can develop friendships of utility is almost infinite, since the ways of being useful are similarly infinite.

It might be thought that the motive of utility debases the very notion and value of friendship, since a friendship of utility appears to be based merely on what one can gain from the other. If this element is the only one present, then only a transaction takes place, not friendship. Certainly a person who merely takes advantage of someone else for selfish gain is no friend at all, as the other person soon discovers. But it is quite possible for persons to be friends who find each other useful in attaining some genuine good in a variety of ways. Since friendship involves willing the good of the other, persons who are useful to each other by helping each other attain some good are rightly regarded as friends. The old saying, "A friend in need is a friend indeed!" bears out this point.

Nevertheless, it is evident that a friendship based *only* on utility is an imperfect sort of friendship. Friends in this way love each other not so much for what each is in himself but for something extrinsic and accidental, namely, the utility itself. Such a friendship can easily dissolve. It does, in fact, as soon as either becomes useless to the other. Furthermore, since what is useful at one time may not be useful at a later time, a person tends to form and break many friendships of this kind during the course of his life. Former friendships are sometimes revived in this way, for a common need may bring persons together again long after their first connection has been broken. Nations do the same sort of thing. They conclude alliances and "treaties of friendship" when the good of both is involved and when each can be useful to the other. The pacts may be dissolved when the utility disappears, and renewed again if the utility re-appears.

The Friendship of Pleasure

Perhaps most persons are friends primarily because each finds pleasure in association with the other. Most friendships, in fact, tend to begin as friendship of pleasure, for we are usually attracted first by what is sensibly pleasant. However, friendship of pleasure is not restricted to pleasure of the senses, although its basis is there. Persons who love each other because of a common enjoyment of games, pleasant exchange of conversation, delight in sharing good humor and wit—in general, delight in various social pastimes—are friends primarily because of pleasure.

The friendship of pleasure is found particularly among young persons, and with reason, for the young tend to love quickly and easily, which is to say, through the senses and the emotions. Children, in fact, experience only the friendship of pleasure. We make friends easily when we are young, since almost any passing fancy may draw two young persons together. For the same reason, friendship of pleasure easily dissolves, for as pleasure changes so does the friendship; and nothing changes as quickly as the enjoyment we experience in a pleasurable object. Moreover, those who are friends only because of pleasure can easily become enemies, for this sort of love easily changes into hate when something unpleasant occurs. Enemies of this kind, however, easily become friends again if they find some common pleasure once more. Young persons who are sworn enemies one week may be bosom friends the next week. They rarely see this fluctuation as inconsistent; in a sense, they are right, for the passions vacillate easily between extremes and are, in fact, inconsistent when left to themselves.

Older persons, of course, also have friendships of pleasure. The pleasure is sometimes of a different type, tending to center in developed interests of one kind or another and extending perhaps to common intellectual interests and pursuits. An evening of conversation among older and more mature persons can be both thoroughly pleasurable and interesting and stimulating. There is, indeed, a need for friendship of pleasure of some kind among persons in the prime of life, for it serves as a needed relaxation from the ordinary strain and concentration of daily work and activity. Persons who are friends in this way often find enjoying plays, motion pictures, concerts and other types of recreation together a relaxing and enjoyable outlet.

The friendship of pleasure concentrates on the present. In this respect it differs from the friendship of utility, which looks to the future when the usefulness will be realized. The concentration on the present characterizes the friendship of pleasure because the emotions are usually stimulated by what is physically present. We thus associate friendship of pleasure with companionship, the delight we experience in the presence of another person. The delight and enjoyment each experiences in the presence of the other most of all characterizes the friendship of pleasure and, at the same time, disposes persons toward true or perfect friendship.

Perfect Friendship

Perfect friendship is realized when two persons love what is best in each of them. The best or highest good in a person, precisely as he is a person, is the character the person has developed. The moral character of a person is best formed, as we have seen, by the development of virtue. Hence, those who are friends because they are alike in virtue and are drawn to each other primarily because of virtue are friends in the most perfect way humanly possible. In the case of perfect friendship, then, we see how friendship at least presupposes virtue, if it is not a distinct virtue itself.

Persons who are friends in this way are *essentially* friends; their friendship does not rest upon any relative or accidental consideration. Compared to friendship based on virtue, friendships of utility and pleasure are relative and imperfect because the good in common in both cases is secondary. Persons formed by virtue are good in themselves, since virtue is the perfection which makes a man good and his actions good. The friendship based on virtue is therefore friendship in the unqualified sense of the term, for in willing the good of each—the indispensable condition of friendship of any kind —persons who are friends in this way love each other because of the truly human good each has, the good formed by virtue.

The friendship of virtue tends to be everlasting. The primary reason for this enduring quality is that virtue itself is a permanent disposition; once acquired, it is difficult to lose. Friendship based on virtue is similarly lasting, persisting through difficulties that would dissolve a friendship based only on utility or pleasure. Pleasures and needs come and go, but the good of virtue remains, and so does perfect friendship.

It should be pointed out, however, that friendship based on virtue normally includes the friendship of utility and of pleasure. If, as we are maintaining, the friendship of virtue is perfect friendship, then it will lack nothing. It will contain all that is in the other kinds of friendship, since perfect friends, being essentially good in themselves, will be good toward each other in all respects. Perfect friends, consequently, are not only essentially good, but essentially useful and essentially pleasing to each other as well. Indeed, precisely as virtuous, such friends are more useful and pleasing than those who are friends only as useful or only as pleasing.

Unlike the other kinds of friendship, the one based on virtue is relatively rare. The principal reason for the infrequency of perfect friendship is that relatively few persons are fully formed in virtue. In saying this, we do not mean to imply that most human beings are necessarily evil and vicious, for persons can achieve a considerable degree of moral goodness without attaining the moral perfection proper to virtue, as we saw in the preceding chapter. We mean, rather, that it is difficult to acquire virtue, and, in some respects, it appears to be a life-long process. The person really formed by virtue can regularly attain the mean of perfection between extremes, not only in justice, but in temperance, fortitude, prudence, and all the other virtues. Such persons do not seem to be numerous, and, as a consequence, neither are the friendships which can be developed only between such persons. Yet, the impression should not be left that perfect friendship is so rare as to seem unattainable. Persons who are on the way to the excellence of virtuous living are on the way to excellence in friendship as well. Perfect friendship, therefore, may be extended to those who are approaching the good of virtue in themselves and in their relation to others. In this broadened sense of the term, perfect friendships are not so rare as might first appear.

There is another reason, however, why perfect friendships are not numerous. It takes a long time to form a friendship based on virtue. It is hardly possible for two persons to become perfect friends at once or even during a short period of time. A certain number of meetings and associations are required in order to come to know each other well enough so that the love based on virtue can develop. Sometimes, it is true, we are immediately impressed by this or that person and wish to form a perfect friendship at once. But this is only the desire for friendship, not yet the attainment of real friendship. Normally, a good deal of time is needed to discern whether the person who appears to be a real friend in fact is one. Consequently, we usually have to begin with a friendship of utility or pleasure, and only after some lapse of time can we form a friendship based on virtue. Since there is only so much time at our disposal, and since friendship based on virtue requires considerable time, it is clear that not many friendships of virtue can be formed. The consolation is that a few friendships of this kind are worth more than countless numbers of other kinds of friendship.

Domestic Friendship

We have already referred to a type of friendship that can and should exist among members of a family. This is not quite the same sort of friendship that we have been discussing so far. The difference arises from the fact that domestic society is a distinct form of life, uniting the members of a family in certain special ways. In the usual sense of the term, friendship rests upon some common agreement in virtue or pleasure or utility. Domestic friendship rests upon the common origin shared by members of a family through their parents, and this common origin is the basis for forming a close mutual love between the members of the family. Obviously, friendships of virtue, pleasure, and utility are also formed among members of a family, but the original basis for the friendship and the motive for developing it are different.

Let us consider, first, the friendship between parents and children. A difficulty about such friendship arises at once, since there is an inequality between parents and children which would seem to preclude the forming of friendship. Nevertheless, this natural inequality between parents and children is not an inequality which eliminates a state of friendship. It is possible for friendship to exist between unequals, but it will exist in a different manner from the way it exists among equals. Friendship among unequals tends to equalize in a proportional manner the relations between them to the extent that a mutual love is formed. There is, in other words, a proportional equality between friends who are unequal in some respect, and this proportional equality suffices for establishing friendship. It is in this way that a father and a son, for example, can be friends, without implying a false and even ridiculous equality whereby the father and the son become "buddies."

By the nature of the case, a parent loves his child more than the child loves his parent, an indication that this kind of friendship rests on proportional equality. Since the child is a natural similitude of the parent, the parent tends to love his child in the manner of loving a part of himself. The basis for the child's love of his parent, on the other hand, is that the parent is a principle and a cause of the child's very being, and the child is aware of this fact in many ways. Consequently, while the parent has a greater love of friendship for the child, the child is more indebted to the parent. If, later in life, the love proper to domestic friendship should greatly diminish or even cease altogether between the son or daughter and the parent, an obligation of justice on the part of the son or daughter would, nevertheless, always remain.

The friendship between children in a family is not a friendship of proportional equality but one of simple equality, since they share equally in the domestic society of which they are members. In addition to their common bond of blood relationship, they should seek to develop friendship resting explicitly on virtue, pleasure, and utility. It is regrettable that friendships of this kind are often not developed explicitly while children are growing up in the family. Somewhat paradoxically, the closeness through blood relation sometimes tends to diminish the mature fostering of genuine friendships among members of a family. Actually, the opposite effect should take place, the developing of friendship in the fullest sense of the term, for the possibilities are normally greatest within a family circle.

The friendship that should exist between husband and wife is a distinct kind known as *conjugal* friendship. Such friendship should be realized to a greater degree than friendship among sons and daughters of the same family, because the union attained through marriage is a better disposition and basis for friendship than even the blood relationship within the family. Here, again, it is regrettable that true friendships frequently are not sought or developed between husbands and wives. It should be quite evident that a perfect friendship, a friendship based on virtue, should be especially developed between husband and wife, for, by the nature of the case, marriage should be a permanent association between two persons based on equally enduring love. How can married love profitably endure without some common basis in virtue, and without the love of each being directed primarily to the good character of the other, by which the common good of married happiness is principally realized? A marriage formed merely on a love of pleasure, similar to a friendship of pleasure, is not likely to last when the pleasure ends. The number of quick marriages and quick divorces suggests that many marriages are based only, or primarily, on love of pleasure.

It may seem strange to speak of the love of friendship between husband and wife, as it seemed strange to speak of friendship among members of a family. The strangeness of the expression seems to arise, again, only because of a narrowed meaning we tend to give to friendship. Actually, a husband and wife should enjoy a special love of friendship, one that combines in a maximum way the love of virtue, pleasure, and utility. They have more to share with each other than any other two human beings, and it is only reasonable to assume that as they go through life together they will tend to increase their love for each other, particularly if their love is rooted in virtue.

It is thus of great practical importance for those who intend to marry to bear in mind that love of utility alone, or love of pleasure alone, is not a sufficient basis for growth in married happiness, which comes only through a complete love of human beings for each other, that is, the mutual love of the well-formed character in each. Each should look primarily for such moral good in the other, for such good alone persists. This point does not mean that moral maturity and perfection must be complete or even highly realized prior to marriage, since marriage itself also promotes the development of virtue. The ordering toward virtue is the minimum basis needed. And it is only such moral good that is capable of continual increase; hence, a married love resting principally on the love of such good can continue to increase as time goes on. It is perhaps well to note, in this connection, the risk in taking "love at first sight" as the reliable approach to married happiness. The love of a person primarily for the person's character is not likely to be revealed at first sight. Perhaps "love at first absence" is a more reliable approach, for then the person in question is apt to be thought of and loved for what he really is, rather than for what he may only appear to be.

REVIEW QUESTIONS

1. Why should friendship be included in a book on ethics?
2. Show how persons of all ages need friendship.
3. How do you distinguish between a friend and an acquaintance?
4. What is a love of benevolence?
5. Is a love of benevolence the same as a love of friendship? Explain
6. What are the three main types of good that human beings love?
7. Define friendship.

8. What are the three principal kinds of friendship?
9. What is a friendship of utility? Explain whether or not it is a good kind of friendship.
10. In what does a friendship of pleasure consist?
11. In what sort of persons are friendships of pleasure more often formed, and why?
12. Describe perfect friendship.
13. Why does friendship based on virtue tend to be enduring?
14. How is friendship based on virtue related to the other kinds?
15. Why is friendship based on virtue relatively rare?
16. Do friendships usually begin as a friendship based on virtue? Why or why not?
17. What is the basis for domestic friendship? In what way does it differ from other types of friendship?
18. Why should the love of parent for child differ from that of child for parent?
19. Describe conjugal friendship.
20. What special practical importance does conjugal friendship have?

SUGGESTED READINGS

Aristotle, *Ethics*, Books VIII-IX.
St. Thomas, *Commentary*, Books VIII-IX.
Plato, *Lysis*.

Cicero, *Essay on Friendship (Laelius De Amicitia)*, translated by A. Inglis. New York: Newton & Cartwright, 1908.
Conway, P., translator, *St. Thomas Aquinas on Aristotle's Love and Friendship*. Providence: Providence College Press, 1951.
Emerson, R., *Love and Friendship*. Philadelphia: Aletmus, 1896.

XIV

The end and the beginning

*E*thics is the study of human happiness and how to achieve it. There is nothing in the preceding chapters that does not bear on human happiness or on some aspect of it. At the very outset we were concerned with establishing *that* there is some ultimate end for which all human beings act. As we noted, men commonly speak of such an end as happiness, at least in the sense of the fulfillment of human desire. The problem of *what* happiness consists in and how it can be attained proved difficult to resolve. It was only partly resolved in Chapter III. It is to this problem that we now return.

We could not return to it before this chapter. Our tentative solution of the problem in Chapter III disclosed that happiness consists in the direction of all our human acts by reason, which is to say, a life of virtue in accordance with reason. We were, accordingly, led to investigate more fully what virtue in general is, the principal means of attaining happiness. To understand virtue thoroughly, we had to distinguish voluntary from involuntary acts. Such considerations enabled us to state precisely when acts are morally good and when morally bad, recognizing right reason as the fundamental intrinsic measure of morality. We were then in a position to consider virtues specifically, ordering them all under the cardinal virtues of fortitude, temperance, justice, and prudence. The life of virtuous action was thus seen to be the kind of life most productive of human happiness. Then law had to be considered, since the happiness of a human being is greatly influenced and formed by an extrinsic measure of moral action.

It is evident, however, that not all human beings lead a life of virtue or act according to the spirit of law. Hence, to give a full account of moral life, it was necessary to examine the kind of life which, though not yet virtuous, was on the way to being virtuous. Such is the life of continence; its opposite, incontinence, was investigated also, since a certain number of human beings tend toward a false realization of happiness without yet being confirmed in vice. Finally, since human beings do not live in a solitary fashion, a special relation of persons to each other is a necessary part of happiness; in ethics, this special relation is considered in terms of friendship, a quality which in its perfect state presumes virtue, or at least the pursuit of virtue, in human beings.

We thus see how ethics reduces primarily to the consideration of human happiness and how to attain it. We are now in a position to take up again the problem still remaining about human happiness and to face three distinct questions raised at the end of Chapter III: (1) Can we attain human happiness? (2) Can we maintain human happiness? (3) Is such happiness complete happiness? We shall take up these questions after first considering some preliminary matters.

The Constituents of Happiness

Let us recall what has been already established about happiness. We have shown that there must be some ultimate end for human action. No human being can act unless something, however implicitly and vaguely, is willed for itself, with everything else willed for it. All men agree, in action if not in word, that happiness is such an ultimate end at least when understood as the satisfaction and fulfillment of all desire. In attempting to determine objectively in what happiness consists, we arrived inductively and analytically at the position that human happiness is primarily a life of virtue in accordance with reason, extending secondarily to goods of the body and external goods.

In the light of what we have studied since the opening chapters, let us try to explain more fully what now seems to constitute human happiness. It must include primarily the good of intellectual and moral virtue—the activity of such virtues as science, understanding, wisdom, art, and prudence, and the cardinal moral virtues of fortitude, temperance, and justice. Along with these goods of the soul and including the good of friendship, human happiness must include such bodily and external goods as health, pleasure, and a degree of wealth.

Human happiness, consequently, is not one ultimate end in the sense that it consists in only one *single* good. Part of the difficulty in trying to solve the problem of what constitutes human happiness has been the supposition that one single object must realize the whole of human happiness; this is an unnecessary complication of the problem, since it is now evident that no single object naturally known and desired could completely satisfy the human quest for happiness. On the other hand, happiness does not consist in a heterogeneous collection of goods either, but in a hierarchical ordering of goods. The sense in which human happiness is one, therefore, consists in the unity of an ordered whole, a unity arising from a natural hierarchy of objective goods. The ordering of these goods into a unified whole according to their relative importance is based upon the natural hierarchy of human powers and the objects specifying their operation. Our vegetative powers, for example, are directed to the good of the body, principally health, and for the good of health we make use of an external good such as wealth. Our powers of sense knowing and desiring are concerned with the good of sense knowing and pleasure, a higher good than physical health in the sense that we are healthy in order to enjoy life, not the reverse. The good of sense pleasure, in turn, is for the sake of the good attained through the will. This latter good is twofold: the good sought by the will in terms of friendship, honor, and the like, and the good sought in the attainment of moral virtue, the moral perfection of our own life. There is, finally, the good proper to the intellect, the good found in knowledge itself, in the understanding and contemplation of all the truths we can know.

The constituents of human happiness, therefore, embrace the following in an ascending order from least important to most important:

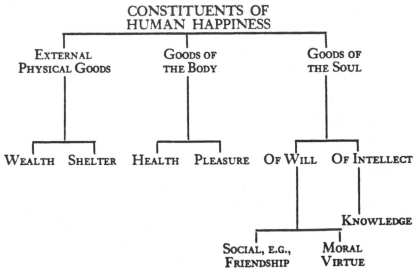

CONSTITUENTS OF
HUMAN HAPPINESS

EXTERNAL PHYSICAL GOODS — GOODS OF THE BODY — GOODS OF THE SOUL

WEALTH   SHELTER   HEALTH   PLEASURE   OF WILL   OF INTELLECT

KNOWLEDGE

SOCIAL, E.G., FRIENDSHIP   MORAL VIRTUE

The Issue of Contemplation vs. Action

It is clear, at our present stage of investigation, that what we are calling "goods of the soul" primarily constitute happiness. There is a question, however, about the importance of the goods of the soul in relation to each other. It is this question which raises the issue of contemplation vs. action. The issue can be stated more precisely by asking which is higher for man: the attaining of intellectual perfection, knowledge and contemplation; or the attaining of moral perfection and good human action, whose principle is the will? This same issue can be put in different terms: does contemplation or moral perfection most of all constitute human happiness? These two questions are not the same, for one asks which is higher for man, while the other asks which most of all constitutes human happiness. In answering both, we can resolve a problem that is important and difficult. This problem arises, it should be noted, only by presuming that both are essential for human happiness. The difficulty lies in trying to determine which one has primacy.

Let us first consider which is higher for man. If happiness consists in the best operation we can perform, and if the operation of reason itself is the highest we have, then the life of reason as it consists in contemplation, especially as it includes a natural knowledge of God, would seem most of all to constitute happiness. This argument rests upon truths drawn from psychology, that the power of reason is higher than that of the will and that we love in terms of what we know. Moreover, the contemplation of truth appears to be the noblest good and therefore the highest good we can attain. Contemplation is also more continuous and more enduring than any other operation we have. It is sought more than anything else for the sake of itself and is most of all self-sufficient. Finally, contemplation perfects man with regard to what his nature specifically is, rationality.

Nevertheless, even granting that contemplation of truth is the highest good man can attain, does it follow that contemplation most of all constitutes happiness for man? What is highest in itself may not make man most happy as a human being. Hence, while it appears to be true that contemplation is the answer to the first question we raised, namely, that a life of contemplation is higher in itself than a life of action, it does not follow that this is the answer to the second question, that it constitutes human happiness more fully. There are, in fact, at least two reasons for thinking that a life of contemplation does not constitute complete happiness for human beings.

The first reason is that contemplation appears to be too high for a human being. Man is rational, but, precisely as rational, he is not wholly intellectual. A life of contemplation, devoted simply to the acquiring of knowledge, characterizes a being that is only and purely intellectual. Human nature is composite—animal as well as rational—hence the satisfaction of man as a whole, as a composite being, will not consist in something pertaining to only a part of him, even if it is the better part. We therefore must recognize that contemplation is above man rather than proper to him. The second reason is based upon the facts of experience. By and large, human beings are not necessarily happiest when they engage in contemplation. Even the most contemplative person needs something else in order to be happy in the way in which human beings are happy. Furthermore, most human beings do not appear to lead a life of contemplation in any developed sense of the term.

The happy life according to the composite nature of a human being, therefore, is realized more in a life of action, that is, in a life of moral perfection originating in the well-ordered will. *Absolutely speaking*, this life of moral virtue is happiness in a secondary sense, for perfect happiness consists in contemplation and the life of reason itself. But life in accordance with virtue seems to be the sort of happiness that befits the composite nature of man. However, a question at once arises. If man is to be happy as man, can the life of moral virtue, which seems to be connected primarily with the will and the passions, satisfy sufficiently the intellectual part of man's composite nature?

This question is answered by recalling that moral virtue is ordered and directed by prudence, a virtue at once intellectual and moral. As we have seen, prudence is both an intellectual virtue and a moral virtue. The life of morally virtuous action, therefore, directed and developed by the intellectual virtue of prudence, is the life most conducive to happiness for a being having the sort of composite nature man has. Thus we recognize that the sort of happiness realizable by man is not the highest degree of happiness realizable; human happiness is not perfect happiness. Nevertheless, through prudence and moral virtue man is disposed to the contemplative life to the degree that he can attain it, and in this way we can say contemplation also constitutes human happiness. As we have been saying from the start, but now more fully and more intelligibly, human happiness is the life of virtue in accordance with reason—that is, a life of morally virtuous action based on prudence along with whatever degree of contemplation is possible for man. All other goods, external and bodily, will be sought secondarily and in proportion as they contribute to achieving human happiness as we now understand it.

Can We Attain Such Happiness?

We can now consider this question, and the two others we raised at the beginning of this chapter. Our first problem is whether all human beings or even most can and do attain happiness as we now understand it. Some persons certainly seem to be excluded from ever reaching such happiness, for example, the insane. Other persons are seriously afflicted most of their lives by great poverty or ill health or heavy burdens of responsibility. We could easily multiply instances illustrating how many human beings, because of varying reasons and circumstances, seem barred from ever really attaining human happiness. Thus the conclusion seems inevitable that a good many persons do not attain human happiness, and we may even wonder to what extent most human beings attain a life of virtue according to reason.

Can We Maintain Such Happiness?

Let us assume, however, that human beings can attain happiness. We might grant that a person is able to rise above the limitations of poor health or heavy misfortune and achieve a real degree of human happiness. We can acknowledge that in many cases insanity can be cured and destitution alleviated. In a word, let us admit that human beings are able to attain happiness at this or that particular time. In making this admission, we only seem to arrive at the more difficult question of whether happiness, once attained, can be maintained.

It is a more difficult question to answer because it seems to be even harder to maintain happiness than to attain it. The difficulty of being able to continue in a real state of happiness is a major one for any human being, no matter how favorable his condition and circumstances. If nothing else, there is always the obscure future and the ubiquitous influence of chance. A man genuinely happy on Monday may be miserable on Tuesday.

Essential and Relative Happiness

We can answer the two foregoing questions to some extent by distinguishing between happiness realized essentially and happiness realized relatively. Human happiness realized essentially is the life of morally virtuous action based on prudence with whatever degree of contemplation is possible. Human happiness realized relatively extends to the enjoyment of external and bodily goods, both for the good they have of themselves and for their utility in realizing the life of essential happiness. We need also to keep in mind the distinction between *objective* happiness, i.e., the objective goods constituting both essential and relative happiness, and *subjective* happiness, the attainment and possession of those goods.

We can answer the first question by saying that human beings can and do *attain* both essential and relative happiness to the extent that they seek what objectively constitutes human happiness. At the same time, we must recognize that objective happiness will be attained in varying degrees by different persons. Objectively, essential and relative happiness are the same for all; subjectively, there is a proportional realization.

Once attained, *essential* happiness can be *maintained*, although we must grant that it is maintained by various persons in proportionate and varying degrees. The life of virtue in accordance with reason, in fact, is as permanent a condition as we can hope to have. The man of right reason and virtuous action is at once as well formed and as permanently constituted in knowing and acting as is humanly possible. All of us can both attain and maintain such a well-formed state in proportion to our ability and powers, for intellectual and moral virtues are permanent qualities of the soul. Nevertheless, as we shall see shortly, we shall have to qualify our answer to the second question. Attaining essential happiness does not necessarily guarantee maintaining it. We must also take into account the theological point of the effect of original sin and the need of supernatural grace in both attaining and maintaining even natural perfection.

Relative happiness, consisting in external and bodily goods which are required for the integrity or fullness of human happiness, may not be maintained. We may not, for example, be able to maintain good health; we may be without sufficient wealth; we may lose a variety of social goods. The loss of some or even most of these goods will doubtless materially affect human happiness, but they need not affect essential human happiness. Indeed, there are times and occasions when the loss of certain external or bodily goods contributes to a finer realization of essential happiness. In any case, while we are not likely to maintain relative happiness fully, we should recognize that although such losses diminish the fullness of human happiness, they need not diminish essential happiness.

Is Human Happiness Complete Happiness?

We come finally to the third question, the question at once the most difficult, the most interesting, and the most important. Is human happiness at its best, embracing as fully as possible both essential and relative happiness, *complete* happiness for a human being?

We can answer this question in one way quite simply. Essential and relative happiness is happiness as complete as it is possible for human happiness to be. It is a happiness completely proportioned to human nature; it serves truly as an end to which human nature tends; it is an end which well-ordered men strive to realize above everything else. It is important to recognize, in this connection, that an ultimate end for human beings is not a static condition; it is not an end achieved fully and completely all at once. Human life is successive, not simultaneous; dynamic, not static. Man's realization of his end, consequently, will be in conformity with the nature he has, a successive and continuing realization. Human happiness is activity taking place in the best way humanly possible. In this respect, then, we can say that there is a completeness to what we have described as human happiness, especially essential human happiness.

Nevertheless, we are still forced to admit that even essential human happiness is not complete happiness in the full and proper sense of the term. We can detect a radical incompleteness of human happiness by turning once again to experience.

We are aware, first of all, that human life at its best and happiest is still quite compatible with the affliction of much evil. As we live our lives, we are quite aware that we are subjected constantly and endlessly to many evils; moreover, these evils can never be wholly eliminated. When some are vanquished, others arise, and some are never wholly removed. There is, for example, the evil constantly affecting the highest part in us, the intellect, the evil of ignorance. We do not mean the ignorance for which we are responsible and which we could remove, but an ignorance arising simply from the limitation of our power of knowing. It is an ignorance we are subjected to necessarily, given the relatively little time we have to know and the almost infinite degree of knowledge we are aware of wanting to attain.

There are the evils arising from inordinate tendencies and movement of the appetite, both the will and the emotions. Even the best ordered human being is not wholly free from some disordered inclinations in his appetite. In a certain respect, in fact, the more ordered morally a human being is, the more he is aware of such inclinations in him, even though he may have rational control over them all or most of the time. Nevertheless, such inordinate inclinations are never wholly vanquished. The facts of experience suggest that there is a natural, perhaps inevitable, contrariety in human nature between appetite and reason. However successful we are in overcoming this contrariety, we have a degree of unhappiness in enduring what seems to be a continual warfare of greater or lesser intensity within our very selves.

Further, we are weighed down by the inevitable ills of the body. To be sure, we may recognize that bodily ills need not touch essential happiness in us, just as we also recognize that the most perfect condition of the body does not guarantee essential happiness. Nevertheless, as we are aware from experience, evils affecting the body do affect us most intimately. The intimate union of body and soul is a sufficient guarantee of our being so affected. There is evidence enough that bodily ills can induce psychological and even moral ills. It would be unrealistic to deny that evils of this kind, even if they do not seriously diminish essential happiness, certainly preclude our being completely happy.

We may summarize the foregoing by saying that there is no guarantee of permanent happiness for us, and certainly in this respect happiness is not complete for us. At any given time, we may be seriously affected by evils afflicting the intellect, the appetite, and the body, successively or at once. Experience amply manifests the tenuousness of our hold on the good condition of intellect, appetite, and body. We did say, earlier in the chapter, that we can maintain essential happiness, thereby implying a permanence in a life of virtue in accordance with reason. But we also noted that this assertion would be subject to qualification. The qualification is that while one may be able to maintain essential happiness for some length of time, still there seems to be no assurance that one can be permanently happy, essentially or relatively. Even the power of reason itself may be damaged or lost through age or illness; and virtue, though difficult to lose once acquired, nevertheless *can* be lost.

There is still another difficulty, even more profound and serious than the lack of permanence. For happiness to be complete in any real sense of the term, it must be realized in such a way as to put to rest all striving and desire. When we say "put to rest all desire" we do not mean the cessation or elimination of desire in the sense of arriving at a state of inertia. We mean, rather, the fulfillment and complete satisfaction of all desire, a state rather of complete actuality. Nothing remains to be desired and there is no desire to seek anything else, precisely because we are achieving an experience of being fully actualized. Such a state of existence certainly would be *complete* happiness, the full possession of all that we could wish for. But the most evident thing we learn from our experience in all periods of life is that we never achieve, or even come close to achieving, such complete satisfaction of all striving and desire. The more we know, the more we desire to know what we do not yet know; the desire to know only increases as we know more things. No person has ever known, or ever could know, in such a way as to satisfy all desire for knowledge. Similarly, there is no object which satisfies completely our love as we now experience love. Like our knowledge, our love only increases as we love the different persons and objects we experience. Both our knowing and our loving, from the standpoint of their capacity, stretch out to something infinite and will not be fully content with anything limited, no matter how great and wonderful it may be.

One might be tempted to despair, confronted with this realization that complete happiness appears to be impossible. There is, of course, the fact of death, and death might seem to be the answer in the sense that it may seem to be one way of bringing to an end all desire and striving. But man naturally revolts at death, and the consideration of death induces sorrow rather than joy and happiness.

For some, death is the end, but at best it is an end only in the sense of being last in a succession of temporal events. It is never a goal. It is never an end in the proper sense of being first in intention, for no human being lives simply for the purpose of dying. Death understood as mere annihilation revolts every tendency in man; no human being *rests* contentedly in the conviction that everything will be as though nothing had ever been, that he who now is will cease to be, as though he had never been. Hence, death cannot be the *answer*.

Absolute and Proportionate Happiness

Our experience brings us to the recognition, sooner or later, that complete happiness (1) is not possible in this life and (2) is possible, but not in this life. We are thus led to see that there must be an eternal life beyond the present life. An eternal life means, first of all, a life of immortality. We can know by reason that man, with respect to the principle of life in him, i.e., the soul, is incorruptible and therefore immortal. In this sense, man survives death, death now understood as the separation of body and soul, the composite principles of a human being. We thus can speak of a natural immortality and can be quite certain of it without, nevertheless, understanding very much about what such a life would be.

But eternal life takes on full and concrete meaning when, enlightened through revelation from God, we understand eternal life in terms of a *supernatural* life. For Christians, this supernatural life is a certainty made known by God through Christ; it is made intelligible through preaching and teaching and is confirmed by signs and miracles. It is a life begun here on earth by living in a state of grace, a state of friendship with God. Natural friendship, as we discussed it in the preceding chapter, does not allow for friendship between God and man, because there is no natural basis for even proportional equality between God and man, but through grace such friendship is possible. The life of friendship with God as we now experience it is, as the name "life" implies, not static but dynamic, just as the life of virtue is, and it culminates in the intellectual vision of God Himself. The "seeing of God face to face" figuratively expresses a mode of knowing and loving infinitely elevated above the natural powers man has. The expression *Beatific Vision* signifies full understanding and joy finally realized. Such happiness is complete and absolute.

We have, of course, moved from the level of philosophy to the level of theology, and, in relation to the question of man's ultimate end, from moral philosophy to moral theology. We have likewise gone from what might be called proportionate happiness to absolute happiness. There is, it must be granted, a leap from one to the other, a leap that could not be known without revelation and could not be attained without the aid of grace. At the same time, however, we can recognize that there is a legitimate sense in which the natural order is open to the supernatural order. The question of man's ultimate happiness opens man's mind to the supernatural order. What now remains to be said depends upon both natural knowledge and knowledge gained through revelation, on both philosophical and theological knowledge. Only in this way can we fully resolve the final questions and difficulties about man's ultimate *ends*.

We have italicized the plural word *ends*. Human nature has two ultimate ends corresponding to two distinct orders, the natural and the supernatural; or it might be said that man has a twofold ultimate end. In this distinction lies the resolution of the problem of man's happiness.

We shall use the phrase *proportionate happiness* to designate man's ultimate natural end, the end proportionate to his nature. As we have seen, it is a life of virtue in accordance with reason, a life of both contemplation and action. We already know that it is a life that can be attained by man in his temporal, terrestrial life, although its permanence is not necessarily assured. It is the only kind of happiness to which man by nature is ordered. He attains this happiness successively throughout a normal span of life, primarily by means of virtue. It is not perfect or absolute happiness, a degree of happiness man is not entitled to, nor would he even conceive such perfect happiness as *realizable* were it not supernaturally revealed. Yet, the facts of our experience reveal a yearning for something that would be perfect happiness, and we thus see again the openness of the natural to the supernatural. Only by comparison with perfect happiness known by faith and realizable in a supernatural way can we speak of natural happiness as "imperfect happiness." This point does not detract from the fact that natural happiness is a true ultimate end in its order and that it is also realizable.

We shall use the phrase *absolute happiness* to designate the complete and perfect happiness enjoyed in the Beatific Vision. It can be attained and maintained by man eternally. It satisfies completely, to a degree infinitely beyond human capacity, all human desire for knowledge and love. It exceeds, in fact, all the qualifications we could think of as necessary for perfect happiness. It is an end given with utter gratuity by God to man.

The Relation of a Natural and a Supernatural End

We have established so far that man has two distinct ultimate ends. Perhaps it is clearer to say that the happiness of man is twofold: the natural happiness that is proportionate to human nature and the supernatural happiness that wholly exceeds human nature. Stated this way, we see that the term "happiness" or "ultimate end" is not univocal, that is, wholly the same in meaning, but analogical. The *difference* in meaning comes from the fact that the object of happiness differs in the two cases. Natural happiness consists in the object to which reason and virtue are directed, along with the goods of the body and external goods, all realized in a hierarchical ordering. The object of supernatural happiness is God Himself, supernaturally known and loved. The *similarity* in meaning is the satisfaction of human desire, naturally and supernaturally.

As we have already indicated, however, compared to the supernatural end, the natural end is imperfect, not with respect to human nature, but with respect to happiness itself. We may go even further when speaking comparatively. Just as God wholly is and the creature as though he is not, so natural happiness is as nothing compared to supernatural happiness. This comparative mode of speaking safeguards two distinct but related truths: (1) Man in fact is not ordered to natural happiness alone and (2) the natural moral order has a genuine ultimate end. Two errors are thereby also excluded: (1) Man's absolute happiness is natural happiness and (2) the happiness of man is *only* supernatural. Consequently, to grasp the whole truth about human happiness, we must see the distinction between the natural and the supernatural order as well as understand that the natural order is redeemed and perfected through the supernatural order.

The Domain of Moral Theology

Under this heading we wish to consider, in a necessarily limited manner, not only the province of moral theology but also its relation to moral philosophy. Our reason for this brief excursion into moral theology is to manifest the distinction between moral theology and moral philosophy, the relation between the two, and the need of both for understanding the moral life completely.

Moral theology is one part of the science of theology. Theology as a science proceeds discursively from truths given by divine revelation to the establishment of conclusions scientifically known in the light of the Faith. Moral theology is that part of theology which judges and directs human acts in their relation to the supernatural end of the Beatific Vision.

As in any practical science, the principles of moral theology come from the end of the science, in this case God supernaturally known and loved. The Beatific Vision, therefore, is the first topic in moral theology, explained as far as we can now understand it from revelation and grasped as that ultimate end to which all natural and supernatural actions are directed. Human acts are then considered and analyzed as voluntary acts ordered to an end, with a consideration of actions and passions. The intrinsic principles of human acts, virtues and vices, are examined in general, as are the extrinsic principles of law and grace. Because of the need of approaching the concrete order as much as possible, the virtues are then taken up in detail, starting with the theological virtues and proceeding on to the moral virtues by means of the cardinal virtues. There is, finally, the consideration of the contemplative and active states of life and the relation between them.

In thus outlining most of the major points in moral theology, we wish to bring out two points in particular. First, the order of treatment in moral theology is different from the order of treatment in ethics, the difference arising from the different ultimate ends. For example, in moral theology we treat the theological virtues, which cannot be treated at all in ethics, after which the intellectual and moral virtues are considered in a descending order. In ethics, we proceed according to what is more known to us. After examining the natural ultimate end and virtue in general, we treat the moral virtues before considering the intellectual virtues and law, with a return to the ultimate end at the conclusion because of the difficulty in establishing in what natural happiness consists.

Secondly, it is important to recognize that a great deal of moral theology depends upon and makes use of matter known and defined in ethics, for example, the notion of end, means, virtue, and human act. Accordingly, we see a necessary distinction between the two, the relation between them, and the need of acquiring the knowledge found in both, in order to understand the complete moral ordering of human acts.

The Adequacy of Ethics

We come, however, to a difficulty that can be raised about the status of ethics as a science of the moral order. This difficulty is one about the adequacy of ethics as a moral science; it arises from the fact that the state of pure, i.e., integral, human nature does not actually exist. Human beings are either in a state of grace, that is, in a state of friendship with God and actually leading a supernatural as well as a natural life, or they are in a state of sin, that is, leading a life that rejects God's grace and His friendship, which are necessary means to both natural and supernatural happiness. In other words, human beings either are in conformity with the supernatural order whose culmination is in the Beatific Vision, or they are opposed to the supernatural order and, in a real sense, to the achievement of the good of the natural order as well. Therefore, it would seem that ethics, as a natural science of morality, is at least inadequate if not false.

In facing this difficulty, we must recall a distinction made in the opening chapter between the formally practical order and the completely practical order. In the completely practical order, the order of concrete existence in which individual acts are done here and now, ethics is inadequate in the sense that human beings need to have supernatural means to achieve a supernatural end, an end which in fact all men have. Moreover, man needs the grace of God to accomplish much of the good even of the natural order, in particular the good of the moral virtues, the ordering to, and practice of which, is hindered as a consequence of original sin. However, it is misleading to speak of ethics as inadequate in this respect, for ethics as a science does not and cannot embrace the completely practical order. But in this same respect, it must be emphasized, moral theology is also insufficient, for no science can include the completely practical order. This is the order of action, not of science. In this order, we can say that natural prudence is not enough, since it is not proportionate to a supernatural end. Only the infused virtue of prudence is sufficient, and similarly with the other virtues.

In the formally practical order, the order of practical science, ethics is distinct from moral theology and is adequate as a science of moral truths established by reason. As we have seen, ethics is a distinct science because it considers a distinct end, the end of natural happiness. Knowledge of such happiness and the means ordered to acquiring such happiness are established by reason and constitute the science of ethics. Moreover,—and this point must be emphasized—such knowledge is necessary for and is presupposed by the science of moral theology. A person cannot be a moral theologian without a grasp of the fundamental definitions and truths established by ethics. Revealed knowledge does not and cannot eliminate the need of acquiring natural knowledge.

Consequently, it is false and misleading to speak of natural moral science as "pagan ethics," if this designation is to imply that ethics is *opposed* to moral theology. The end considered in ethics is in no way opposed to the supernatural end; rather, the former is subordinated to the latter. The phrase "Christian Ethics" can also be misleading, since a study of morality which is based on revealed principles, is not ethics but moral theology. Christian revelation proposes divine grace and the infused virtues, not merely to help man achieve more easily what he could achieve anyway by his mere natural powers, but to make it possible for him to achieve a good that is absolutely impossible without them. Properly speaking, therefore, ethics is neither pagan nor Christian but the natural moral doctrine needed to understand man's moral life and necessary for the science of moral theology.

The Openness of Ethics

In noting that revealed knowledge does not eliminate the need of acquiring natural knowledge, we should stress likewise the openness of ethics to moral theology. If, on the one hand, moral theology presupposes the grasp of natural moral truth, on the other hand, the fulfillment of the knowledge established in ethics is attained in moral theology, through knowledge of the supernatural end to which mankind is ultimately ordered. In this sense, ethics is an introduction to moral theology. In this sense, the end of ethics is the beginning of moral theology.

Ethics is also an introduction to other moral knowledge, not of a supernatural kind, but to another branch of moral knowledge in the natural order. This other branch of natural moral knowledge is politics, the practical science concerned with the social and political common good. Here again, though obviously different from the relationship to moral theology, ethics is, on the one hand, presupposed by political science and, on the other hand, furthered and fulfilled by knowledge about the political and social common good to which mankind is ordered. In this sense, the end of ethics is the beginning of political philosophy.

Ethics thus ends by opening out into two different directions: toward the political common good of the natural order, and toward the common good of the supernatural order, God as known and loved in the Beatific Vision.

REVIEW QUESTIONS

1. Is there one single object constituting the ultimate end which is human happiness? Explain.
2. What is a hierarchical ordering of goods? What is the basis for such a hierarchy?
3. What are the principal constituents making up human happiness?
4. State the issue of contemplation vs. action.

5. Is contemplation human happiness? Why or why not?

6. Does human happiness consist in a life of moral virtue? Why or why not?

7. What is essential human happiness?

8. What is relative human happiness?

9. Can happiness be attained by most human beings at some time during their life? Explain.

10. Is there any permanence to human happiness? Why or why not?

11. Can human happiness in any way be considered complete happiness?

12. What facts of experience suggest that human happiness cannot be complete and perfect happiness?

13. Explain the meaning of *eternal life*. Is it the same as a supernatural life? Explain.

14. What is proportionate happiness? Can it be an ultimate end?

15. What is absolute happiness? Is it realizable by man?

16. In relation to a natural and a supernatural end, show how the meaning of "happiness" is analogical.

17. Summarize the content of moral theology.

18. How does the order of treatment in moral theology differ from that of ethics?

19. Is ethics adequate as a science of morality? Explain.

20. How is ethics as a science both an end and a beginning?

DISCUSSION

1. Happiness is said to be the ultimate end which human beings strive to attain. But an ultimate end, to be truly an end, must be realized in some single object. No single object, however, naturally satisfies all human desire. Therefore, there can be no ultimate end, but, at best, a plurality of ends corresponding to a plurality of objects.

2. Give an argument supporting the position that human happiness consists in contemplation. Evaluate the argument.

3. Give an argument opposing the position that human happiness consists in contemplation. Evaluate the argument.

4. Give an argument supporting the position that the life of morally virtuous action constitutes human happiness. Evaluate the argument.

5. It is generally admitted that the ultimate end has to consist in complete satisfaction of all striving and desire. But as long as a human being lives, there is not complete satisfaction, for there is always something more a human being still wishes for and seeks. Only death brings an end to human striving. Death is therefore the ultimate end of human activity.

6. An ultimate end has to be one in the sense that it is something for the sake of which we will everything else. We learn through revelation from God that the ultimate end of man is supernatural. Consequently, there can be no ultimate natural end for man.

7. In the objective sense of the term, no ultimate end can be found within the natural order. The reason is that no good of the natural order can satisfy perfectly man's desire. Only knowing and loving God can perfectly satisfy the desire of human beings. But God is supernatural. Therefore, man has only a supernatural ultimate end.

8. The natural order is distinct from the supernatural order. Each order has its ultimate end. A human being, therefore, can be ordered to the natural ultimate end without being ordered to the supernatural ultimate end.

9. In the completely practical order, man is ordered only to a supernatural ultimate end, the Beatific Vision. The ultimate end of the natural order, therefore, is only analytically distinct from the supernatural ultimate end. Consequently, there is no practical significance to a natural ultimate end.

10. Comment: Ethics is inadequate as a science of morality since human beings need supernatural aid to attain not only a supernatural end, but even the good of the natural order.

SUGGESTED READINGS

Aristotle, *Ethics*, Book X, esp. chaps. 6–9.
St. Thomas, *Commentary*, Book X, esp. Lessons IX–XVI.
St. Thomas, *Summa Contra Gentiles*, Book III, chaps. 37–40; 47–48; 51–63.
St. Augustine, *The City of God*, Book XIX, chaps. 4, 14, 17, 25, 27; Book XXII, chaps. 29–30.

Garrigou-LaGrange, R., *The Three Ages of the Interior Life*. St. Louis, Herder, 1947, chap. III, pp. 48–66.
Hume, *An Enquiry Concerning the Principles of Morals*, Appendix I. Consult Melden, A., *Ethical Theories*, pp. 281–286.

Kant, *Foundation of the Metaphysics of Morals*, third sec. Consult Melden, A., *Ethical Theories*, pp .335-340.

Maritain, *Science and Wisdom.* New York: Charles Scribner's Sons, 1940, Part II, pp. 137-241.

Pritchard, H., "Does Moral Philosophy Rest on a Mistake?" Consult Melden, A., *Ethical Theories*, pp. 469-481.

Renard, *The Philosophy of Morality*, Epilogue, pp. 242-247.

Stevenson, *Ethics and Language*, chap. XV, pp. 319-336.

Tsanoff, *Ethics*, chap. 18, pp. 360-379.

Ward, *Christian Ethics*, chap. 4, pp. 43-56.

Index